The Swiss Banks

T. R. FEHRENBACH

The Swiss Banks

McGRAW-HILL BOOK COMPANY

New York   *London*   *Toronto*

CONTENTS

PREFACE

The facts, cases, incidents, and stories related in this book are true.

The civil codes of most Atlantic nations provide for the right of individuals and business firms to be left alone. Public figures, such as dictator Juan Perón of Argentina or Yul Brynner of Switzerland and Hollywood, are fair game. Anyone may tell the truth about their private affairs. But ordinary businessmen, such as Signor Agnelli, the Italian auto-maker, his money, his lawyers, and his banks, are not. Rich men, corporations, corporation lawyers, and their banks all enjoy a legal right to privacy.

But the world also has a right to know about Swiss banks. To tell the whole story, it has been necessary in some cases in this book to alter circumstances or dates, and even to change names to protect the innocent. In any event, many names are not important. What happened—and is still happening—is important.

Many men contributed to the writing of this book: Swiss bankers, lawyers, businessmen, police, and officials. People from various parts of the world assisted. But Interpol detectives, Treasury agents, and Department of Justice lawyers, as well as ordinary European businessmen, do not like their names made public. In a few instances any open acknowledgment might be embarrassing; it would pinpoint whence the story came. So no acknowledgments will be made, but I am grateful to everyone who helped.

Finally it is hoped that an honest attempt to show Swiss banks as they really are—and the world around them which supports them as it actually is—will be considered by no one, even the Swiss bankers themselves, as unfair.

T. R. F.

Gott regiert im Himel und s Gält uf Erde.
Für Gält tanzet sogar de Tüüfel.
(God rules in Heaven, and money on earth.
Even the Devil dances for gold.)

Zürich Proverb

INTRODUCTION

In recent years Swiss banks have been very much in world news.

In 1954 the government of Israel charged that huge sums of money deposited by Jewish families killed in Hitler's death camps still resided in Zurich. Under Swiss law, after twenty years this money would revert to the Swiss banks. Israel claimed at least $30 million was at stake, and various Jewish world organizations began court proceedings to make the banks disgorge. But there was one problem; it was almost impossible to prove that such deposits did in fact exist.

In 1957 American newspapers carried the news that notorious proxy raider Leopold Silberstein had used Swiss banks to buy up big chunks of Fairbanks, Morse Company stock in his undercover battle to gain control of that corporation.

Also in 1957 Louis Lefkowitz, the Attorney General of New York, accused three Swiss trusts of stock fraud amounting to $8 million. The trusts were administered through Swiss banks. Lefkowitz complained there was nothing he, the state of New York, or even the federal government could do about this. No US regulatory or governmental agency had jurisdiction or control over foreign businesses headquartered abroad, even if they operated in New York state and took money from American citizens.

The same year the Senate of the United States began hearings to determine what influence Swiss banks wielded in American financial affairs. Securities Exchange Commission Chairman J. Sinclair Armstrong was called to testify. He stated it was quite possible for SEC rules to be flouted and American taxes evaded by individuals buying and selling American securities through Swiss banks. He further stated it might be possible for Communist nations to use Swiss banks as agents to buy control of vital US industries.

What most irritated Armstrong was the fact that most stocks and bonds purchased by foreigners in the United States were bought through Swiss banks, and under Swiss law all bank transactions remained closed to the government of the US. Unlike American banks, Swiss banks could act all over the world as stockbrokers for clients whose names were protected from revelation by Swiss law. For this reason alone the Senate investigation of 1957 was able to prove, or even investigate, very little of the problem.

In 1958 Senator Dennis Chavez, Democrat of New Mexico, attacked Swiss bank secrecy on the Senate floor. Chavez said the system permitted "crooks and swindlers" and even Communists to buy American defense stocks. He implied that the managers of Swiss banks, no matter how unsavory the client, would do anything the client desired, for a profit.

The chairman of the Senate Judiciary Committee on Banking and Currency, South Carolina's Olin Johnston, went so far as to inform the managers of the three largest Swiss banks of his intention to call them as witnesses. This proved impossible, since no Senate subpoena could be served in Switzerland.

On July 18, 1958, *The New York Times* quoted the American ambassador to the Swiss Confederation, Mr. Henry J. Taylor, as follows: "There has been a heavy increase in financial transactions in Bern in connection with the narcotic traffic from Communist China to the Western world," and "there is reason to believe that Communists send out an average of $1,000,000 a week from Switzerland to spies, provocateurs, and contraband agents for their work in the Western democracies."

To all this the New York *Journal-American* editorialized: *It is one thing to protect the funds of refugees from Communist lands and Nazis back in World War II. But it is something else to run a business that caters to international vice racketeers, Communists in their infiltration activities, financial operators evading American law and SEC rules, and American income tax dodgers. These are criminal activities.*

In 1959 *Newsweek* ran an article on Swiss banking. Among other things, it reported that ex-strong man Juan Domingo Perón of Argentina had $15 million in Swiss vaults. Fulgencio Batista, former President of Cuba, was said to have at least $3 million. Exiled King Farouk of Egypt, the former Red boss of Guatemala, Jácobo Arbenz, and the murdered King of Iraq, Feisal, were all claimed to have concealed enormous fortunes somewhere in

Switzerland. It was said that Feisal's relatives could not touch his money, and that Perón himself was unable to get at some $60 million carted off to Geneva by his dead wife, Little Eva—who had inconveniently failed to open a joint account.

Also in 1959, the French government angrily accused Swiss banks of financing major arms deals for Algerian rebels, using Egyptian and other Arab money. But because of bank secrecy, not even the Swiss government could interfere.

Newsweek further announced that purchases of American stocks by Swiss banks acting as agents for anonymous clients had been $30 million in 1950. Mysteriously, the annual amount had jumped to $500 million by 1959.

Not long afterward, European newspapers printed that Premier Moise Tshombe's first stop after leaving the Congo was his Swiss bank.

Another news item of the early 1960s was that the heirs, legitimate and otherwise, of the late Dominican dictator Rafael Leónidas Trujillo had brought suit against certain Swiss banks to gain control of the Dominican gross national product, reputedly deposited there over a period of thirty years. The papers also reported that Trujillo's direct heirs had as little chance of getting this money as the new government of Santo Domingo, which felt it also had a claim.

Newspapers in Milan and Rome stated that the most important event in the lives of Italian businessmen was not weekly visits to their mistresses but their annual or semiannual jaunts to Lugano just over the Swiss border. Lugano had three major attractions: it was close, it was in the hard Swiss franc area, and it was conveniently beyond the reach of the Italian tax collector.

German government journals mourned private hoarding and the loss of German gold in 1963. One repeated a modern German proverb: *Money alone can't bring happiness—unless you've got it in a Swiss bank.*

In 1964 when the British pound teetered on the brink, the *Manchester Guardian* reported Labour ministers were convinced Swiss banks were deliberately undermining sterling. In London government and financial circles Zurich had become a dirty word.

For more than ten years the daily press, periodicals, and

journals of the Western world have revealed the existence of a smoldering, half-hidden resentment toward the institution of Swiss banking. The Swiss, everyone admits, are a decent, democratic people, who make superb watches and fine chocolate and bother no one. The country of Switzerland is highly admired. But the Swiss banker, to the press, is something else.

The rancor is widespread. It permeates Senators and cynics, liberals and labor, editors and economists, bankers and bureaucrats. Very few people have ever met a Swiss banker—but a great many who never have don't like them.

In New York the Swiss bank manager is a wily crook, one of whose minor crimes is the concealing of Nazi assets in World War II. In Tel Aviv he is a ghoul, who robs defenseless orphans of their rightful means. In Washington, he is sometimes a smug and protesting son-of-a-bitch who works hand in glove with international gangsters when not too busy counting Communist cash.

The liberal press of Latin America paints him as a soulless, Protestant Shylock, accepting blood-stained money with no questions asked. In London the Swiss banker is a well-fed Zurcher, paunchy and cold-eyed and dressed in black, who smiles toothily each morning after breakfast while figuring out how to sell sterling—and the British Empire—short.

Meanwhile, the thought of what may lie in his steel-and-granite vaults gives every conscientious taxman nightmares.

The press, the governments, and the bureaus of the Western world have brought five major accusations against Swiss banks:

1. They allow Communists to buy control of free-world defense industries.

2. They furnish the agencies through which Communist powers pay their spies and purchase forbidden strategic materials in Western nations.

3. They offer a hiding place for stolen or looted money.

4. They provide a screen for proxy raiders, stock manipulators, and shady promoters—and have been involved in every smelly deal from the Penn-Texas–Fairbanks, Morse showdown to the sacking of Chrysler's Colbert.

5. They help tax evaders conceal both income and assets.

These are serious charges.

But there is another side to the picture. Switzerland and its banks hold a great fascination. No one can deny that the anonymous or numbered account has become both the most subtle and the most sophisticated status symbol in the modern world.

From the gray antiseptic corridors of the US Internal Revenue Service to the sun-sprayed cafés of the Via Veneto hardly any subject produces more interest than what goes on in Swiss banks.

Very few people, however, know much about them. It is possible to become quite ignorant, reading only the papers.

People have asked, what is so special about a Swiss bank? What does Swiss bank secrecy mean?

What is a numbered account? What does it mean to have one? How can I get one?

What kind of people have them, and how much does it take?

What's all this talk about dope peddlers, vice racketeers, Communists, and *caudillos?* Is any of it true?

Do Swiss banks really sit on millions in unclaimed funds?

Are they actually important in the world of finance, and if so how did this happen?

In short, what goes on here?

That, in short, is what this book is all about.

Banker's Blood

ON NOVEMBER 25, 1964, a youngish Labour member of Parliament walked out of a lobby in the House of Commons. He was very angry. He paused, struck his fist into a cupped palm. He said: "The bloody international bankers! The goddam bloody international bankers!"

There was an air of quiet crisis in the lobbies of the House. A deep uneasiness had spread through the British financial center, the City of London. The pound sterling was in serious trouble.

As the immediate result of a wave of heavy selling of sterling on the continental money exchanges sterling had slipped to 2.78⅝ dollars, a record low. Much more of this kind of battering would force an official devaluation. If this happened, everything imported into Britain would become more expensive, since British money would buy less. A sterling crisis was not so spectacular as German U-boats lurking off the coasts—but in its way it was just as dangerous.

The reasons for the crisis were varied and controversial. They included the effects of a reactionary labor movement and a nonprofessional industrial management in England as well as government spending policies. Basically, in terms of world trade, the greatest trading nation in the world was spending more than it took up and paying its subjects wages and benefits they had not earned. British goods were out of date or overpriced. There was a serious imbalance of trade and a loss of gold.

The new Labour government, elected in October, had not

created the crisis, but they had inherited it—and even in a way precipitated it. Labour had come to power not with a new austerity program but on promises to spend more on various welfare measures.

Whatever the human values and social justice involved, such measures could only increase the cost of British goods and make the situation worse. And Britain, an island, had to trade to live. The old Conservative government had been drifting with the tide and making up its international deficits through international borrowing, getting credit from the continent. The Labour regime, with its socialist policies, suddenly found the credit windows closed.

Worse, the banks in Amsterdam, Paris, Zurich, and Geneva began to unload sterling. The people who held sterling or sterling credits ordered their bankers to sell, and to sell short, as confidence in the British government and British money weakened.

There was a strong and bitter feeling among British government Ministers that the pound was the victim of deliberate sabotage by Swiss bankers. This was not, of course, wholly true. The only people who could sink the pound were the British themselves. The selling by international bankers was a symptom, not a cause, of sterling's decline. But George Brown, Economic Minister and Number Two man in Prime Minister Harold Wilson's cabinet came out of a meeting and snapped: "The gnomes of Zurich are at work again."

The remark was widely repeated in the lobbies of the House as bitterness against the "international bankers" rose.

In a night meeting November 24, Douglas Houghton, Minister for Social Policy, told Labour back-benchers that the crisis ruled out the promised payment of increased old-age pensions. The new MPs were stunned, then angry. The meeting became noisy and bitter. MP John Mendelson sparked a back-bench revolt.

He told the unhappy and squirming Labour Ministers assembled at the meeting, "It is improper for the Government to prove its financial respectability to the international bankers and the IMF by denying the means of livelihood to the old-age pensioners!"

Mendelson immediately circulated a round robin, or petition, designed to make the government reconsider. Emanuel Shinwell, party chairman, emphatically called for party unity, solidarity, and secrecy—none of which he got.

The blow was too bitter. The Labourites, with a shaky majority of three in the House, had confidently expected to offer the increased pensions to the voters as a sort of Christmas bonus. Even worse than this disappointment was the chilling disillusionment in the realization that the "international bankers" were in the driver's seat.

Britain had to have more loans—and Britain could only get them by creating confidence in British credit. The government had applied to the IMF—the International Monetary Fund in Basel—for $1,000,000,000 in standby credits. The money was available. But the bankers managing the Fund told the British government bluntly to hold up all further expenditures on social services until the British house was in order.

Prime Minister Wilson was a realist even if some of his supporters were not. Wilson gave the word to do what the bankers advised, and to knock off this unfortunate "gnomes of Zurich" talk.

Meanwhile, the American government had become alarmed at the decline of sterling. The pound was the world's second most important reserve currency, after the dollar. In international payments the pound served the same way gold or dollar credits did, as an international currency. Its collapse would not only put pressure on the US dollar itself, it would also create financial turmoil in the Atlantic trading community. The United States, now the great stabilizer in world politics, determined to help bail the British out.

With a series of phone calls to the continent, Washington arranged an immense standby fund of $3,000,000,000 to shore up the pound. So long as this sum lasted, sterling would be held to a level price. The very size of the fund engendered confidence, and it precluded any hope of success by money manipulators interested in devaluing the pound for their own purposes.

But the US did not put up all the money. Two thirds of it came from continental bankers, the men in Amsterdam, Paris, and the "gnomes of Zurich" themselves who quickly pledged large sums.

If the dark-suited men behind the geranium-boxed windows in Basel and Zurich had driven the pound down, they now moved quickly to shore it up. The French bankers, not Anglophiles but understanding the nature of the interconnected Atlantic financial community, raised $500 million. The Swiss came in heavily; the rescue operation was in their own interests. Bankers live off healthy commercial operations, not financial chaos.

But the faceless men behind the great banks wanted a certain security for their loans; all bankers do. In this case the collateral was complete financial orthodoxy in British monetary affairs. The bank rate, or basic interest rate, had to rise, making all loans more expensive in Great Britain and keeping inflation down. There had to be heavier taxes, surcharges on imports, and cuts in government spending on "unprofitable" measures such as social services.

With no course open except to go along, Labour politicians went through the corridors of Parliament cursing international bankers and damning men whose names they did not know.

It was a disillusioning thing for men newly come to power in Britain to learn how powerful international money really was. That money, and the power it created, entered the back rooms of Westminster; it sobered Whitehall. Neither MPs nor Ministers could ignore it—above all, not when Britain was overdrawn at the bank.

What most infuriated Economic Minister George Brown, and Labour MPs such as John Mendelson and Ian Mikardo— doctrinaire socialists who hated banks and bankers on principle —was that the men they disparaged as the "gnomes of Zurich" were really giants.

Money, even in the age of A-bombs and superpowers, is still power. Because they have or control vast amounts of money, Swiss banks are powerful. It is a power which operates in the gray, dim, unseen world of international finance. Only a few people are aware of it, but it affects everyone. Swiss money builds Norwegian chemical plants, modernizes Swedish communications systems, stabilizes the Dutch guilder, and salvages the British pound.

It reaches into Wall Street, and Swiss loans to the World Bank have strengthened the American dollar.

The solid-silver Swiss franc, backed by gold reserves of more than 135 per cent, is not an international currency like the dollar or sterling. But its influence in other ways reaches almost everywhere in the non-Communist world—and sometimes behind the Iron Curtain.

All this is amazing because, on paper, Switzerland should be one of the weakest, poorest, and least influential nations in the world.

The Confederation of Switzerland, in existence since 1291 and fully made in its modern form in 1815, is not even a nation-state in the modern Western sense. It is composed of three separate, and rather hostile, language and ethnic groups—Germanic, French, and Italian. There are only 5.8 million people in all, far fewer men and women than live in New York or London. They live in an area of only 41,288 square kilometers, of which less than 7 per cent is farmable. The soil of Switzerland throughout its history has never fed its population. And, unique in Europe, that soil contains no minerals. Switzerland has never had any coal, iron, petroleum, gas—all the things a modern nation needs—nor even any seaports through which to get them.

Resource-poor Switzerland should be a desperately impoverished country. It is instead more industrialized than Belgium, and its people enjoy the third or fourth highest standard of living in the world.

Switzerland has the loosest form of national organization of any modern nation, and the weakest central government in the West. Its tiny area is divided into twenty-five sovereign cantons, each of which retains real powers. The federal capital at Bern manages foreign affairs, controls arms and alcohol, regulates the currency, and runs the mails and railroads. Almost everything else is left to the several states. The President of the Confederation is a figurehead, selected annually from a federal Cabinet of seven, whose powers overall are small. There are two legislative houses, the *Nationalrat* and *Ständerat,* modeled on the American House and Senate. Both houses must issue bills to make them law—but any law can be voided by popular initiative and national referendum, and some have been. The federal judiciary has no powers of legislative review.

Yet Switzerland has never had a serious civil war or national revolution, and has the most stable society and government in the Western world.

It is traditionally neutral, a neutrality recognized by all international law and treaties since 1815. It has no standing army and takes no initiative in international affairs. It fought in neither world war and has made no alliances since.

Switzerland thus has none of the sources or tools of national power and prestige. But few nations have more prestige in the world at large, and few societies are more influential beyond their borders. The reason is not the superb Swiss watches or Swiss chocolate, both the world's best, or even the famed and genuine Swiss direct democracy, in which every male Swiss participates.

It is "Swiss" money, of which the banks of Switzerland manage or control an immense amount.

Millions of tourists visit the Alps each year, or sit in the sunny sidewalk cafés of Lugano or Geneva. Millions of people have admired the clear air of Davos, enjoyed the sparkling blue waters of Lakes Luzern and Leman, or tried the fashionable snow slopes of St. Moritz. Few places on earth pack more natural beauty into a small area, a beauty the sensible Swiss have cannily exploited. Swiss are almost pathologically clean, hard-working, and honest. They are the hoteliers *par excellence* of the world; anyone who has been to Switzerland enjoys going back.

Yet the Switzerland of red-cheeked maids, yodeling mountaineers, superb hotels and expensive ski lodges, and costumed villagers voting in the *Gemeinde* square is as representative of modern Switzerland as cowboys roping steers in Texas or a Frontier Days parade in Santa Barbara, California, is of the present United States.

There is another Switzerland, centered along Bahnhofstrasse in Zurich and near the old city of Geneva, which only certain kinds of tourist see. This is the Switzerland of barred bank windows, of gray-uniformed bank porters, and tiny offices where men from all over the earth talk casually in millions over tea.

This is where the heads of multimillion-dollar corporations come borrowing, where a frown can frighten the elected governments of entire nations. This is where other men come to leave their money, and where banks can *charge* interest on deposits and still obtain more money than they know what to do with.

This is the weird world of Swiss banks, which are in some ways like no other banks on earth.

The beginnings of Swiss banking are inextricably intertwined into the history of the Confederation, which began in the thirteenth century as a military alliance (not a political union) between certain forest and mountain cantons of Upper Germany and the medieval towns situated along the alpine waterways. The alliance began with three forest districts—Uri, Unterwalden, and Schwyz, from whose name came Swiss and Switzerland. These three cantons were populated by historically free Alemannic tribesmen speaking a form of German called *Schwyzerdutch*, and their elders banded together and swore an eternal alliance against the feudal claims of the House of Habsburg in 1291.

The land of the Swiss was rocky and poor, and sharply compartmentalized by horrendous mountains. It was a country which made the formation of large estates or large political territories impractical. Each family, each valley community, was thrown very much on its own resources to survive. Survival required hard work, and it bred a singular independence and a deep-seated desire to be left alone. Mountaineers everywhere tend to be clannish, aloof, hardheaded, and wanting little to do with foreigners —and foreigners are people from outside the glen. They are traditionally hospitable, but hospitality and political contacts are two different things. The character of William Tell, the legendary Swiss national hero who lived only in literature, reveals the nature of the Swiss people, past and present. Tell was pragmatic, independent, self-reliant, and unconcerned with moral or ideological problems. He wanted to be left alone. When Rudolf of Habsburg's tax collectors interfered with him and put his son's life in danger, Tell fought back. He is every Swiss' secret hero.

Uri, Schwyz, and Unterwalden fought the power of Austria savagely, and in a century-long war established their independence. The Swiss cantons were the only free tribal groupings in Western Europe which successfully resisted incorporation into the feudal system. An old Germanic form of communal democracy was carried on unchanged, and this was an immensely important factor in Swiss history. Certain towns of Upper Germany (Luzern, Zug, Zurich, and Bern, which had their own troubles with the feudal dukes) made alliance with them, forming what was called the Everlasting League. It was not a true political union. Each district and town remained sovereign. But the alliance was so effective militarily that its power grew and its territory expanded. Other cities and cantons were taken in or attached themselves to the Swiss as allies, protectorates, or dependencies. In the fifteenth century the Swiss alliance took on the three greatest powers of Europe—Charles the Bold's Burgundy, France, and the Holy Roman Empire—and defeated each in turn. The league then made a disastrous foreign alliance with the Pope, entered an Italian war, and was badly mauled at Marignano in 1515.

After this the Swiss renounced all foreign adventures, the first European people to do so. Their neutrality was recognized by every European court. Almost from the first, then, the Swiss nation was in Europe, but not really a part of Europe or the collective European experience.

While the medieval foresters and alpine herdsmen were successfully resisting incorporation into the Middle Ages, Swiss townsmen were leaving them by a different route. The Swiss towns lay directly on the German–Mediterranean trade route, the first great trade route in modern Europe. Their location made them the first European entrepôts. Swiss burghers handled sugar and salt, spices and silk. They quickly learned to discount Rhenish silver to Venetian gold. They were businessmen. In time, the cults, polities, and policies of the European Middle Ages ceased to make sense to them.

The Swiss townsman was just as clannish and hardheaded as the forester, and even more practical and unphilosophic. His life hinged on monetary profit. He put silver in the vault, and as soon as he had, the systems, organizations, and pretensions of the middle-European feudalism were no more logical to him than to the free farmers scrabbling for a living in the rocky Swiss dirt.

The quarrel was profound. The alpine farmers merely wanted political freedom; the Swiss burghers went further. They hated Christendom. In its flower medieval Christendom denigrated individual effort; every Swiss burgher lived by it. Christendom, an agrarian society, condemned the love of money; the Swiss merchant lived for it. Swiss businessmen, sweatily turning goods for gold, had to listen to sermons about the curse of Eve at the same time they had to band together to fight off the pretensions of an armed feudal "leisure class."

When John Calvin and Ulrich Zwingli arrived on the Swiss scene calling gold the sober gift of God and comparing work to holiness, Protestantism swept the Swiss cities by storm. The forest cantons had already won their war with Europe, and they stayed Catholic and conservative. But the growing cities, with greater population, wealth, and energies released by new doctrines, soon came to dominate the League.

Here the modern business ethic, already in being, was formally born.

Calvin in Geneva, at this time a French-speaking protectorate of Bern, spoiled men's fun. He also established doctrines and polities, completely outside the rigid Calvinist theology, which shaped the modern business world.

Calvin argued salvation by the sweat of men's brows, and that not only by their works but by their visible rewards you shall know the elect. Gold was God's gift for pleasing work, of which man was a mere steward—not to spend, but to gather and husband. Men had no more right to squander gold, in Calvin's eyes, than they had to refuse to work for it.

Out of this came an ethic no American can fail to recognize:

Work is a virtue, not a necessity. Only bums fail to work.

Wealth is a reasonable, if not the only reasonable, measure of status.

Savings are a must.

Visible poverty offended both God and God's elect.

After Calvin, people in Evangelical lands could still be poor, and most of them continued to be. But they could never again pretend they were proud of it. There is no understanding the energy of seventeenth-century Amsterdam, present *haute société Protestante* in France, or the social and economic history of the United States without John Calvin. For while Calvin lost Switzerland itself to Zwingli, his missionaries carried his doctrines westward, and they became the basis for the Reformed churches and societies of Holland, Scotland, the United States, and France.

Ulrich Zwingli was born in St. Gallen, the only Reformer great who was a native Swiss. Like most of the Reformers, Zwingli was a Catholic theologian who arrived at his Protestantism independently. But unlike many others, Zwingli was a teacher who could consciously pick and choose. He seems to have deliberately set about selecting and organizing a religion and an ethic which fitted the Swiss businessman's hardheaded nature while he served as people's priest at Zurich.

Zwingli agreed with Luther and Calvin on the uselessness of popes and prelates, on the virtues of hard work and puritanical living. But he backed away from Luther's rather aristocratic social notions, and above all from Luther's evident disdain for business. This would never fit in bustling, bourgeois Zurich.

He retreated even farther from Calvin's preoccupation with hellfire, trying to organize the enduring Swiss notions toward God, man, and state which had already grown up along the trade routes. What came finally from Zwingli was a loose, rational, hardhead sort of Protestantism, *echt-Schwyz* and superbly fitted for the culture it permeated:

Duty, work, and the rewards of work are holy.

Honesty is the best business policy.

You get what you pay for, and you should expect to pay for what you get.

Hell may or may not exist, but the conservative view of anything is safer.

It is permissible to sin, but not to enjoy it.

Moral ambiguity is necessary in life, but should never be admitted.

God—and, above all, one's neighbors—are watching.

Zwinglianism, which came to dominate the cities of Switzerland except Luzern and Geneva, was thus a prudent, puritanical, inherently practical and decent code. Its stress was on work, caution, and honesty. But it completely lacked any kind of moral imperative; it was the bourgeois banking ethic for all time.

Four hundred years after Zwingli's death, both Protestant bankers in Basel and Roman Catholic herdsmen in Schwyz are deeply puritanical, pathologically hardworking, capable of a certain internal moral duplicity—though never outright dishonesty—

and convinced that God owes them nothing they cannot earn.

The banker may—and usually does—keep a silk-stockinged mistress in Bern; the farmer may covet one; both feel guilty because they do. Sometimes their major concern is that their neighbors, who are exactly the same, may ferret out their terrible secrets.

Sociologists generally agree that banking and high finance are Protestant fine arts. Zwinglianism did not reconcile Christ and Mammon. Zwingli and his rational spiritual descendants never saw any conflict. The Swiss did not learn to love money. That is a misconception. The Swiss *respects* money, a very different thing. Respecting it, a Swiss pursues, handles, and husbands money as an end in itself, which is utterly different from German materialism with its emphasis upon *things* or American status-seeking, with its drive for power or prestige. A Zurich millionaire of today lives hardly any differently from his grandfather—at work before eight, in sober dress, fretting over every franc as if it were personally vital. In Basel or Bern it is impossible to distinguish between first-generation and sixth-generation banking rich. There are thousands of playboys in Switzerland, but they usually have Arab or Hispanic names.

Respecting money, the Swiss made its handling not a miserly trait but more a priestly calling. He erected ritual rooms and bare confessionals, guarded one and gave the other secrecy.

As early as the seventeenth century Swiss industry, Swiss neutrality, and Swiss Protestant ethic had begun to pay off handsomely. The Swiss internal situation, in spite of its extreme parochialism (each city, each canton maintained its own armed forces, flew its own flag, and coined its own money), was remarkably stable. What was later described as the unique Swiss tolerance was only the reverse of the coin that every Swiss wanted to be left alone. Feeling this way, he was willing to grant the same desire to others. Swiss did fight among themselves but, compared with other peoples—and compared with the mauling the famous Swiss mercenaries gave other troops—these brawls were mild. Hardheaded and pragmatic, the Swiss never had any interest, like the rest of Europe, in grandiose schemes of conquest or ultrarational goals like the propagation of politics or religion.

No true businessman, of any nationality, ever does. As a Swiss historian once remarked, it has never been proved that such things are good for business or likely to turn a profit, which was after all the Swiss' true goal upon this earth.

Significantly, the *two million* Swiss military mercenaries who left the cantons and fought in every European war between the Middle Ages and the eighteenth century fought for money. Switzerland was in Europe, but never quite a part of it, from the first.

Given Swiss neutrality, tolerance, and internal stability, it was natural that the capital now being formed in neighboring areas of France, the Germanies, and northern Italy in time of war should pass over into Switzerland. Swiss towns provided ready refuge for war victims and, above all, their money. Each European attempt at standardization or consolidation, with its ensuing turmoil and persecution, thrust new people, new skills, and fresh coin across the Alps.

The French Protestants, after the revocation of the Edict of Nantes in 1685, brought both watchmaking and the nucleus of the great French banking houses to Geneva. Later, with the French Revolution, most of the money of the French nobility followed them, some never to return. After that revolution, a great many moneyed Frenchmen never again trusted any Gallic government. The great banking families of Geneva, most of them originally French Huguenots, were made.

In 1802 Napoleon recognized a fact that all the statesmen who followed him also honored: a neutral enclave in the heart of Europe was useful. Napoleon guaranteed Swiss independence and neutrality after French revolutionaries had briefly invaded the cantons. But Napoleon's logical latinate mind could not bear the utter informality of the Swiss arrangements. Under his guidance the great, loose association of cantons, dependencies, protectorates revolving about each other was tightened. The Grisons, St. Gallen, Thurgau, Ticino, and Vaud—all regions which had been politically Swiss for centuries—became full-fledged cantons or states. The Peace of Vienna, which ended the Napoleonic period, added three more—Geneva, Valais, and Neuchâtel—while it formally guaranteed Swiss neutrality. Territorially, Switzerland was complete in 1815.

But each sovereign canton still hoisted its own flag, raised its own army, and issued its separate money. This arrangement stood in the face of two European improvements of immense consequence to the economic and industrial revolution which had now begun: modern railways and modern national monetary systems.

Twenty-five separate currencies made money-handling bewildering even for a Swiss whose ancestors had been exchanging European coins for generations, and the mere idea of building or operating a single rail system across twenty-five independent nations made financiers and engineers alike throw up their hands. After brilliant seventeenth and eighteenth centuries, economic progress in Switzerland ground to a halt.

The Swiss population was increasing, but the market for mercenaries was much depressed; the stability in nineteenth-century Europe was keeping foreign capital home; in the absence of rails, the industrial revolution was passing the cantons by.

Under pressure of the urban business classes—the farmers were notably reluctant—and leaning heavily on the example of the United States, a Swiss federal constitution was drawn up in 1847. After some brief and almost bloodless strife between the rural and city cantons, it was adopted in 1848. This created the modern Confederation of Helvetia, or the Swiss republic.

The federal government was given only those powers— money, foreign affairs, post, rails—essential to create and run a modern economy. Government generally was allowed no other powers. The dominant Swiss city groups were consciously bent on improving business, not trying to build a newfangled nation.

Real political power remained in the hands of the citizenry to a remarkable extent. The old plutocracy and guild system which had ruled the towns by the last half of the nineteenth century shifted to universal male suffrage, but without causing incisive social change. Power was very diffuse, scattered through four thousand small communities or *Gemeinden,* twenty-five cantons, and a loose federal structure. No element in the cantons possessed the power to make real change, even if such change had been desired. The system worked. It worked because the Swiss were and are an intensely ordered and self-disciplined people who require almost no outside coercion. They are bound by that same tension between personal liberty and public order which marks Anglo-Saxon societies, although in Switzerland order always wins.

Otherwise, the weak governmental structure allowed the Swiss to operate splendidly because government never embarked on a program of requiring Swiss to do anything they did not approve. Long ago the Swiss collectively decided to fight no foreign wars, launch no domestic crusades, build no single society, and pursue no national goals. The business of Switzerland is business. The Swiss skull is remarkably hard: new ideas, unless obviously practical and demonstrably profitable, are distrusted. The Swiss who rejected feudalism as bad for business took the same attitude toward despotism, centralism, nationalism, socialism, Marxism, and female suffrage in turn.

To a businessman in Zurich, forced to make a living from foreigners and able to see only so far as the surrounding Alps, none of the enthusiasms which continually sweep over Europe and the world make much sense, whether they concern the brotherhood of man or the notion that what is good for a Swiss might be good for everyone.

Very few of the recurring European passions can be proven profitable.

The very genuine Swiss democracy has nothing to do with equality or fraternity. Swiss society remained graduated, class- and title-conscious, all structured on money rather than birth. Even education follows wealth, since very few lower-middle-class families can afford a university education. Swiss democracy guaranteed not that Swiss were equal, but that they would be treated equally by law and government and fairly by all elements. Above all it never meant that the Swiss would like each other.

It usually surprises outsiders to discover the depth to which Swiss despise one another. Parochialism is strong. The Schwyzer distrusted the black-clad Zurcher with whom he was allied in the Middle Ages and has never changed his attitude. The Zurcher despises the Bernese, who detests the French-speaking Genevois. French and Germanic Swiss regard the Italians with contempt, just as every Swiss feels an almost instinctive contempt for any countryman who earns less money than he does. But this is a hatred and contempt which is freely expressed and may not be practiced; under the dominant ethic no Swiss has the right to interfere with any other or to treat him unfairly.

It is an ethic—not a law—which works but it is not exportable.

Swiss workers have long been unionized, and they extract the highest wages on the continent. But the Swiss attitude toward fairness is a subtle, powerful thing: it permeates all classes. Swiss workers expect to pay through the nose for every benefit they get—and do, by hard work. Switzerland has the only strong labor movement in the world which held a national referendum on the forty-four-hour week and voted it down. Swiss employers do not know what to do with their money. But Swiss workers are frightened by the thought of idleness, or something for nothing: both are immoral.

Inside Switzerland, it merely looks like part of the Western world. Things are subtly different.

George Washington, returning to present-day America, would be lost. The ideas of current Presidents would probably appall him. He would be told that things have changed and had to change; you could not apply eighteenth-century forms and practices and ideas to a modern, industrial United States. Similarly, Queen Victoria would probably find her present Ministers and present subjects somewhat distasteful.

But if the legendary William Tell came back to the Swiss mountains, sparkling with new factories, he would feel at home. He would exchange his old crossbow for a shining new *Sturmgewehr*—the machine gun issued to the militia—with pleasure; he would see its advantages at once. But he would never think of using it for anything but target practice unless some new invader entered his Alps. He would find that Swiss society, Swiss industry, and Swiss government, including Swiss taxes, are still structured to leave him independent, and very much alone.

Remembering the trouble Rudolf of Habsburg had, no Swiss government has ever made evasion of taxes a crime.

The bearded Zurcher merchant who moved his spices and silks over the Zurich-See and nodded to Zwingli's sermons in *Schwyzerdutch* would require only a tailor, a shave, and a brief orientation on modern money before getting back into business. The blue-and-white flag he once saw over the harbor gates still flies along Bahnhofstrasse, and Zurich still deals in exports and coin.

Other nations, other peoples have gone through wars, revolutions, and crises with all their social erosions. They have come out subtly changed. The Swiss have not. Switzerland built a seemingly modern society and an industrial plant more efficient than Britain's in the twentieth century. But it is still the last pre-feudal farming society in Europe, in armed alliance and in armed truce with the last prestatist and pre-Marxist town bourgeoisie on earth.

This kind of sanity has not meant stasis or stagnation. Over the centuries it has always meant money in the bank.

Big Banks
and Small,
Bad Times
and Good

IRONICALLY, modern banking was late arriving in Switzerland. The old wealthy private houses were usually not true banks but depositories of coin, discount houses, or centers of exchange attached to mercantile businesses. They stored or exchanged money but rarely loaned it.

Banks in the modern sense only came to Switzerland after the middle of the nineteenth century. Modern banking concepts were developed elsewhere—in England, France, and Holland, as part of the expanding capitalist economy of Europe in the early industrial age. But just as Switzerland had been ripe for the Protestant ethic, the forms and practices of capitalism invented in other countries found nowhere a more secure or lasting home.

As with religion, Zurchers never really gave a damn about the theory. It was a lovely technique, and it worked.

The greatest need of the Swiss at the middle of the nineteenth century was for transportation. This meant railroads, for by 1850 without rails no industrial or trading system could keep pace or even be built. European commerce had already begun to pass around the Alps by rails running to the east or west, or by water transport powered by steam. Railroads would permit not only a through commerce but a Swiss industry. But before they could be built the money first had to be found. What was needed was a new kind of Swiss bank.

There was plenty of gold and silver buried in Switzerland. The problem was how to get it out of the ground and to work financing industry. The joint-stock company did not provide the answer. It was impractical to float a stock or bond issue every time some railroad-construction company ran out of ready cash.

The answer was first found in France. It was the modern commercial bank, which engages in business and makes vast loans as well as stores money or exchanges it.

The Credit Mobilier, founded in Paris in 1852 by the Pereire Brothers, paved the way for all Europe. The Credit Mobilier was organized not only as a bank to collect capital; it was expressly set up to participate in certain new industries such as railroads and manufacturing. It used the proceeds of its own bond sales to buy shares in supported industries—then a radical notion. It could also hold the shares of new or growing industries until the time seemed ripe for public sale. The idea was sound, and the Paris Credit Mobilier at first made dazzling profits. However, a basically sound idea was pushed ever onward with Gallic élan, beyond the realm of reason into the wildest sort of speculation. The Credit Mobilier eventually collapsed in a tangle of ruin and scandal. But the basic idea took Europe by storm.

The Swiss would not likely have thought up such a complicated scheme. But they seized upon it as the solution to their credit and financing problems. The story of Alfred Escher and the Swiss Credit Bank, which became the biggest bank in Switzerland, is representative of the most successful credit mobiliers.

Alfred Escher came from an old Zurich military and merchant family, and he was representative of the class and thinking which now drove Zurich on to the preëminent rank among Swiss cities. Escher combined a keen grasp of Swiss politics with a good business brain. He was a demon for work, a member of the new Federal Council in 1848, and served for a time as burgomaster.

The Swiss upper class was not an aristocracy. There had never been a country gentry, and the men who controlled the cities (and with them the Confederation) were businessmen. Offices and cantonal power since the Middle Ages had been in the hands of the merchant rich—but a family which lost its business lost the source of its power. With the end of wealth came the end of office, honor, titles, everything. This fact made the Swiss *Patrizier* a working plutocrat rather than a patrician on the English or Roman scale.

Being first and last a businessman—the offices and governmental functions, though important, were incidental—the Swiss *Patrizier* had to have two qualities: one was energy; the other was the ability to predict what was going to happen, or to judge trends. No businessman could survive without them. And this nature of the Swiss plutocrat was significant for Swiss development: he could and did change, in a basically changeless society. He could adopt new artifacts and ideas—if they made business sense—happily. He could help break the hampering guild system and even accept the coming mass democracy with reasonable grace, for in some ways each change enhanced his business.

The Swiss merchant or banker was different from his counterparts in Germany or England in two important ways. First, he was *the* upper class. Therefore he was deeply involved in government on the highest level, even though he was bourgeois. Second, there was no aristocratic group above him with which he could fuse or by whom he could be infected with genuinely patrician notions. In both Germany and England the industrial upper-middle classes were almost feudalized by the twentieth century and came into the modern world alienated from the working world from which they had sprung. The Swiss patrician not only had no way of becoming, or trying to become, a gentleman; he also suffered no such decay but rather infused the populace working for him with his own ideas.

Zurich in 1850 sat where it always had, squarely in the heart of central Europe, but the mountains which had helped protect the town in the Middle Ages now cut if off from the mainstream of European commerce. Zurich in 1850 contained only 17,000 people, and it had never been so important as Geneva, Basel, or even Lausanne, which were more accessible. Escher and a few other Zurchers like him saw that Zurich had to have rails. Escher began to dream of a great rail system linking France and Austria through Switzerland, and carrying goods from Germany over the horrendous St. Gotthard Pass down to the Lombard plain. Zurich would be at this system's heart.

But a project like this needed far more than vision or even construction engineers. It needed credit. And there were only two banks in Zurich, one private, the other a discount house for foreign traders. Neither was in the lending business. But Escher, a politician and statesman as well as a businessman, was determined his rails would be Swiss-financed, or at least Swiss-controlled.

The answer was a Swiss credit mobilier. A German firm, the Allgemeine Deutsche Creditanstalt of Leipzig, was willing to subscribe 7.5 million Swiss francs to such a bank, half the amount needed, without seeking control. French money, which was also ready to come in, was rejected because the French would not eschew such control. With half the money ready in Germany, Escher had to raise the rest in Switzerland.

Now he put his family and personal prestige to work. He gathered around him a solid core of Swiss *Patriziere*—professors at the university, colonels who were also manufacturers, members of the cantonal government, booksellers, merchants, and small private bankers. Escher made sure that there was not a speculator or promoter among them. They were all solid men, not subject to any kind of get-rich-quick fever. Most Swiss historians credit what now happened to this fact.

Escher and his bearded, frock-coated colleagues drew up the articles for a Swiss Credit Bank (Kreditanstalt). Control by Swiss citizens was specified in the charter, and the powers of the organization were purposely made very wide. The articles of the new bank allowed it to

1. grant loans or credits
2. form industrial or other companies and conduct these for its own account
3. participate in both new and old enterprises
4. issue securities and its own bonds
5. buy and sell precious metals, stocks, or merchandise
6. discount bills
7. accept deposits.

Escher's group made certain, however, that the trap the Paris Credit Mobilier fell into would be avoided: the Kreditanstalt of Zurich was not permitted to issue bonds in excess of its subscribed capital.

This was the modern *banque d'affaires*, no longer a mere depository and trading house for gold and silver coin or for discounting notes. It was equipped to be a powerful and positive force in the business and industrial world.

Escher's group took 3 million francs of the new bank's capital themselves. But the cantonal government of Zurich refused to subscribe to the shares Escher set aside for it. Escher then added these to those set aside for the Swiss public. And on July 17, 1856, with some trepidation, these pioneer capitalists offered 9000 shares in the Swiss Credit Bank, worth 4.5 million gold francs, for public sale.

The subscriptions sought were an enormous sum for a town of fewer than 20,000. But outside the proposed bank's offices on the Kleiner Tiefenhof there was a near-riot, as stovepipe-hatted Zurchers pushed and shoved each other to sign their names first to the subscription list. Ten per cent of the purchase price had to be paid down, to reserve the stock, but this did not slow the sales at all.

Three days later Escher closed the subscription lists. He had orders for 436,539 shares at a par value of 218,269,500 gold francs —against a public offering of only 9000 shares.

The idea of the credit mobilier, and the prestige of Escher's group, had brought money buried in Zurich since the Middle Ages out of hiding and put it to work. Zurich was suddenly in the banking business. Escher could now put cash behind his dreams.

Escher lived to see it all come true. In 1882 the amazing Gotthard Tunnel was opened. The Alps were pierced; a trip which had not only been dangerous but had taken weeks could now be completed in minutes. Zurich was again no longer a backwater town, but suddenly at the nerve center of Europe. By 1900 it had increased its population eleven fold. By 1950 it had passed from Swiss parochialism to international urban elegance, and to domination of the Swiss financial scene. By the middle of the century one in every five Swiss lived in Zurich or its environs, and if Bern was the federal capital Zurich ran the real business of Switzerland —business.

The first Kreditanstalt was widely imitated. Soon there were similar banks in all large Swiss towns. Basel and Geneva followed Zurich's growth—though they never caught up to it—and in a few years every rustic community sought, and many got, its own credit bank. No idea could be more appealing to such a money-conscious race.

From the first, then, the connection between Swiss modern

banking and Swiss industrialization was complete. The banks came first, before the industries, but there could not have been one without the other. Bank directors in Switzerland from the first were not just specialists in finance but entrepreneurs in their own right. They were deeply involved in railroads, factories, and exports. Bankers created the Swiss insurance industry, which became one of the largest in the world. Escher's Kreditanstalt took the lead in forming the Swiss Reinsurance Company, still the biggest of its kind. The bank helped Oerlikon, Brown Boveri, and countless other smaller companies grow. At the same time, Basel's banks and Basel's burgeoning chemical complex grew up side by side. Each would have been impossible without the other.

Zurich was one of the first financial centers to begin issuing overdrafts and unsecured loans. The Swiss traditionally bet on men, not ideas. Most of the Zurchers who had battled to get their names on Escher's subscription lists knew nothing about credit mobiliers—but they knew Escher and his men. Swiss bankers, starting what other European bankers called a radical practice, soon discovered that the unsecured business loan was better business than that based on brilliant balance sheets. If a man was honest, hard-working, money-respecting, and determined to succeed, these qualities were security enough. The bank invariably got its money back with interest. If a man—or corporation, or nation—lacked any of these qualities, no matter what goods secured the loan, it was inherently more risky.

The Swiss scrutiny of men and companies was often brutal; they applied Swiss standards. But it was rarely wrong. If Zurich bankers did not care for habits, attitudes, or ethic of a man's, company's, or nation's business they preferred not to back it—a habit they acquired early and never lost.

By the end of the nineteenth century Zurich, Basel, and Geneva were issuing drafts payable in Paris or London, for all European capital development during this period was closely interconnected. The British had forced both the gold standard and free trade down the industrial world's throat, but the world had not choked on it. There was for the first time in history a recognized international currency—gold—and money as well as people and goods flowed from places where there was an oversupply to where all three was needed. International borders had not yet got in the way. German credit backed Swiss banks and German artisans settled in Switzerland, while British money entered Basel and formed giant insurance companies. This involved international money settlements and transactions, and Swiss banks, like all continental banks, had to make arrangement abroad for handling foreign drafts.

In this era Swiss banks could be partially capitalized out of France or Germany and freely lend credit to both England and Romania. In this formative period there was nothing whatever unusual about the Swiss banks. Their practices, bylaws, and business resembled those of banks everywhere in the Western world. Swiss banks had a place, but until 1914 it was actually a very small place. Switzerland was a minuscule nation compared to the capitalistic giants surrounding it. Swiss banks could hardly be a challenge or even competition to the huge banks of London, Paris, Germany, and Holland—so long as all followed a common European course.

Meanwhile, the Swiss had discovered that the blue waters of the alpine lakes, the snow slopes of their mountains, and their clear air brought in the same foreign exchange other nations had to proletarianize their populations, pollute their air and water, begrime their landscapes, and fight bitter trade wars to earn. The Swiss, through tourism, got both money and good will.

In industry, Swiss emphasis gradually shifted out of watchmaking and embroidery to chemicals, metal-working, and engineering. Swiss craftsmanship in these chosen fields gained a reputation as second to none. The Zwinglian ethic brought a finely grained discipline to any project a Swiss attacked. That ethic permitted the Swiss to achieve both the social discipline and the tolerance of others and the indifference to everything not connected with business the modern industrial world demands. And each new industry fitted nicely into the old scheme of things.

The time from 1848 to 1873 was the great stage of corporation- and industry-building, not only in Switzerland but all over the Western world. The ideas and ethic—capitalism—were everywhere dominant and very much the same. During this time the modern industrial world was made—but it was of this period of Swiss history that the historian Ernst Gagliardi wrote: "It was the time most devoid of ideas in the modern history of the Confederation." (Historians like many other intellectuals often take dim views of eras whose primary goals are money or work for the sake of work itself, and Swiss historians are no exception.)

The first great European boom ended abruptly in 1873. Excessive speculation killed it. Men were playing with and riding financial forces they did not yet understand, and on May 9, Black Friday, the Vienna Stock Exchange collapsed amid wild disorder. The crash, like all such crashes, was felt across borders and shook the whole capitalist world. The end of stock speculation—the business anticycle was then unknown—threw a chill over European economic growth for twenty years.

This meant bad times in Switzerland. The bigger banks retrenched and survived. Many smaller or newer banks, operating valiantly and foolishly as *banques d'affaires*, collapsed with the industries to which they were tied. Others failed to pay dividends for long periods.

By 1893 this depression had run its course, and a new era of industry-building began. But the disasters of the 1870s had left a lasting mark: there was fear of small financial or industrial institutions. Small businesses had failed in hard times faster than big ones. Now, the trend was strongly toward industrial consolidation. Industries formed cartels and trusts, big business getting rapidly bigger. Banks followed the trend. Bigger and bigger business demanded bigger and better banks, and the bigger the bank the safer it seemed, also. Banks began to merge, or buy one another up. The Kreditanstalt, the strongest, expanded enormously. The Union Bank of Switzerland, originally a bank in Winterthur, followed the same pattern. The large Commercial Bank of Basel, the Swiss People's Bank (ironically begun in 1869 as a bank for the "little man"), and the Swiss Bank Corporation came into being through giant mergers between different banks in different Swiss cities.

But this bank concentration could not proceed so far in Switzerland as it did in England, for example. Five British banks—Barclays, Lloyds, Midland, National Provincial, Westminster—the survivors of many dozens, came to dominate all British banking. But in confederate Switzerland, divided into sovereign cantons, banking could not quite follow the path of unitary England or metropolitan France. Cantonal political separation and the strongly ingrained idea of separatism took a heavy and healthy toll of late nineteenth-century consolidation fever.

Local cantonal banks were established by law, and these could not be driven out. And a certain feeling pervaded all Swiss bank directors—money should be freely accepted from outside cantonal borders but should be spent at home. Unlike other banking structures in Europe, the five biggest commercial banks in Switzerland did not acquire more than about one third the assets of all Swiss banking.

During the boom period 1893–1912, the general shape of the modern Swiss bank structure took form. It was similar to continental systems but not to the American.

The Swiss National Bank—corresponding to the Bank of England or the US Federal Reserve—was created only in 1907. This bank only obtained a monopoly on the issuance of banknotes in 1910; the Swiss Confederation was the last advanced nation to consolidate and centralize its banknote and credit system. And even here there was a difference. The National Bank, although rigidly controlled by federal statute, remained a private institution. Half its shares were held by other banks, half by private parties—who had, however, to be Swiss. The Swiss National Bank was empowered to regulate monetary and credit policies, serve as a national clearing house, and stockpile the national gold reserve.

The National Bank also kept and issued records on all other Swiss banks, which it classified into seven types. These classifications are, like the Swiss mind, more practical than precise. And the Swiss, unlike Germans or Americans, always have had a positive dislike for statistics. Some classes of Swiss banks are not required to publish balance sheets; all National Bank audits are kept secret, even from government, and vast amounts of the money managed by banks are not required to show in the admitted assets of any bank. All these policies were firm and in force before 1912, which was long before Swiss banks had any international importance. Critics who later claimed Swiss banks geared their policies to attract foreign money simply never had any understanding of either Swiss banking history or the Swiss mind. Swiss banking law and policy grew up bent by the almost neurotic Swiss desire for personal privacy and determination of the individual to be left alone, not only by his neighbors but by his own government as well.

While banks gradually changed from private businesses to public trusts in other countries, Swiss bankers jealously guarded ownership and control of their own institutions. They were successful only because banking in Switzerland was conducted with skill, pragmatic business sense, and—above all—restraint. While Swiss banks, like Swiss business generally, grew into and stayed a maze of interlocking directorates, family corporations, and close-held trusts (by 1900 almost every enterprise was part of a monopoly or trust), the whole structure continued to tick as sweetly as a Rolex watch.

Another striking feature of this system was that banker and businessman, always deeply involved in government as was Alfred Escher, stayed involved. The Swiss *Patrizier* was called to work and business by necessity, but he was also called into government by a sense of Zwinglian duty and plain good sense, both of which were remarkably lacking in some other nations. Surprisingly, the United States, with its gradually overwhelming federal government, far more powerful and pervasive than the Swiss, and the homogeneous, unitary British grew to be far more compartmentalized philosophically and socially than diverse Switzerland.

A serious dichotomy between business and government in Switzerland is almost unthinkable.

The actual structure of Swiss banking is fairly simple; it is not interesting to outsiders. The important thing about it is that until January 1, 1964, it remained remarkably free of any kind of governmental restriction. All banks were examined by the National Bank and all had to pass rigid liquidity and capital requirements. Outside of that, most of them were on their own.

The seven classes of Swiss banks are Cantonal Banks, Big Banks, Local Banks, Savings Banks, Loan Associations, Other Banks, and Private Banks.

Cantonal Banks developed from the desire of each canton to have its own "national bank." Some have private participation, but most are state-owned. They operate as commercial banks, but the bulk of their business is mortgage loans and cantonal financing. There were twenty-eight such banks in 1964, holding one third the admitted assets of all Swiss banks.

The Big Banks are members of the Cartel of Swiss Banks. This cartel, or trust, sets interest rates and general policies for all, but otherwise its members compete keenly. There were once eight Big Banks, but three, including the once-notorious Commercial Bank of Basel, fell "victim to changing times." The five Big Banks own one third the admitted assets of Swiss banking and dominate the commercial field.

Bank	Admitted Assets in 1963 (Sw. Fr.)
Swiss Credit Bank (Zurich)	7.910 billion
Union Bank of Switzerland (Zurich)	7.895 billion
Swiss Bank Corporation (Basel)	7.777 billion
People's Bank of Switzerland (Bern)	3.444 billion
Bank Leu & Company, Ltd. (Zurich)	668 million

All these banks began as individual institutions, then merged or bought up other banks. Bank Leu was originally private and began in 1755, the Bank Corporation as a merger between Basel and Zurich banks to finance the chemical industry.

The functions of Big Banks were always very broad. They accepted deposits and loaned money like any bank. But they also functioned like American stock-brokerage houses and financial underwriting institutions. They bought and sold all Swiss and foreign securities on their own and private account; they bought and sold foreign exchange. They provided investment counsel and tax advice. They underwrote Swiss and foreign companies and even governments. They formed corporations, trusts, and holding companies, and owned and managed great investment trusts, or mutual funds. Their ownership and influence ran and still runs deeply through Swiss utilities, insurance, mortgage loan, and real estate affairs.

The admitted assets of the three largest banks put them only in about fiftieth place in the international hierarchy of great banks —but their balance sheets do not reflect the enormous sums in currency, securities, and gold they hold or manage for private account. About one half of all Big Bank business is the management of gold, money, or stocks on private account.

Local Banks specialize in mortgage loans, or are what would be called in the United States "country banks." Again the classification is not precise: all Swiss banks deal in mortgages, and some

Local Banks are located in large cities and own assets larger than the smallest Big Banks. Some, like the Banca della Svizzera Italiana, are of international importance.

Savings Banks are what the name indicates, although again all Swiss banks accept some form of savings account. The true savings bank, however, is aimed at the small depositor. It pays less interest on accounts over 20,000 francs. Savings banks in Switzerland also deal in securities and mortgages. The most interesting thing about Swiss savings accounts is the fact that in 1964 there were almost 7 million savings books issued to the Swiss population of 5.8 millions. Swiss children are taught from birth to save money and not to ask why.

Loan Associations would be called System Raiffeissen in Germany, credit unions in the United States. These are organized on regional rather than fraternal or occupational lines; nearly every small community has one. This allows almost every spare franc, even in remote hamlets, to be put to work in the capitalist system. The money is used locally.

The Other Banks are simply banks established as Swiss corporations inside Switzerland under Swiss law but are owned by foreigners and do most of their business outside the Confederation. These are a recent innovation; they became numerous only after World War II. Twenty-eight were opened in Geneva between 1945 and 1964, and some, like the new Israeli-owned banks, have grown bigger than small Big Banks.

Private banks are the oldest of all, and in many ways the most interesting. Private banks are not incorporated; they are not required to publish balance sheets or any other figures. They have very little importance to the financial structure of Switzerland itself—but these banks were to acquire tremendous influence in the field of world finance. There were sixty of these banks in 1964.

Other than dealing in securities, Swiss banks have another feature which makes them different from American banks. Inside Switzerland the personal checking account is almost unknown. The Swiss developed a similar clearing system, but administer it through the federal post office. This is called the *giro account*. Most Swiss people and businesses maintain one; Swiss stores send money orders with their bills. The post office then transfers money from one giro account to another, acting exactly like a bank. If a payee or payor has no account, the post office accepts or delivers banknotes. Money can be sent anywhere in one day or less; the system works. Oddly, in the most overbanked nation on earth, the post office is also in what most foreigners would consider the banking business.

This Swiss system of banking resembled the German. Neither it nor the capitalist structure of which it was an essential part differed markedly from any European system until 1914.

The year 1914 was the turning point. For the enormous changes made elsewhere during and after the first world war never came about in Switzerland. The Swiss avoided the century's great trap and never left the Golden Age.

And this was when the world's money began to move to Switzerland.

THREE

The Plain
Brown Envelope

IN THE fall of 1920 a fleshy, well-dressed Swiss citizen of about thirty-five crossed the border from Basel into France. His name was Guizot, and he was an employee of the Basler Handelsbank, also known as the Banque Commerciale de Basle. M. Guizot carried many papers with him, but these were unintelligible and uninteresting to French customs officers. They were in no way negotiable and looked unimportant. Bankers were always crossing borders in Europe; Guizot was passed without incident and with due respect.

He rode the train to Paris, keeping to himself in the European manner, looking at the passing rich brown countryside and sometimes smoking a small Swiss cigar. He arrived at the Gare de l'Est and hired a taxi to drive him through a murky drizzle to a small, clean, respectable hotel, inexpensive and a great favorite among the Swiss.

Guizot ate a quiet, enormous dinner, which it was once again possible to find in Paris. Later, he visited a brothel which had been recommended to him in Basel. Guizot felt most expansive; Paris compared to Basel's chemical haze and stodgy habits, was a wonderful city, even in the rain.

The following morning M. Guizot was up early. He bought two dozen French postage stamps from the concierge and took them to his room. Here he carefully affixed them to a number of plain, unprinted manila envelopes he had brought in his brief case. Then, in neat black ink he addressed the envelopes. He did not consult a little black book, but wrote the names and addresses from memory. Ernst Guizot had a good memory and a good head for figures. In his business he had to.

When the envelopes were addressed and drying, he took various sheafs of papers, also penned in neat black ink, from his bag, scanned the lightly penciled digits in the corner of each page, then folded the papers and put them into the proper envelope. Some of the papers carried columns of figures, others seemed merely letters. There were no names on any of them until Guizot wrote them out.

When Guizot had finished sealing the last envelope, he took the lot to the nearest post and mailed them personally. Most of the letters went to Paris, a few to outlying provinces, some close to the Swiss border. No one handling or receiving them would have any indication that they were correspondence from a big Swiss bank.

There were other ways to have mail carried across the border in bulk and mailed with a French postmark and stamp. Guizot had handled these letters and statements for a few chosen customers because he was coming to Paris anyway. Guizot was a member of a new profession European authorities had not yet caught on to—the traveling Swiss bank agent.

Now, he used the antiquated telephone system of Paris to make his appointments. It was still rather revolutionary to telephone direct, but Guizot made contact quickly. He was generally expected. He was emphatically not welcome at several offices— but he was invited to visit certain homes in the evening, preferably after nine.

One of the men he called on was a manufacturer who had a beautiful home in the environs of Paris. This man was war-rich but worried. He took Guizot into his study, closed the door, and offered cigars, which the Swiss accepted.

Looking harassed, the Frenchman told Guizot he had to get his money out of France. The Socialists were taking over the country, and they were going to tax all prudent Frenchmen to death.

In his fluent but rather awful Basler French Guizot agreed with the prognosis. But he remarked that franc accounts were blocked, and it was rather difficult to transfer funds since the

war. Impatiently his host said he did not have currency in mind
—he wanted to get his capital out of France. He took Guizot to a
wall safe and showed him a great pile of securities and certificates. Some were worthless, some dubious, but others were very
valuable indeed. They would be negotiable anywhere in the
Western world short of a complete Bolshevik revolution—which
some men confidently expected in 1920.

The Frenchman, biting his lip, also mentioned he could put
his hands on some ten thousand gold napoleons. He would not
feel secure until all of this money was where no French government could reach it.

Guizot estimated rapidly; the securities were worth an estimated six or seven hundred thousand Swiss francs; the ten thousand gold coins came to two hundred thousand francs. It was all
told nearly a million Swiss francs, or about two hundred thousand dollars. Guizot became a bit excited. He liked substantial
deals.

He was quite aware that it was against the current laws of the
French Republic to remove either capital or gold. He was also
certain that his host had either come by the money somewhat
illegally or through the black market, or owed taxes on it. All
rich Frenchmen owed taxes. Neither idea bothered Ernst Guizot.
It was not against Swiss law to import gold or money, and in
Switzerland even the evasion of Swiss taxes was not a crime. The
Banque Commerciale de Basle was very circumspect; it never
broke any Swiss laws or allowed its representatives to do so. The
hasty, arbitrary, and often ill-advised laws of the panicky and
often inexperienced European governments bordering Switzerland were, of course, another matter.

The bank's main interest was in serving its clients.

Guizot agreed to assist his customer get his capital out of
France. He told the Frenchman that he could carry the securities
out himself. It would be disastrous to be caught—but there was
very little to fear on that score. Bank agents were careful. The
gold was a little more difficult to handle. It was too heavy to
carry, but Guizot said he would make certain arrangements with
Banque Commerciale representatives in France. There were ways
of getting it across the Rhine into Basel.

He accepted the sheaf of certificates and gave the Frenchman a short, cryptic receipt. The Frenchman hardly looked at it. One thing every Frenchman knew was that the banks of Switzerland, and their agents, were more trustworthy than any possible government of France. That night the rich Frenchman slept well, and he slept well for many years afterward.

Guizot left Paris two days later on the night train for Basel. He too slept well, dreaming of the bonus he was sure to make. Business, after what had been some quite hard years for Swiss bankers, was very good.

The great flood of gold to Switzerland began in 1920. It began because Europe changed and Switzerland did not.

European business, finance, and industry had everywhere been largely private concerns in 1914. But World War I was fought not only on the battlefields between battalions; entire nations were mobilized and engaged. This meant that business and industry were mobilized and spent as well as men. Modern war and modern industry and finance were inseparable, and by 1917 all national governments were waging industry as well as war.

The principal and enormous problem nineteenth-century economics faced in the twentieth century was not recurring cycles of boom and bust. The trouble was that truly free economics and free money could not be applied to nationalistic policies. The gold standard insured hard money, worth the same everywhere. But the gold standard was not only incompatible with wars, which required fantastic financing at a level unheard of before, but with policies of national self-sufficiency as well. The adherence to the gold standard, or any other standard of recognized value and limited supply, meant that a nation had a means of exchange with the world or it did not, depending on its luck, national resources, organization, and working habits. The British, becoming the first industrial and worldwide commercial nation, with products everyone needed, insisted upon and finally enforced the gold standard and free trade. It favored them. But when their trade was ruined and their resources shot up during the war and the policy worked against them, they were quick to desert both. It was always true that the true gold standard and the later dollar and pound reserve standard had real faults. There was never quite enough gold or dollars or reserve sterling to go around—there couldn't be, in human terms, if the standard was worth having. This meant some nations would always have the advantage of others; some would be living high and others pulling in their belts to get in shape to live high again. The so-called crisis in liquidity international bankers are always talking about is nothing different from the troubles many people go through each month when their bills come due. But an individual, hard up for cash, either quits spending or works to get more. He cannot borrow indefinitely or manipulate his credit.

But with increasing mass sovereignty or popular democracy in the Western world, twentieth-century politicians found this kind of discipline intolerable.

With gold, whether it is valued at $20, $35, or $300 an ounce, there is very little room to play around, and none at all in which to manipulate currency. In hard-currency systems governments tend to be bound by forces they cannot control, at least not quickly or by simple fiat. It is natural that both politicians and nationalist-minded economists shuddered away from this kind of straitjacket.

The prosecution of the Great War effectively bankrupted most European nations in real terms. They shot up their national treasuries and their natural resources. Both could be replaced in time—but the real tragedy of World War I was that it settled nothing. Pervading hostility, fear, and instability followed the war, not real peace. Most thinking men—though it was politically impractical to say so—were keenly aware that the European power struggle would be pursued again. No European nation had been economically self-sufficient in 1914. When borders, markets, and resources had been cut off by war, every nation suffered severely. In 1919, the leaders of most nations were determined not to be caught short again.

In this kind of atmosphere a return to the mercantilism of the seventeenth century was almost assured. Each government tried to keep its own gold and resources at home while trying to get all it could abroad. Ironically, the terrible war merely damaged the world business community. It was the new autarky and the new nationalist restrictions which stayed in force following the war that wrecked it. The gold standard, under which men and money and goods had moved freely without regard to *Weltpolitik* or national boundaries had had its limitations. But what replaced it was chaos.

Autarky, or complete national self-sufficiency, never made any *economic* sense. And industrial Europe was, and had to be, an economic community. There was no reason any European country needed to be self-sufficient, unless it was moved by ultra-rational ideas of grandeur or scheming to lay its neighbors by the heels, or afraid its neighbors were doing so.

Money had always been the lifeblood of world as well as national commerce. But where once German banks financed Swiss credit mobiliers and Scottish financiers helped build the American cattle industry, by 1920 every country put restrictions on the export of its capital. These were extremely short-sighted policies, made by men who did not really understand the nature of money. Capital markets became increasingly isolated from each other in an interdependent world. A great depression was virtually assured.

Switzerland had to trade to live, and it ran into bad times during and immediately after the war. Swiss banks had already grown too big to prosper financing the limited Swiss market alone. During the early part of the war, these banks made paper profits loaning hard currency abroad. Swiss banks had assets of $8 billion in 1918. But by 1920 the amount had shrunk by about half because foreign currencies were going bad everywhere.

The Big Banks, which were geared to do business outside of Switzerland were in serious trouble. But ironically, the processes which began about 1920 not only saved them but also made them some of the most important banks in the world.

The Swiss avoided the physical damages of the war as well as the war's social and ideological damages by staying neutral. Swiss government, Swiss institutions, Swiss impartial justice, Swiss honest administration, and Swiss money came through the war completely intact.

In 1920 the Swiss franc was still good as gold. In fact, the Swiss were still using gold. Swiss public finance was sound, while the economies of Germany, Austria, France, Italy, and most smaller nations descended into chaos. Separated from gold, the French franc, German mark, Austrian crown, and Italian lira became almost worthless overnight.

Switzerland was the only country in Europe which did not impose restrictions on foreign exchange. Capital, gold, and currencies were as free to move in or out as British capital, for example, had been in 1912.

The fact that Switzerland had been involved in no armed conflict for more than a hundred years and seemed likely never to be involved again suddenly took on new meaning. Switzerland had become an island of sanity and permanence in the midst of a European hurricane. Even if the Swiss had been the world's worst bankers, French, German, Austrian, Italian, and Bulgarian money would still have rushed to try to convert itself into solid Swiss francs. This was the most logical way to avoid the erosion of rampant inflation.

And there were other powerful and compelling reasons why Switzerland was suddenly attractive to everyone with money. The trouble with the business of controlled assets, blocked accounts, confiscatory taxation, artificial inflation, and ordered devaluation—all the manipulation of money in general—which all European governments tried after World War I was that men who either had capital or the ability to make it had no patience with such interference. Such manipulation either frightened them or outraged them.

Men who make money tend to regard it as theirs once made. They do not think of it as a friable commodity permitted them by government whim. Traditionally, governments printed or coined money and assured its authenticity and value. There, in classic economic theory, government control ended. And there many of Europe's rich thought it should end. It was perfectly normal that when weak, inexperienced, or socialistic regimes in postwar Europe panicked at the wreckage the war had caused and took steps to control or keep liquid capital at home, the immediate result was the flight of capital in all its forms to Switzerland.

European money soon proved that it had a life of its own, completely outside race, religion, political philosophy, or national citizenship. The sad corollary of the modern age was that thousands of wealthy families by 1920 trusted the Swiss government and the Swiss banks for more than they trusted their own, and with reason.

This was not "hot" or, for the most part, illegal money. It was the savings of the widows of German generals, French industrialists, Italian steel magnates, Austrian landowners. It is hard for Americans, whose twentieth-century inflations have been gradual and usually accompanied by a rise in real income and who never saw their currency turn to wallpaper overnight or their society collapse, to understand the fears which panicked almost all European rentiers and businessmen. Many families in many countries had thousands or hundreds of thousands of gold marks, lire, or francs in the bank in 1918. By 1920 their life savings were worthless.

A hundred French francs were not worth what one had been, and in Germany a billion new marks did not equal one former gold coin. In Austria one prominent family discovered its money holdings, once a million gold crowns, now would not buy a ride on the Vienna transit system.

Added to fears of inflation was the prevailing mood of fear. Society seemed to be dissolving, frightening everyone, but most of all the people who had been at the apex of it, the moneyed upper class. The Bolshevist revolution seemed destined to sweep all Europe; there were Communist regimes in Hungary and parts of Germany. The old Austrian empire, which had stabilized east Europe, was torn apart in economic ruin and massacre. There was political crisis in Italy and the beginning of a perennial mess in France. There were, everywhere, a great many new governments, some free, some tyrannical, all doing economically stupid things.

European families began to visit Switzerland and increasingly to try to take their money with them. Switzerland was a haven from war fear, revolution, confiscation, and inflation. It was the one place French auto makers, German chemical executives, and Italian counts, fearful of labor movements, inflation, or taxation, could all relax. It was not at all remarkable that so much of modern European literature in the 1920s—and again in the 1950s—reflected a Swiss setting.

Millions of dollars in currency, stock certificates, bonds, foreign exchange credits, and gold were smuggled into the Confederation. Europeans smuggled it through in lunch boxes on trains, slipped it through the mails, entered with negotiable paper sewn in their clothing. Women crossed the border in brassières padded with banknotes. Touring cars were packed with gold. Some of the flow was intercepted by alert border guards, but most of it got through.

Operating legally, virtually every German corporation doing business abroad opened a Swiss bank account and channeled most of its foreign exchange there. Every German company which could put its executive pension plan in the hands of a Swiss bank or trust. Workers were paid in inflated marks which had to be rushed to the store and spent the same day they were received, if they could be spent at all—but by using Swiss banks as cash boxes, German industries were able to build up impressive hard-currency credits outside Germany. This did two things: it got around Allied reparation demands, and it created a solid financial basis for German industry in spite of the social and political dissolution in Germany—which later served the German war machine very well.

The Swiss banks, which had been pinched for liquid funds in 1918, were suddenly faced with a whole new world. They had done nothing to make it—but it was a new world they faced not only bravely but ingeniously. Swiss hospitality was not strained.

Many outsiders have never understood the dominant Swiss outlook toward Europe and the world. Swiss have never felt bound in any way by dominant social or political trends outside the Confederation. In 1685, after the revocation of the Edict of Nantes, Swiss bankers helped French Huguenots flee France and bring their assets with them—in fact, the entire Protestant banking structure of France shifted from Paris to Geneva. In the eighteenth century it went back into France, operating out of Switzerland. The Swiss also gave refuge to French aristocrats fleeing the guillotine; many of them left money deposited in Geneva. In the nineteenth century the Swiss allowed almost anyone entry. Elizabeth, the Empress of Austria, and Luccheni, the anarchist who murdered her, both found asylum behind the Alps. Lenin left Switzerland on his famous train to Russia.

Swiss never saw any essential difference between Louis XIV's persecutions of Protestants and later persecutions of money. Both French religious persecution and modern taxation were enacted by a French national government backed by a French national consensus. The Swiss approved of neither. They regulated neither religion nor money—in fact, they considered a man's money as important, and as private, as his soul. They were not bound by any other nation's panics or prejudices toward either.

Now Swiss bankers rose to the occasion. The cartel of Big Banks soon opened new branches in every Swiss city. They furnished these with luxurious appointments and helpful, multilingual officers. They steeped themselves in the psychology, outlook, and idiosyncrasies of every Swiss neighbor. They were very much aware they were sitting on a gold mine.

The Swiss historian Gagliardi wrote sneeringly of early Zurich: "Anything circular circulated." This had always been true. When they handled the north-south European trade in the Middle Ages Swiss learned to discount, or respect, denare and ducats, scudi and soldi, grossi and gulden. Their descendants had no trouble finding the intricate ways between paper Reichsmarks and securities payable in sterling. It had never been, and never would be, illegal or even immoral to accept foreign cash—French cash, German cash, Protestant cash, Jewish cash—in the Confederation. Within a very short time the big Swiss banks were managing immense blocks of foreign securities out of their trust departments, and had on deposit more foreign exchange than they knew what to do with.

The unstable and panic-prone governments from which this capital was bleeding tried to stop it. They blocked accounts, froze exchange, and searched every citizen leaving for Switzerland. They passed laws making it illegal to own money outside the country or to do business with a Swiss bank.

But the Swiss banks, with ears and representatives to the ground all over Europe, stayed a step ahead. It was no longer necessary for clients to enter Switzerland at all; bank agents called at convenient times, like insurance salesmen. Swiss banks invented the numbered account, in which no names were involved, and began the use of the plain brown envelope. Swiss bank correspondence became as discreet as the traffic in manuals on married sex.

Mail to foreign customers was carried in bulk across borders and mailed with domestic stamps. Bank agents advised clients how to transfer assets to Switzerland, and delivered statements and other correspondence in person. A few banks, among them the Banque Commerciale de Basle, even helped clients smuggle gold or securities into Switzerland.

Few banks, however, would do anything illegal under Swiss or even international law. They did not call on criminals, but on doctors, lawyers, nobility, industrialists, and cabinet ministers, men of the highest social standing. Ironically, in Europe some of the biggest official complainers about Swiss bank practices have been Swiss bank customers who knew a good thing when they saw it. Money in Switzerland was *safe*.

Germany, France, and Italy all put severe diplomatic pressure on the government either to stop accepting deposits or to disclose deposits made. Both the Swiss federal and cantonal governments had the good sense not to interfere. Their attitude was that this was private enterprise; besides, in the Swiss view, what was illegal today in France might be tomorrow's honored practice. Banking itself had once been illegal, before the Reformation. Later, it was unlawful in much of Europe to be a Protestant or a Jew. The Swiss were doing nothing that had been illegal anywhere in 1913. It was not incumbent on Swiss authorities to enforce, or even assist the enforcement, of foreign laws as they changed from year to year.

The Swiss extended to foreigners' money exactly the same courtesy, privacy, and respect they had always shown for his individual religion. If other nations refused to recognize banking as a priestly calling or to admit that bankers' offices and vaults should have the same sanctity as the confessional, that was their problem.

Of course the fact that the Swiss needed outside capital to live and finance their own industry reinforced the Swiss attitude. The stream of gold and foreign credits, and the entire vast estates removed to Swiss control, gave Swiss banks both liquidity and power beyond Swiss borders. They meant rising gold balances in the Swiss National Bank, greater banking activity and therefore greater employment and a rising standard of Swiss living. Even the fact that rich people flocked into Switzerland to bank meant larger revenues for the government from resorts and hotel taxes. Everyone benefited.

The fact that the Swiss benefited from European instability

caused many outsiders to regard the Swiss attitude Olympian sophistry.

In 1924 Paul Jaberg, an officer of the Union Bank of Switzerland, said: "Today the major Swiss banks could not live on their Swiss business alone." He had a palliative for any Swiss citizen who tended to worry about this. "Swiss customers [of our banks] benefit by the high terms abroad, since if it were not for these the charges for domestic lending would have to be increased."

Jaberg, whose bank liked to refer to him in documents as a "simple Swiss," became Chairman of the Board, and in 1945 repeated: "No branch of industry or insurance can today contain itself to Switzerland alone, and what applies to those fields is even more true of banking."

For obvious reasons, no Swiss government was eager to interfere with the banking trade, and none did until January 1, 1964.

But critics of the Swiss attitude and actions always ran up against one prickly fact—not Swiss duplicity or sharp practices but foreign instability and fear made Swiss banks irresistibly attractive. If all European nations had continued to act after World War I exactly as they had before it, no money would have ever fled to Switzerland.

Once foreign money had surmounted the various problems inherent in getting inside the Confederation, whether it came from Spain or England, its owners faced one more problem.

Foreign depositors in the early years did not completely trust the Swiss government. Its honesty or efficient administration was never in question. But foreign customers were concerned that the Swiss might succumb to outside pressures and tax, regulate, or worst of all, publish names of foreign investors in the Confederation.

Any kind of publication of names or informing of outside governments which of their nationals had money in Swiss banks would have been catastrophic. Almost every French industrialist, German exporter, or Spanish cabinet minister who had money in a Swiss bank was in some way delinquent at home. Most of them had evaded some kind of tax, flaunted currency restrictions, or broken actual criminal codes by the removal of capital to Switzerland.

An answer to this problem was found in the Swiss holding company and the Swiss personal corporation, two things of flexibility and beauty in the financial world.

One chill spring day in the 1920s, in the canton of Zug, a careful country lawyer named Hermann Streuli-Schmitt was called to a conference in the private office of the managing director of the local branch of one of the three largest Swiss banks. After a few minutes spent following the normal course of *Schwyzerdutch* politeness, the manager, Herr Grubenmann, asked his secretary to prepare tea. Then, because they both were Swiss, the two men got down to business. Grubenmann passed over to Streuli-Schmitt several documents he had recently received from Zurich.

The lawyer was somewhat rumpled and untidily barbered compared to Grubenmann's tailored elegance. He was slightly fat, approaching late middle age, and had keen blue eyes and a precise mouth. He was completely undistinguished and unobtrusive, the kind of local businessman one sees in all the towns of central Europe. Few people in Switzerland, or even in the canton, had ever heard his name. But Streuli-Schmitt was one of a breed of modest, hard-working, scrupulously honest, and competent backwoods lawyers which had grown up in Switzerland—he was an expert on international corporate law and the corporate, tax, and civil codes of twenty-two cantons and four European nations. For several years Dr. Iur. Hermann Streuli-Schmitt had had no need to wear out his life on deeds and wills and mortage transfers.

Reading the papers, he began to nod rapidly. He knew the name at once. It was that of a well-known Italian corporation headquartered in Milan, owned in its entirety by a well-known Italian industrial family. Once, when he reached certain figures, he whistled almost soundlessly and looked up at Grubenmann. Herr Dr. Streuli-Schmitt was impressed.

The deal involved twenty million Swiss francs, or about five million dollars, a lot of money in 1925.

The papers, which had been referred to the local bank by the main office in Zurich, contained everything the lawyer needed: name, nature, and the desires of his client, whom he would never see. There had been some instructions to a Swiss bank agent a few weeks before. The bank agent had assured the client it was all feasible, and that his bank, in return for certain charges and the privilege of managing the estate at the regular custodial fees, would take care of everything.

In Zurich the men whose job it was to take care of things knew immediately which canton to approach. Just as some American states, notably Delaware and New Jersey—deliberately wrote their corporate codes to attract industry during the formative period of American capitalism, certain cantons in Switzerland had begun competing with one another to obtain as many firms incorporated under their statutes as possible. The issuance of cantonal corporate charters—there were no federal charters —was good business. The fees were modest, but enough of them solved many of the problems of raising cantonal revenue.

The fees of country lawyers were modest, too—infinitesimal compared to London or New York.

"We have great confidence in your ability to handle this matter," Grubenmann told the lawyer.

"*Merci vielmals,*" Streuli-Schmitt said politely. "It's an interesting, but still a routine, case."

He arranged to have another conference with Grubenmann in a week.

Streuli-Schmitt, attending to the business himself, then drew up a proposed charter for a cantonal corporation which he called Ajax, A.G. When he was satisfied with the last penstrokes of this, he attacked the formation of a second, personal corporation. He made sure both charters were quite legal and very tight.

When he came back to see Grubenmann again he was ready to discuss names. Corporations needed directors, and Swiss corporations had to have Swiss directors, certain qualifying Swiss stockholders, and above all, a Swiss address. The address was no problem; in drawing the papers Streuli-Schmitt had used his own. Legal residence was thus acquired. Getting the directors was no greater problem. Streuli-Schmitt proposed that his clerk be one and asked Grubenmann to name two employees of the bank, which Grubenmann was glad to do. Two other dummy directors were found from a list of men also glad to serve. The title *Herr Direktor* was legal; the new officers could put it on their cards, perhaps sometimes collect directors' fees. More important, it gave a man prestige to be a director in several important international corporations. Hardly anyone approached the right way ever turned the opportunity down. Quite a few citizens of Zug were already directors in important-sounding firms, not one of which did any business inside the Confederation.

The stockholding arrangements were equally neat and careful. Each director had to own stock, of course, and would be allowed to purchase the legally required amount at a very reasonable price. But the voting arrangements had been carefully drawn, with weighted voting shares. The dummy directors would never control Ajax, A.G.

More important, Ajax would be capitalized by shares of the second corporation, which was organized as a personal holding company. This was perfectly proper under cantonal law. This capitalization meant that control of Ajax was vested in the second corporation.

Streuli-Schmitt went over this carefully with Herr Grubenmann, who was impressed.

"The problem," the lawyer instructed, "is not here. It is to slip the transfer of assets from Milan."

Grubenmann, who had been in contact with Zurich, which had been in close contact with another legal firm with close connections in Italy, stated he was assured that this was taken care of.

"Splendid!" Streuli-Schmitt said, and went off to get the charter. He had no trouble at all with the cantonal authorities; he had even used his law-office address as the legal residence of a corporation eight or ten times before. The cantonal clerks did not have to look it up. Besides, they knew Herr Dr. Iur. Streuli-Schmitt and respected his standing. He had never been accused of doing anything shady or illegal in his life.

For the payment of a few francs' fee, the charter was quickly granted for both corporations. They were both in business, *echt-Schwyz.*

Now, Grubenmann and the lawyer conferred again. It was a matter of timing. There was a brief discussion of strategy, a couple of long-distance telephone calls—then, quietly, legally, and completely anonymously the ownership of a huge Italian fortune changed hands. It was transferred from an Italian corporation owned by an Italian family to a Swiss corporation with a diverse group of stockholders who purchased the shares with money pledged by another Swiss corporation. On paper, Ajax, A.G., was now worth five million dollars.

The assets themselves did not even have to leave Italy. They could remain where they were—but under international law they were now completely Swiss, protected by Swiss and international law. Ajax's papers could be produced at any time to prove the fact.

What need never be produced publicly was another set of papers wrapped in a neat blue ribbon which now rested in a safety-deposit box of one of the biggest Swiss banks. These certificates proved that Ajax belonged in its entirety to a company which was owned by an Italian family which had never left Milan. The family would never pay a cent on it in Italian domestic taxes, and Ajax's assets would be transferred in time to joint beneficiaries, undiminished in any way through inheritance tax or death duties.

In this same way, with certain quirks and variations, Dr. Streuli-Schmitt in all transferred some fourteen major Italian, German, or French family fortunes. He never became really famous except in a few circles, but he grew quite rich. The foreign nations involved sometimes investigated, and sometimes brought action. It was possible in some countries such as Spain to put the owner of a "Swiss corporation" in jail—but not to recover the assets legally without the greatest uproar and trouble in the courts of international corporate law.

None of this process would have been possible without the services of a good Swiss bank. It was vital that important papers remain in Swiss bank vaults and that essential conferences take place there, making both privileged information. No Swiss bank was required to reveal names, amounts, shares, or anything which had transpired to anyone, including the Swiss government. Not even the federal government could open a Swiss bank box. Long before 1920, and again in 1930, the Swiss Supreme Court ruled that it was not only immaterial whether any specific agreement concerning secrecy was made between bank and client but that in all cases unless authorized specifically by the customer the bank was *under obligation* to preserve secrecy. Swiss law recognized secrecy as an unwritten but essential feature of the bank-customer relationship years before such ideas were codified into statutes.

Actually, the civil codes of almost all advanced countries read the same, with one enormous exception: the "independent" judiciaries of France, Great Britain, Sweden, Germany, or the United States never dared to include the government itself under the ban of bank secrecy.

This banning of information to the Swiss government, federal or cantonal, was disturbing to many foreigners, especially foreign bureaucrats trying to follow the muddy trail of lost assets in the maze of Swiss corporate law. Many governments felt this interpretation of law was aimed at foreign governments. But it grew out of divergent Swiss definitions of public and private property and the powers of government itself.

In Switzerland there was no such thing as "national" or "public" money. Once money was printed, the Swiss authorities retained no umbilical cord to it. Private property in Switzerland was private property, and there was no theoretical or any other kind of nonsense about an individual holding it or using it for the good of the nation as a whole or for the general welfare. Developing neither an aristocracy nor a genuine national bureaucracy, Switzerland was never subject to such pressures. A sense of nationhood, common destiny, or blood and soil has to precede such ideas, and Switzerland had none of them except on local levels. There were no Rockefeller Foundations or Huntington Libraries in Switzerland, which many Swiss themselves have regretted. But on the other hand there were never anything approaching Huntingtons or Rockefellers, only small and bigger bourgeoisie. There were many millionaires—the banking families of Bär, Vontobel, Pictet, Bordier, Mirabaud are examples. But hardly anyone thought, or thinks, of them as millionaires unless they are trying to borrow money at the family banks.

It is hard to get excited about—or do away with—millionaires who live and act no different from anyone else. This was always a form of protective coloration which French, Italian, and other millionaires have found more distasteful than any danger of control or confiscation they might face.

No Swiss would ever dream that the "nation" or the "people"

had any rights or privileges where M. Pictet's or Herr Vontobel's money is concerned—an attitude Swiss law generously extended to foreigners: the purest example of true democracy and tolerance available.

There were times Herr Dr. Streuli-Schmitt and his kind formed as many as a dozen different corporations, each capitalizing the other, in a kind of circle. This made the trail of assets escaping foreign countries impossible to follow. The path led to the Kreditanstalt, the Union Bank, or the Bank Corporation, and there it stopped. When foreign powers requested Swiss courts to investigate they received polite replies, but never any action.

Under its own rulings, the Supreme Court itself could not force its way into a Swiss bank box—except in certain criminal cases in which definite Swiss law had been broken.

Honest men like Dr. Streuli-Schmitt hardly ever broke Swiss laws. They made the Swiss bank-personal corporation symbiosis a thing of international beauty to important European families. The lawyers were busily employed, and made money. The banks charged steep custodial fees, and made profits from estate management. The customers usually saved so much escaping taxes or other harassment they would have gladly paid double for the service.

The Swiss corporation, canton to canton, was also flexible. It could come into being easily and likewise go out of existence without a whimper. In one interesting case, lawyers in Vaud transferred an enormous block of assets from Italian to Swiss control five minutes after a cantonal charter was granted. These Swiss assets were then moved immediately to a Netherlands corporation; from there, no one except the owner and his lawyers know. The Swiss company was liquidated over satisfied smiles and a good cigar all around. Its total life had been just over one hour. But in that time it had handled more net worth than most corporations see in a generation and it was retired sentimentally and with honor.

This kind of business, and the urgent necessity for managing and reinvesting huge chunks of capital abroad, forced the major banks to open foreign branches. The Swiss Bank Corporation began to maintain offices in both New York and London, not to receive money but to get rid of it. The Swiss Credit Bank, Alfred

Escher's giant, even opened its own securities and brokerage house in Wall Street.

Between 1920 and 1939, when war came again and sterling became inconvertible, a dozen London brokerage firms grew fat on the orders of millions of pounds by the local office of the Union Bank of Switzerland. The brokers happily filling these buy orders knew that not more than 2 or 3 per cent of the amounts could have been initiated by or for bona-fide Swiss citizens, based on experience before the war. This was a revelation not of Swiss financial chicanery, but of the appalling financial, moral, and social chaos into which between-wars Europe fell.

For the same reasons, the same kind of thing followed World War II—only by then Switzerland was doing business not just with Europe but with most of the world. The Swiss banks soon had competitors. People always try to imitate a good thing and bankers are no exception. Banks on the Swiss order soon sprouted in Beirut, Lebanon; in the Bahamas, Montevideo, and in other less important places. All of these offered sharp international lawyers, financial freedom, and advertised bank secrecy. Lebanon went so far as to study and deliberately copy Swiss banking law and to institute the numbered account. They had some success; admittedly, Near Eastern traders have always been sharp with money. But that, ironically, was one of their problems.

The Beirut, Bahaman, and Montevideo banks grew up exotically. They were hothouse corporate refuges and storage banks. They did not grow out of a solid banking philosophy and national ethic like Swiss institutions. Some who organized and ran them more often loved than respected money, and they would take any kind of money. Men with that attitude are sometimes not above sharping the customer as well as the tax collector, and most of the substantial rich people of the world realized this. Unlike the Swiss, the other exotic banks did not stem from a national consensus, nor did they have an honest, hard-working, stable society behind them. Most of them have always been on shaky ground, and the customers know it.

Much of the money they get is money the Swiss will not take, for various reasons.

Swiss banks and Swiss banking practices were completely formed by 1912. What came after that were only minor alterations or inventions to meet changing world conditions. Before World War I very little foreign money entered Switzerland except to be invested in Swiss industries or on loan. If money has flooded the Confederation since, if thousands of men and women in many countries are willing to smuggle, evade, and break their own laws to transfer their money into Swiss hands, the entire answer cannot be found in the numbered account or the plain brown envelope. It lies in social attitudes and sicknesses in the world at large.

Very little of the money that fled to Switzerland was ever criminal money; it was frightened capital. More modern governments than not have proved themselves inept at management, shaky from war, or thoroughly untrustworthy in tax or social policy. In a world without war, with limited and reasonable taxation even of the rich, with liberal economic policies, with stable politics and sound money—in short, if all the world were like Switzerland—many Swiss citizens who came to sit behind impressive bank desks might have gone on making cheese.

Cloaks without Daggers

GEORG HANNES THOMAE in 1934 was a member of the German *Geheime Staats Polizei*—a Gestapo agent. He had the methodical mind and grubby past which characterized most early Nazis. His middle-class family had apprenticed him to a bank and tried to make a gentleman of him. But Thomae hated the atmosphere of a bank—the icy formality, the stiffness of the starch-collared Herr Direktor, the whole damned system. He ceased being regularly employed sometime in 1928 and took up what the Germans call *bummeln*—bumming around. By 1929 he had company.

It was logical that he join the Nazi Party. It gave Georg Thomae both goals and purpose, and the Nazis hated the whole system, too. Thomae could be a charming fellow when he tried, and he had a keen mind in some channels which held his interest. He got into Party undercover work, and when Hitler arrived at power he came into the Secret Police through the back door—political favoritism.

In January 1934 Agent Thomae was given a special assignment in the Confederation of Switzerland. He was picked for one reason: he had worked in a bank.

Adolf Hitler was contemptuous of both "Aryan" and "non-Aryan" banking and business. The symbiosis between German capital and Swiss banks had long irritated him, and in 1933 the Nazi regime ordered every German citizen with foreign holdings to declare them. The penalty for noncompliance was death. The Nazis never really trusted any German with outside connections, and even the commercial partnership with Switzerland, into which politics never entered, was suspect.

German industry and Swiss industry had grown up together in the nineteenth century; Germany was always Switzerland's biggest customer, and German coal, iron, and wheat supplied Switzerland's lack of all three. German capitalization of Swiss banks was common, and Swiss bank loans to German industry were the norm. Several of the largest Swiss banks made most of their investment in Germany. Between Zurich and Basel and German capitalists there had grown up almost the same kind of relationship that developed between the bankers of Geneva and the wealthy families of France after the French Revolution. Politics, religion, or nationalism never entered the picture. Just as French bishops advised French Roman Catholics to bank with the Calvinists of Geneva, Germans of various political persuasions had delicate arrangements with the democratic bankers of Switzerland. It was a purely business relationship, nothing else. For this reason, both the French-Swiss and German-Swiss symbiosis survived wars, revolutions, and calamities virtually unchanged.

But it was a relationship Hitler was determined to control. He also had a brooding suspicion that thousands of Jews and others were getting their money out of Germany through Swiss banks. Georg Thomae was called to Berlin and briefed on the situation. His superiors told him that while thousands of loyal German citizens and corporations had declared their holdings abroad, there were "certain Jews and other swine masquerading as Germans" who concealed them. Thomae was given a list of names of people who were suspected of having secret deposits in Swiss banks. His job was to enter Switzerland and ferret these accounts out.

With all the power and resources of the German state behind him, Thomae acquired a new passport, received orders placing him on detached service, and was tendered a fat expense account —every pfennig of which he must strictly account for. One reason so much is known of the internal operations of the Nazi regime was due to the German compulsion to keep tidy records. Thomae bought tourist clothes and took the night train to Zurich.

Here he established residence, posing as a vacationing rentier, a man with a private income. There were approximately two hundred thousand German nationals living or working in the Confederation at this time, and he was completely unnoticeable. He opened accounts in several large Swiss banks, making it a point to meet as many minor employees as he could. In a very short time he had formed a close friendship with one lonely young counter clerk from Basel and a sleeping relationship with a *fräulein* in another bank. In the accepted Swiss manner, however, the girl continued to work and earn her own way.

Swiss working in a foreign canton were always vulnerable to foreign friendships. Baslers or others employed in Zurich revealed themselves as outsiders by their accent and were regarded coolly. Swiss adults are normally cold and reserved with each other and uncomfortable in the normal relationships which spring up naturally and easily elsewhere. Oddly enough, however, this reserve seldom applies to genuine foreigners from outside the Confederation. Swiss frequently formed more lasting friendships with foreigners than with their own kind.

Georg Thomae entered the patterns of Zurich life—sober, hard-working weeks punctuated by an almost cataclysmic breaking of tension on the rip-roaring Saturday nights—which are a feature of all deeply puritanical societies. Thomae ate, sang, and got roaring drunk with his new friends. He had fun, and he picked up an enormous amount of information as to how Swiss banks operated, both in bed and over café tables.

Gestapo agent Thomae became one of the first men ever to crack the secrets of a Swiss bank.

One method he used was tried and true: simple bribery. As he enlarged his acquaintance among bank employees, he found here and there the right man. He was in a position to offer more money than some hard-pressed young family men could turn down for what seemed rather innocuous information. For a few thousand Swiss francs Thomae gained the name of more than one German depositor at the Kreditanstalt.

The other thing Thomae did had a touch of genius. He began to approach banks with a respectable sum of money, trying to deposit it to the account of certain names. In 1934 neither Switzerland nor its banks were prepared for the Gestapo agent and his bag of tricks. Everything depended upon the immediate judgment of counter clerks and minor bank officials when confronted with this situation—and some, tragically, guessed wrong.

In one case Thomae entered the Swiss Bank Corporation and tried to deposit a sum of 20,000 francs—$5000—in the name of Anton Fabricius of Hannover, Germany. The young teller he approached was nonplused at first, then made his first mistake. The teller failed to call the Zurich police.

He turned Thomae over to an under official. Thomae, utterly plausible, completely charming, and looking like anything but a Nazi agent, explained to this official that he had carried the money over the border for Herr Fabricius. It was obviously impossible for Fabricius to leave Germany, or to have any direct contact with the bank, considering the present state of affairs. The bank officer did not quite know what to do, and now a second and fatal mistake was made. The officer conferred with another official who, unaware of what was going on, established the fact that Anton Fabricius of Hannover did have a Bank Corporation account. It no longer mattered whether the bank now accepted the money or turned it back—Agent Thomae had been told all he needed to know.

The bank would never have given any information in the face of a direct demand; no Swiss bank would. But the situation for German depositors in Swiss banks—of which there were thousands—had become chaotic. Every means of electronic communication between Switzerland and Germany and the mails were watched. Communication had broken down. In this situation, it was not always possible for banks to follow strictly customers' instructions made years before. Almost all German customers were now using third parties or Swiss agents to handle their business. Thomae's offered deposit might very well have been a legitimate one, and it might seriously inconvenience Fabricius if the bank failed to take it. The bank took the money.

That night Thomae communicated with Germany, and two hours later Anton Fabricius of Hannover disappeared. Three days later a complicated cable was received at the Bank Corporation, requesting in proper form the repatriation of all Fabricius' money. German records do not reveal what was done to the Hannover businessman to extract the necessary information.

Thomae had hit pay dirt. The gambit was passed on to other Gestapo agents in Switzerland, who used it before the banks could understand what was happening. It did not usually work; most Swiss bankers were inherently cautious. But the trick gained the Gestapo needed information in a dozen cases. Many Germans with Swiss accounts were smoked out.

The kind of information Thomae got would have been useless to any government in a country with impartial justice. But German justice was already corrupt in treason cases, and completely arbitrary. German justice was able to use threats, night arrests, and torture on men who had, or were strongly suspected of having, Swiss accounts. Under torture or the threat of it, Germans with money in Swiss banks revealed bank names, amounts, numbers, cable codes, everything.

If the depositor was prominent or highly placed, and some were, a mere visit from the Gestapo usually was enough to bring him around. He confessed and got off lightly, with a fine or confiscation. If the depositor were a Jew, or more stubborn, he was in serious trouble. The least he faced was a concentration camp. Three Germans whose accounts were ferreted out by the Gestapo were brought to public trial in Germany, and executed.

As the domestic German authorities began to use the data fed them by Thomae and his colleagues, Swiss banks began to be deluged with frantic phone calls from Germany. Depositors called and begged for money to be sent home. Often a German official was listening in, or sitting in the same room. German agents turned up at banks armed with passbooks, codes, and account numbers, demanding money. Wires arrived from Germany, properly coded, requesting the return of all deposits or their payment to certain accounts known to belong to the German government. In other cases the depositor himself entered the bank, where he was sometimes well known, with a bulky stranger in tow, and asked to close out his account.

But the banks reacted swiftly to the situation. The big banks refused to surrender any funds requested by phone or wire until discreet inquiries were made through the Swiss consulates or Swiss business firms in Germany. If a wire arrived from a depositor who had recently dropped out of sight or who could not be contacted in person by a trusted representative, the banks refused to forward money. The Swiss Banker's Association made it a firm rule that no depositor was to be given his money, or have business discussed with him, in the presence of an unknown third party. Swiss banks, by agreement among themselves, neither paid nor acknowledged communications until bank officers had assured themselves that no pressure was placed against the depositor.

The moral pressures against Swiss bankers meanwhile were terrible. They were being asked to play God. If a wire arrived at a bank, properly coded and sent, anything they did could be a disaster to their depositor. A mere reply could sentence him to death under Nazi law; the forwarding of money was prima facie evidence of guilt. But the withholding of funds—legitimately the depositor's—on the grounds that he was being forced to ask for them also could result in hideous and protracted torture of the customer involved. Finally, the Banker's Association issued instructions that in any case of doubt the bank should do nothing and admit nothing.

The banks could not prevent what was happening to their depositors in Germany—but they could prevent the Nazis from ever getting their hands on the money.

The execution of the three Germans in 1934 brought the whole desperate game to light. What had been a secret, underground struggle between banks, depositors, and Gestapo entered the Swiss newspapers. Swiss public opinion was outraged. There were heated speeches in the Nationalrat. The Swiss police began to crack down.

Georg Hannes Thomae had outlived his usefulness in Zurich. He returned home, was later employed in France, then in Denmark. He survived the war, and after 1950 was able to re-enter government service. In his own mind he had never done anything wrong, since it had all been done in the service of his country.

Georg Thomae and others like him succeeded in getting many Germans jailed, tortured, or killed, and more than a few Swiss citizens, caught succumbing to bribes, disgraced. But more important, Thomae was to have a profound and lasting effect on the institution of Swiss banking. His actions produced the Banking Code of 1934.

The reaction of the Swiss government to the Gestapo's determined efforts to crack Swiss banks was swift, sure, and in character. The National Council ratified a new Swiss banking code, which for the first time in history put the principle of bank secrecy under the official protection of the penal law.

Bank secrecy had been general practice in Switzerland, and in 1930 the Swiss Supreme Court had upheld it in a celebrated case. The idea of bank secrecy was vital to Swiss international banking after 1920, and every bank executive and Nationalrat member knew it. But the civil code itself was hardly proof against the kind of pressures and stratagems the German Gestapo employed. Thomae and his kind hit Swiss banking where it hurt. He had damaged the trust and confidence which had always existed between bank and foreign depositor.

Not only Germans, but other foreign customers as well no longer felt safe. What the Gestapo had done was always possible for the French Second Bureau, the Italian Secret Service, or even British Intelligence or the American Treasury to imitate. In an angry, furious session, the Swiss Nationalrat gave all Swiss and foreign bank customers the protection of Swiss criminal law.

Codifying bank secrecy into law served three immediate purposes. First, it put Switzerland on record before the world and its governments: foreign deposits would be protected. Second, it protected the banker, and gave him a legal as well as moral code to stand by: he was ordered not to talk, and punished if he did. Third, and too many outsiders overlooked this, the codification of bank secrecy satisfied many fears among native Swiss about their own government as well. Few Swiss ever really trusted the bureaucrats they employed in Bern.

Few people are aware that the principle of bank secrecy is far older in law and custom than nonsecrecy. In fact, the opening of private financial affairs to outsiders is a recent innovation, an outgrowth of the modern "national" society. Bank secrecy was written into Roman law as the *actio iniuriarum,* and in Germanic civil law as the *lex Visigothorum,* or law of the Visigoths. In northern Italy, where banking revived in the late Middle Ages, bank secrecy was provided for among early statutes. Among these were the rules of the Bank of St. Ambrosius of Milan, which stipulated severe punishment for anyone in the bank who revealed information about clients without the client's permission. Up through the eighteenth century it was taken for granted everywhere in Europe that no bank would willingly reveal any pertinent information concerning clients to anyone. More than one banker was put to the torture by petty despots to gain such information.

A Swiss Master of Arts thesis once summed up the subject concisely: "The entire concept is based on the ethical law of secrecy for all those professions where facts and conditions of a personal nature must be disclosed by the client. It is obvious that the banker is more or less in the same position as a lawyer, doctor, or clergyman, each of which must guard the personal interests of the client. Much of the confidence which a customer must place in his banker, as regards his business and finance, is based on the knowledge that the facts related to the banker will be kept in strict confidence."

The law courts of a number of European nations have ruled that secrecy is an essential part of the banker-client relationship. German and American law have generally considered any breach of confidence actionable at civil law; the customer can, and has, recovered damages. Any US banker can be sued for being too talkative, although American society does not take financial privacy seriously.

In the United States any recognized department store or business credit manager can obtain information from banks, including whether or not a customer has an account, how long he has had it, and even its approximate size. American bankers are quite talkative in terms of "low six figures" or "high three figures." This is shocking to many Europeans. But it is only a reflection of the necessities of the American system of widespread personal consumer credit and of the American disregard for privacy in general. Any American citizen, for about two hundred dollars, can discover almost anything he wants to know about any other: past history, credit rating, record of convictions or arrests, drinking habits, current income, and sex life.

But while Europeans profess to be horrified by this, most Europeans—and all Swiss—live in much smaller countries, with relatively immobile populations. For the purposes of society, most Europeans know their customers or employees well enough, sometimes for generations. Europeans who sneer at the American unconcern for privacy, or express horror at the fact most Americans will willingly tell anyone how much they make, do not enjoy quite so much privacy as they fondly hope. People in Europe watch their neighbors much more closely than in America.

This very watchfulness, probably, is what has ingrained such deep desires for legal privacy among the Swiss.

Bank secrecy, then, was historic and recognized in every country's legal code. But the enormous difference between ordinary bank secrecy and the Swiss code promulgated in 1934 was that Swiss secrecy was written into *penal* law, and it was *specifically and deliberately applied to all government*.

Article 47 of the Code stated:

Whosoever as agent, official, employee of a bank, or as accountant or accountant's assistant, or as a member of the Banking Commission, or as a clerk or employee of its secretariat, violates the duty of absolute silence in respect to a professional secret, or whosoever induces or attempts to induce others to do so, will be punished with a fine of up to 20,000 francs, or with imprisonment of up to six months or both. If such an act is due to negligence, the penalty shall be a fine not exceeding 10,000 francs.

The federal law fixed penalties for a crime it did not attempt to define. However, the cantonal codes of every Swiss state defined the banking secret comprehensively, and in legal terms the passage of the federal law made all cantonal laws *leges perfectae*, iron-clad.

All banking information was defined as "trade secrets" and the definition was upheld by the courts. Trade secrets also included virtually any commercial, financial, or industrial fact which its owner considers worth keeping from public knowledge. The Swiss Criminal Code, under Article 273, was framed as follows:

Whosoever explores trade secrets in order to make them accessible to foreign governments or foreign enterprises or foreign organizations or their agents, and whosoever makes such trade secrets accessible to foreign governments or organizations or private enterprises or to agents thereof, will be punished by imprisonment....

The Swiss had had enough of Gestapo men and foreign snoopers. Under Article 47, and particularly Article 273, a number of Swiss citizens were jailed after 1934. No small number of foreigners have been expelled.

A bank manager could be jailed for merely revealing the existence of a bank account without its owner's permission. The law would apply if the person he revealed it to was the President of the Confederation.

No Swiss government has tried to repeal this law or to exempt agencies of the Swiss federal or cantonal governments from it. Any such attempt would be blocked in the Nationalrat by the banking interests. Even more decisively, Swiss polls have shown that even if the Nationalrat passed such a bill, it would be overwhelmingly overturned by national referendum. Every Swiss citizen has at least one bank or savings account, and whether he has in it a hundred francs or a hundred million he considers this none of the government's business. Genuine democracy obviously has definite disadvantages for bureaucratic government that representative government does not pose.

Bank secrecy was codified because of Nazi pressures, but it grew out of Swiss nature. It is always possible for a Swiss to authorize his bank to give out certain information to the tax collector, but few prefer to do so.

This universal application of the banking secret has been widely criticized in other nations, paticularly those whose governments have sought information on their own subjects. Some of these fail to understand that the Swiss authorities are powerless to change it even if they want to.

Bank secrecy has to yield to the provisions of Swiss criminal law, however. Courts have held it may not be invoked to conceal stolen money or crimes committed under Swiss criminal codes. In such cases, banks must comply with Swiss court orders to produce information. But here arises a matter which has been the extreme irritation and cause of bad feeling between the Swiss and many other governments: *tax matters, in Switzerland, while they come under the civil or criminal law in theory in most cantons are handled as administrative details between the citizen and state.*

Swiss democracy, which trusts every able-bodied male with a modern machine gun or Army rifle in his kitchen cabinet, trusts him to pay his taxes too.

Since domestic tax questions are not normally prosecuted under the criminal or civil law, the Swiss Supreme Court ruled that no Swiss court may assist any foreign authority in any proceeding based on revenue, tax, foreign exchange, or political offenses.

This is perfectly logical. No American court would convict, or assist in any way in the conviction, of a Russian citizen who had committed no crime in the United States but had broken Soviet law. What causes the trouble is that foreign governments, including the American, are often highly impatient with the peculiarities of Swiss domestic law.

In actual practice, foreign governments frequently request pertinent information from Swiss authorities, especially in the case of criminal proceedings where the offense is contrary to both Swiss and the foreign law. Bank robbery or swindling is such a case. Informed of a bank robbery or the suspected smuggling of stolen money into Switzerland, Swiss authorities have always cooperated. But the information requested must have no connection in any way with foreign fiscal or tax matters.

For example, in the 1950s some of the proceeds from a Canadian bank robbery found their way to Switzerland. Informed of the serial numbers, Swiss police notified all banks. When some of the bills turned up, the bank involved notified the police, who informed Interpol. From this cooperation the Swiss depositor was traced, and eventually the crime was solved and the robbers brought to justice. The Swiss were delighted to assist. Bank robbery in Switzerland is understandably a very serious offense.

But when the United States government slapped a tax lien on all of convicted swindler Billie Sol Estes' missing assets, it automatically removed any hope of Swiss cooperation in finding them. Some seven million dollars of the Texas promoter's alleged profits were never found. There is strong suspicion that some of them were whisked away to Swiss banks. But the imposition of the tax lien made the whole thing a fiscal or revenue matter under Swiss law, and placed it under the Swiss banking secret.

The Swiss banking code has other interesting quirks. A husband can request data on his wife and get it if any community property is concerned. But no wife, for any reason, can get such information on her husband without his express consent. This is another law the Swiss, who have never allowed women to vote, have no intention of changing.

In the case of Swiss bankruptcy proceedings, or even foreign bankruptcy cases, cantonal courts are empowered to seek certain information. But this information, once obtained, is for the use of the court. No third parties, even lawyers, are allowed to see it. In the case of a legal judgment rendered against a bank depositor, the law has not been clearly settled. It has not been definitely established whether a bank should reveal the existence of an account, let alone surrender the money. In Switzerland some bank-ruptcy cases have been dragging on for years.

In inheritance matters, if all of the heirs of an estate request a banker to reveal information he must do so. But if even one re-fuses to request the information, he must not. This has caused a great deal of trouble over the years, and much publicity, as heirs —most of whom do not know exactly who is an heir and who is not—carry cases through cantonal courts and make a great public clamor over being cheated.

Finally, the courts have taken the position that in any case where a banker has any doubt as to what he should do, he should refuse any and all information. Even in criminal cases under Swiss law, involving Swiss citizens, it is difficult to open a Swiss bank vault or get a Swiss bank statement. These involve local courts, and some cases have been known to take more than eight years. If a good Swiss lawyer opposes the obtaining of such infor-mation, it is usually far harder to get into a Swiss bank box than it was for the state of California to execute Caryl Chessman. The Swiss themselves prefer not to discuss this feature with outsiders, and in defense of bank secrecy in general are frequently hypo-critical about it.

The truth is, no Swiss likes the idea of anyone, for any reason, having access to his bank account, and this prejudice permeates all Swiss society.

The vogue of numbered or anonymous accounts illustrates this. Swiss bankers invented the numbered account as a means of giving a client a little more privacy, particularly a client in a for-eign country where Swiss banking was a crime. Instead of his name, a four-digit number was assigned to his records; instead of José López of Barcelona or Alfonse Schlumberger of Paris he be-came Number 4040. Of course the bank had to know the custom-er's name and address, but this information was limited to two, or at most three, bank officers. It was closely guarded from clerks and other employees of the bank. In this sense there was no such thing as a truly "anonymous" account, but this system greatly reduced the chances of either bribed or accidental betrayal of a foreign customer by a bank employee. The number appeared on all statements and balance sheets, and this number, written out in script, became the customer's banking signature. He used it for both correspondence and checks. It was often elaborated on for use in cables from overseas, so that even the number itself would be unidentifiable to anyone without the proper code.

When agent Thomae and other Gestapo men became active in Switzerland the numbered account began to have obvious attractions. The German government was not the only one which sent agents into Switzerland, nor was Thomae the last to use the attempted-deposit gambit. In 1958, an attaché of the Communist Romanian delegation was expelled from Switzerland. He had a list of suspected Romanian depositors and was making the round of big Swiss banks.

The fact that only top officers knew the name corresponding to a numbered account made it immensely more difficult for foreign agents or tax men to get any information at all, while the law of 1934 made them subject to immediate arrest. The numbered-accounts appeal to foreigners was immediate—but it became a great favorite in Switzerland for Swiss customers, too.

Swiss banks did not escape the consequences of the worldwide depression of 1929. Swiss banks were in much better shape and much better managed than either American or German—the Swiss were conservative, even toward booms—and only approximately sixty of the four hundred Swiss banks got into difficulties or failed.

But even this relatively small number of bank failures caused severe hardship in the Confederation, and it produced a sense of shock much more profound than in America, where banks had always failed. Swiss public opinion was aroused, and for the first time a law was passed requiring banks to be audited. Typically, the Swiss did not involve any agency of government in this. The law, passed in 1933, required bank audits by independent accountants outside the banking structure, who then turned the results over to the National Bank and Banking Commission for any indicated action. These agencies had the power to discipline or close any bank which was out of line, even though they were private bodies.

But the very people who were concerned and demanded bank audits for their own protection were also very reluctant to allow any parties outside banks to have access to privileged information.

Swiss courts had already ruled that the banking structure had to observe bank secrecy, but these decisions did not apply to outside accountants. There was no law or recognized rule which prevented an accountant from passing on certain information he had observed. In Swiss eyes this was unthinkable. The numbered account came into great favor. Changing names to numbers meant that Swiss auditors never had any idea whose accounts they were checking. Later, in 1934, the banking secret was extended to include accountants and their staffs, but the vogue for numbered accounts continued.

No other feature has brought more calumny or criticism on Swiss banking than the banking secret and the use of the numbered account. But the claim that both were devised to shield foreign criminals and foreign shenanigans is nonsense. The Swiss themselves would continue both practices if every dollar in outside money were withdrawn. Both practices are not unknown elsewhere.

The banking secret is written into a number of legal codes in Europe and in the Near East, although none makes its breach a criminal offense, and none applies it to government. Banks in Canada offer numbered accounts, as do those in Lebanon. West German banks have offered the service for years, particularly to customers coming from East Germany. And a number of American-owned banks abroad, including the Banque de Depots in Geneva and the Bank of America branch in Beirut, have regularly advertised the service of *comptes numerotés* in newspapers. Austrian banks allow savings accounts to be held under numbers instead of names.

The Swiss have always felt that financial privacy falls within the privileges of personal liberty. One enormous social benefit of bank privacy is that there is virtually no hoarded money in Switzerland, as there is in Germany and France. All Swiss cash goes into banks, and from the banks is put to work in the Swiss economy. Almost all Swiss citizens approve of the fact that no one is ever going to get into a Swiss bank box without a court order, and that court orders are almost impossible to get. They really cannot help it if thousands of foreigners find the idea irresistibly attractive, too.

The system does have faults. It does permit some foreigners to evade legitimate taxes at home and some to escape the consequences of bankruptcy actions. The trail of a number of shady transactions ends at a Swiss bank.

But the Swiss are not going to change the system, and that is that.

A Squeeze
by Any
Other Name

SWISS BANK secrecy faced its severest test not from the methods of the Gestapo but from the demands of the United States government at the close of World War II.

Hitler was not the only one worried about German depositors in Switzerland. For a number of years the matter deeply concerned the American Secretary of the Treasury, Henry Morgenthau. The question of Jewish and other German assets in Swiss banks got the Swiss people into trouble with the Nazi regime. Conversely, the problem of German assets in the same banks almost caused a war with Washington.

The friction started during 1940, when President Roosevelt and his Cabinet realized that war with Nazi Germany was inevitable and began to make plans for it. Many Americans were never aware that the United States entered the war after Pearl Harbor well on the way to mobilization, with strategic plans for economic and financial warfare well drawn. The vision of the Roosevelt administration in 1940 and 1941 tended to exceed its political courage in the face of American reluctance to become involved. No American during this period was more active in or more responsible for US preparedness than Henry Morgenthau. Morgenthau not only organized the Treasury to finance the war, but for some months actually operated the US War Department, with FDR's concurrence and without general public knowledge.

Even before US entry, Morgenthau saw that one way to hurt the Nazi war effort was by restricting and blocking its trading overseas. In 1940, German trade passed mainly through the neutral nations of Sweden and Switzerland. The Germans could not trade directly outside Europe; the British blockade swept German commerce off the seas. Both Sweden and the Confederation sold finished goods to the Germans, and the Swedes provided iron ores which the Swiss made into precision timing devices for the German war machine. No one, not even the worst Swissophobe, suggested that the Swiss people approved of the Nazi ideology any more than the Swedes did. But these nations were Germany's traditional and natural trading partners, and Switzerland, particularly, had to have German wheat and coal to live. No industrial society can survive without coal, petroleum, and metals; in 1938 Switzerland had imported 167,000 carloads of food. This had to continue during the war.

The Swiss mobilized, manned the mountain passes, and kept one quarter of their men of military age on active duty for years. These measures may have prevented a German invasion; it is known that German contingency plans existed to cross the Rhine at Basel. But Switzerland also had to live by the rule of *primum vivere:* the first duty of any society is to survive. Swiss survival meant selling the Nazis electric power, precision tools from Winterthur, and timing devices from Geneva in return for food and fuel. The Swiss did not profit on the trade. It was impossible to do business with Hitler on any but his terms, and after the fall of France Germans set the prices and squeezed everything they could.

Morgenthau and the American Treasury understood the necessity of the Swiss trade with Germany. But what concerned American officialdom was that the trust and cartel network of Germany and Switzerland stretched across the border. There were Swiss-owned German companies, and there were German-owned Swiss corporations. First to avoid rampant inflation, and afterward to avoid anti-German sentiment in many parts of the world, many German firms had taken to channeling most of their foreign operations through the Swiss.

It was almost impossible for German enemies to discover the extent of this symbiosis and, because of the nature of Swiss corporate law, to ascertain if certain international companies were

Nazi-owned or genuinely Swiss. Swiss lawyers, operating behind bank secrecy, had made any unraveling extremely difficult.

Some wartime operations were quite involved. For example, a Swiss firm got a license from the German government to penetrate the German counterblockade of Britain. This firm sold the British machine tools which were badly needed by the British aircraft industry in 1940. But the Swiss demanded refined copper in payment, and got it. The copper ended up in Germany, where it was needed almost as badly as the British RAF needed Spitfires.

Allied businessmen and governments were deeply concerned that many Swiss businessmen were working for, or fronting for, the Nazi war industries.

To combat this, on April 10, 1940, President Roosevelt signed Executive Order 8389, which empowered the Treasury Department to control both German nationals and their property within the United States, and to regulate also any non-Germans suspected of acting for German interests. The Treasury immediately drew up a blacklist of world firms doing business with Germany, and it began secret moves to block the funds of all potentially hostile countries which had been sent to New York for safekeeping.

At the beginning of the war in 1939, the United States as well as Switzerland attracted a great deal of frightened capital. Much of this even came from such Axis nations as Japan.

The old Trading with the Enemy Act, still on the books from World War I, was revised and amended to fit the modern situation. And since a number of Swiss firms were on the blacklist, American Treasury agents were ordered to investigate their activities inside the United States.

There was no bank secrecy in America. Treasury men could easily demand to see banks' records, and they began to go through banks in the New York area looking for foreign money. This tipped their hand immediately. Seeing what was in the wind, the German, Japanese, and Italian governments withdrew all liquid capital from the United States long before Washington could move to freeze or block it.

The Swiss made no move to pull assets back from America after the investigations began. They saw no reason to. There had always been the highest regard and friendship between the two nations; they were both democratic, and even their national outlooks were much alike. The Swiss did not anticipate trouble with the United States. In fact, after the fall of France the Swiss government transferred its gold reserves to New York to avoid their capture in the event of a Nazi invasion. Also, the war completely hampered most Swiss banking operations around the world. To continue those with Africa and South America—where Swiss money had gone in significant amounts—the big Swiss banks began a large-scale inside-the-US business for the first time. In 1941 New York was a far easier place to operate out of than Basel or Bern.

With these bank branches the Swiss sent in large amounts of money. The under-officials in the Treasury tended to regard this as suspicious.

Many Washington bureaus of the 1940s were salted with men who were actively suspicious if not openly hostile toward most big business, foreign or domestic. Many of these men looked on the Swiss corporate structure, with its holding companies, lack of antitrust laws, and complete freedom from government regulation with distaste, or even considered it immoral. From this general bias came a feeling—which soon turned into an *idée fixe*—that Nazis and Nazi collaboraters were using Swiss banks to cover up their global operations. As these men saw it, Switzerland and its banks provided a beautiful setup: the Swiss had a good image and could cover nicely for the more unsavory Nazi one. If Germany won the war, the Swiss would then merely return assets and money to Germany. If Germany lost, the assets were safe in neutral hands, even though Germans would continue to own them.

There was a certain amount of this going on—but it never approached the extent which Treasury officials darkly imagined. Ironically enough, the problem was Nazi officialdom. The Nazis were always almost pathologically suspicious of their own people's dealings through Swiss banks or Swiss fronts, and permitted it to take place only under limited circumstances. The Nazi mentality was even more anti-free-enterprise than some of the sentiment in Washington.

Swiss banks would have been immensely useful to German businesses during the war if the Nazi regime would have let German businessmen use them. But only men with political influence, or industrial giants like I. G. Farben, could get carte blanche to do so, and then only in exceptional cases.

The thing American officials forgot was that once a German national got money or assets channeled into Switzerland they were completely beyond the reach of the Nazis, too.

By 1941, however, Swiss bank branches operating in New York held about a billion dollars in dollar accounts. Treasury men entered these banks and requested records on deposits, transactions, withdrawals, and the like, trying to trace the actual ownership of certain Swiss money. Operating under US law, these banks had to turn such records over the same as American banks.

But the Treasury men were uniformly frustrated in uncovering any real information. Every Swiss dollar held in American branches or affiliates, and every Swiss stock certificate or bar of gold, was not held in the name of individuals but for the account of banks in Basel, Bern, Zurich, or Geneva. Swiss banks always operated this way. Every Swiss stock purchase in Wall Street, for example, was made in the name of one of the three largest Swiss banks, never in the name of the actual customer for whom the bank was buying. Therefore the T-men hit a stone wall.

Further inquiries to the banks themselves in Switzerland established the fact that no Swiss bank would cooperate with American authorities in revealing names of depositors or principals. The Swiss banking code of 1934 expressly forbade it. But this answer was not acceptable to the Treasury, which tried to get the Swiss government to take action and open the banks. When the Swiss indignantly refused to amend their established laws, the Treasury retaliated by freezing or blocking all Swiss assets in the United States on June 14, 1941.

This was six months before the United States entered the war.

That the act was punitive as well as precautionary was evident from the fact that the Swiss national gold reserves, whose ownership was never in question, were also frozen by the order.

The Swiss government immediately protested. The Swiss stated that this was no way for one friendly government to treat another. The protest was rejected on Morgenthau's strong recommendation.

The freeze did not stop the Swiss from doing business in the

United States, but it did prevent them from transferring any assets abroad or repatriating any dollars in the United States to Switzerland. It hampered their operations and made New York a much less effective base than they had hoped. But the Swiss banks and affiliates stayed in business in New York, and actually, over the next four years, piled up large profits.

During 1941, 1942, and right up to the end of the war, US Treasury agents kept trying to penetrate the secrets of the Swiss banks and uncover the German trade. They were completely unsuccessful in getting any evidence which would stand up in an impartial court. Meanwhile, the general blacklist of suspected firms was put into effect, barring them from trading or operating anywhere within the Allied world. This blacklist did damage German attempts to trade. It also damaged the Swiss exporters, including some who were completely innocent of any Nazi connections.

As the war progressed toward conclusion the American economic planners grew more and more concerned with the danger that Nazi interests and assets would be protected behind "Swiss" ownership. The experience of the 1920s was disturbing. Then, millions of dollars in German assets had been transferred to Swiss corporations or Swiss banks, avoiding both reparations and the disastrous German inflation. This not only kept a firm German capital base intact and kept German industry in business but also provided the foreign exchange which Hitler needed when the Nazi came to power. The German industrialists and others who had transferred their money into Swiss banks had not been thinking of a greater German Reich at the time. They had been merely protecting their own interests—but this, in time, had served the interests of the German war machine. Because German industry, during a time of German collapse and Allied occupation, had been able to operate out of a foreign hard-currency area it had been able to rebuild, profit, and finally to furnish the material basis for the Nazi conquest of Europe. American planners were determined never to let this happen again.

But what worried them was the question of how many German patents, licenses, and processes—more important to modern war than mere money—would prove to be officially "Swiss" when the war ended, and thus removed from any kind of Allied control or seizure. The discoveries of new German techniques in metallurgy and jet aircraft, and the possible German work with nuclear energy, frightened both London and Washington. If certain German patents and secret techniques, as well as huge sums of German gold, escaped into Switzerland, what happened after World War I—when a prostrate Germany recovered sooner than the apparent victors—might happen again.

By 1945, all Allied planners had made up their minds that there was to be *no* German recovery after the war. This was, of course, a short-sighted view, but understandable during a war in which fifty million people died and at a time when Nazi crimes all over Europe were coming to light.

A decision was made inside the US Treasury Department that all German assets, public and private, must be seized on Germany's defeat *no matter where they might be located*. This was more drastic than it might seem. It meant that the United States, with the President's backing, intended to seize the property of German nationals in Stockholm, Basel, or even Buenos Aires if it could be located. The purpose officially stated was not vengeance or even reparations, but to assure that any possible base for a resurgence of Nazism was destroyed.

This scheme violated international law. It should also be noted that Henry Morgenthau, whose immense services to the United States during the war cannot be denigrated, also helped concoct and got Roosevelt to initial the morally satisfying but intellectually idiotic Morgenthau Plan for an agricultural Germany. This kind of thinking permeated certain quarters of American government. While the Morgenthau Plan was never implemented, and was by 1948 officially repudiated, the fact that President Roosevelt initialed and approved it at Quebec in 1943 was to hamper, confuse, and delay American policy in central Europe for many years.

The Swiss government never had any argument with the Allies over the purpose behind American plans for German assets. The Nazis had put severe pressures on the Swiss; they had threatened them with invasion for three years and had taken great advantage of them economically when Nazi power surrounded the entire Swiss enclave. German actions in Europe had turned the entire Swiss population against the Nazis. Pro-German sentiment was scarce in democratic Switzerland, and no Allied government believed that the Swiss Republic was in any way corrupt or would willingly serve as a Nazi tool. The last thing any Swiss businessman or banker wanted was a Nazi revival following the war. Nothing could be worse for European commerce and industry, which the Swiss, as a trading nation, wanted to have restored to an even keel.

But a combination of several factors embittered Swiss-American relations for many years. One was the attitude of the US Treasury when it began to discuss the question of German assets with the Swiss. Some Treasury men were rude, suspicious, adamant in their stands, self-righteous, and many snorted at Swiss pretensions to neutrality, hitting the sorest of all Swiss nerves. The Swiss expected, and got, bureaucratic arrogance from the Nazis. But they never expected it from a nation they greatly admired, the greatest democracy on earth.

Swiss banking, like all Swiss trade and industry, suffered enormous disruption during the war. Banks which were not completely on a sound footing in 1939 did not survive. The depression, however, had been a blessing in disguise. The bad times which followed 1929 threw Swiss banks back on their own resources, for the immense flood of foreign money slowed. The fact that sixty banks got into trouble made all banks put their houses in order, and they were operating on an austere, sound, and practical basis long before German armies entered Poland.

World War II took no one in the business community by surprise. Therefore there were no immediate large withdrawals from Swiss banks by either Swiss or foreign depositors. In fact, most foreigners preferred to leave their money where it was, and by 1940 Swiss bank deposits had again begun to rise. The balance sheets of the Swiss Credit Bank rose by 500 million francs between 1939 and 1945. Some of this was the result of inevitable wartime inflation, but most of it represented a real gain. This money was useful to the Swiss government since by 1944, because of Swiss mobilization and defense measures, claims of national, cantonal, and local governments comprised 32 per cent of the Kreditanstalt's total balance sheet. The war measures were not financed without inroads into Switzerland's stored capital.

But unlike most other nations, the business-dominated Swiss quickly paid off all war debts after 1945.

Foreign exchange, a big business with Swiss banks, was stifled after 1939. The trade in foreign securities dried up, and the exchange and securities business of the banks collapsed. Portuguese money was about the only commodity tradable after 1939, and it had a limited appeal. With wartime taxes and inflation, costs rose while income fell. Foreign assets and all dollar accounts were blocked, and Swiss overseas affiliates were isolated.

All these factors, plus the disruption of the tourist trade, income from foreign investment, and import business, cramped all Swiss banks. Regulations restricted them. The managing director of the Union Bank of Switzerland spoke for all Swiss bankers when he told a 1944 board meeting:

"Almost every banking transaction carried out today is much more complicated than formerly ... we need only cast our minds back to the happy days when all currencies could be freely dealt in, when there were no clearing offices, when coupons could be paid and bonds redeemed without an affidavit and without any deduction, and when the triumvirate of the Coupon, Defense and Anticipatory Taxes, as well as taxes on bank interest payments and deposit books, the Bill Stamp Duty and the Stock Exchange Turnover Tax were totally unknown." He also complained because the banks were required to withhold all these taxes, costing millions of francs in labor, without any extra compensation.

War brought controls, even in Switzerland. But the enormous difference between the Confederation and the outside world was that again Swiss society survived intact and unchanged. In 1945, the whole nation only wanted to get back to the business interrupted in 1939. Switzerland was almost unique at the end of the European fighting. It maintained full conscription and certain forms of price control, with food rationing, but immediately took off all other business controls. This was in great contrast with the United States, which had also come through the war physically untouched, but not completely unchanged.

All was not dark. In 1938 the major Swiss banks combined profits amounted to 25.5 million francs. They were still 21.2 million in 1944. There was still a lot of money inside Switzerland.

And Swiss banks were among the leading creditors of the world. They not only had money, but they were owed vastly more money.

While Washington officials were brooding about possible Nazi capital in Switzerland, some Swiss banks were in grave trouble because of the flow of Swiss capital toward Germany. The flow had begun in the 1920s, as part of a general trend in which the United States also participated. The close connection between Swiss and German banks, insurance companies, and industries since the nineteenth century meant that much Swiss capital went back to Germany during the era of the Weimar Republic. Neither the Nazi regime nor the war liquidated all of it; in fact, Swiss credits grew.

But with the imminent defeat of Germany, Swiss banks were holding a very empty bag. The Banque Commerciale de Basle, or Basler Handelsbank, which got into trouble in 1935 over the size of its German claims, went into federal Swiss receivership in 1945. Its German paper was worthless, and it was liquidated. Another big bank, the Federal Bank in Zurich, had large German interests and was also facing ruin. Shareholders began to demand an investigation. The directors of the Federal Bank agreed to a quick merger with the strong Union Bank of Switzerland in the interests of Swiss banking; the German assets of the Federal Bank were segregated upon merger. A third Big Bank, Leu & Company, was also shaky, for the same reasons as the other two. But Leu issued a statement that all its German liabilities were covered by Swiss assets, and Leu survived. Meanwhile, the federal government and the National Bank kept their hands off Swiss banks unless one actually failed—on the sacred Swiss principle that banks were still private businesses.

At the beginning of 1945 Swiss banks and businesses held approximately a billion francs in German credits, which were rapidly turning into liabilities. Another five billion in banking and industrial investment was in the process of being written off. Most of the billion francs in credits were for Swiss goods which had been shipped to Germany during the war, and for which the Germans had not paid. In addition to these staggering financial losses, some four thousand Swiss businessmen doing business with or in Germany were wiped out.

But this was the price of doing international business. The Swiss had lost before, and would again.

Their major worries, as the end of the war grew clearly visible in 1944, were the blocked dollar accounts in New York, which the banks badly needed, and the still-enforced blacklist, which included thirteen hundred Swiss firms—every firm which had ever sold any kind of goods to Germany. The Swiss banks particularly needed to free the frozen dollar assets in New York to rebuild their world business.

The Swiss Banker's Association held a high-level conference and agreed to a compromise with the Americans. The banks would report to the US government which of the accounts in New York were honest Swiss and which were held for Germans or other foreigners. The Banker's Association of Basel—from which most German accounts stemmed—was appointed the certifying agency. No Swiss bank had ever done this kind of thing before, and it was done with distaste. The top bankers regarded it as a major concession. They could do it without contravening the banking secret since the accounts were in the United States.

Armed with this concession, a delegation of the Banker's Association flew to Washington in December 1944. They hoped this would lead to a thaw of Swiss assets in New York.

They met, however, a very cool reception, and one problem no one in Switzerland had anticipated. The Treasury Department of the United States refused to meet with them in any kind of plenary session because all of the delegation were private Swiss citizens and not officials. To begin with, Treasury officials were huffy about meeting with a bunch of private bankers. They neither understood nor approved of the banking-government relationship in Switzerland.

The Treasury informed the delegation that the United States would not be a party to any deal to which Swiss private bankers were a party. They did not trust the Swiss bankers at all. The Treasury would accept certification of the dollar assets only by the Swiss federal government, or at the very least by the National Bank, which had official status.

Government officials in the United States would sit down only with government officials in Switzerland, and the bankers themselves were to have no right to sit in on any meeting.

There was a certain logic to the US position, certainly. But whether the Treasury understood the fact or not, it was asking that Swiss federal law be set aside. The federal government in Bern had no right to request any kind of information on depositors from any bank. And if the National Bank obtained this kind of data, it would be liable to both criminal and civil action in each Swiss canton. The directors of the National Bank angrily refused to consider entering the controversy. The federal Finance Department—which in the Confederation had limited powers—declined to touch the matter for the same reasons.

Several messages were passed, which reaffirmed the determination of the Treasury to deal with Swiss bureaucrats or no one and which re-emphasized the position of Swiss bureaucracy that it had no powers to deal with the situation. Both sides suggested the other was being unreasonable. The Americans grew more certain that the Swiss were trying to conceal something. It was difficult for Americans, who had given government broad powers over money and private business, to accept the view that to allow the Swiss government to enter a Swiss bank was much the same as letting FBI men sit in on confessionals in America.

However, a number of influential Swiss bankers proposed that the Confederation would have to make some concessions. The Swiss were aware that the United States was now not just a distant great power, but the dominant power in Europe. In this sense, the United States had replaced the Germans. In banks and in the Nationalrat it was agreed that the banking secret could be breached in some respects due to the unusual circumstances. Public—and not just banking—opinion in Switzerland was strongly against any breaking of bank secrecy. But public opinion was also behind the American purpose, which was final destruction of the Nazi empire.

Already, however, there was a deep divergence which few people recognized. The Swiss had never been emotionally committed in the war beyond a sincere determination to defend their homeland and keep out of trouble. They tended to look upon the events of World War II with a historic perspective gained over the ages. Hitler, like Rudolf of Habsburg, Napoleon, and all the other would-be conquerors would pass. France after Napoleon continued to be Switzerland's biggest bank depositor. The Swiss quite logically saw that Germany, after Hitler, would continue to be Switzerland's biggest customer for industrial products. They took an economic, rather than a political or ultrarational, view at the very time when economic views of history had reached their nadir in the West.

The Swiss felt the war ended the day the shooting ceased, and they wanted to forget the whole thing and get back to business. They were ready to do business with Germany—and even, after staggering losses, invest in Germany again. They considered Germany the economic and industrial hub of Europe, and realized it would not go away.

But a vastly different viewpoint pervaded Allied thought. There was a powerful sentiment either to destroy Germany or keep it as a sort of European economic pesthole, based completely on nonbusiness reasons. The case of I. G. Farben shares a short time after the fall of Germany was an illustration. Germans and some Swiss began buying these securities up. Immediately the US Military Government in Germany banned all such trading. A high US official in Germany stated flatly: "Germans are betting that Farben will come back. We are going to prove it won't."

Just what would be proved by this, unfortunately, had never been thought out on American government levels. General Lucius Clay, diplomat Robert Murphy, and other Americans eventually ended this kind of economic nonsense, but these men were not in command of the situation in 1945.

However, when the United States sent negotiator Lauchlin Currie, who was known as President Roosevelt's "economic blitzman," to Bern in February 1945, the Swiss federal government agreed:

1. To freeze all German assets, including those of Swiss holding companies, in Switzerland.

2. To impound all German bank balances.

3. To halt all war commerce with Germany at once.

4. To cut off all electric current furnished Germans.

5. To stop all shipments of German gold into Switzerland.

6. To certify the blocked accounts in New York with the Swiss Clearing Office, an agency which had supervised all Swiss-German trade during the war, and which had semiofficial status.

7. To begin a census of all German assets in Switzerland by the same organization.

This seemed a reasonable compromise, and here the matter

rested while American, Russian, and British armies overran Germany in the spring of 1945. No one really expected any further trouble.

But within days after the fighting ended in Germany, a large team of US Treasury agents was flown to Europe. This team went into action in Germany as soon as the American military had taken over. The US Treasury Department has never been accused of being corrupt; it was one of the least corrupt such agencies in the world. Its people were never dishonest. But in 1945 a number of the heads of the Department were somewhat over-zealous. Secretary Morgenthau and his second-echelon officials had never lost their notion that vast amounts of German money had escaped into Switzerland. The idea certainly leaked to agents as they were briefed to go into Germany; they were told that such assets existed, and it was their job to find them. Also, and while this was understandable and completely appropriate to Treasury operations inside the USA, a rather unfortunate "cops-and-robbers" attitude pervaded T-man ranks. They were the cops; therefore the other side had to be the robbers. This was very different from the relationship between Swiss citizens and their government.

Arriving in Germany, the T-men had a wonderfully free hand. In the chaos of the collapse they were bound only by their judgment. There were no real rules or hampering restrictions. They could acquire evidence in any practical way, and they could force German bankers to open any and all records. As such records were rather scattered, the agents relied in many cases on oral German statements. In the spring and summer of 1945 a great many German bankers were eager, if not desperate, to please. Understandably, while a great deal of solid evidence of German assets in Switzerland was compiled, a high proportion of innuendo, rumor, and hearsay, from bank underlings and others, went into the record and was accepted as fact.

In the aftermath of the war and in the atmosphere of 1945 there was a tendency to look on all Swiss-German transactions as shady, even those which took place in 1925.

Further, all Treasury evidence compiled in Germany was placed under a strict classification of secrecy. Written or oral, it was never divulged to anyone outside the Treasury. If the Swiss attitude was that private business was strictly private and public business public, the Washington attitude seemed completely the reverse.

In the fall of 1945, the Swiss Clearing Office confidently announced that a survey of all German assets in Switzerland showed the amount to be $250 million. The Treasury immediately rebutted this. Its own evidence, it announced, showed the amount to be three times this figure. The Treasury, in diplomatic language, had called the Swiss Clearing Office liars.

Here a little love was lost.

What happened was that both sides were giving themselves the benefit of the doubt. The Swiss Clearing Office bent over backwards not to breach bank secrecy; it did not go into banks except in rare cases without bankers' permission. Swiss banks were queried as to how much they held in German assets. If the bank gave the Clearing Office a list, then bank boxes were opened. If the bank stated no such deposits existed, the Office took its word. If the T-men were accepting some imaginative and arbitrary evidence, the Swiss unquestionably overlooked some solid evidence on their side of the border.

The Swiss now asked to see the Treasury evidence to assist their investigation. The US officials stated all its sources were confidential. They hinted that US officers should be permitted to enter Switzerland, and this blew both Bern and the Nationalrat sky high.

There were outside pressures on both governments, in fact. A number of influential Americans hoped to get control of profitable Swiss business held by Swiss-German corporations, particularly in the lucrative patent field. If these firms could be tainted with the Nazi brush, the job would be relatively simple. Other Allied businessmen hoped to rid themselves of painful competiton by putting some Swiss businesses with international connections out of action. Both hard Swiss francs and valuable licenses were at stake in a very hungry marketplace.

But at the same time quite a few Swiss bankers and industrialists with longstanding German connections—which had nothing to do with politics—put pressure on Bern for their own reasons. The Zurich-Basel industrial-financial complex controlled the Nationalrat in practice, and business-banker influence was profound in Swiss government. Banks which had profits at stake found it easy to become vehement defending Swiss principles.

Unfortunately, in October 1945 an ill-considered and badly worded decree of the Four Power Allied Control Council which had been set up in Berlin further inflamed Swiss opinion. This was the infamous Public Law Number 5—a decree which gave the Council's External Control Commission ownership not only of all German governmental assets outside of Germany proper, but control of all such property belonging to private German citizens as well.

In their determination to destroy any possible base for Nazi resurgence, the Four Power Council was in effect contravening international law. Governmental property outside Germany could be construed to come under the Council's jurisdiction, since the occupying powers had replaced the Nazi regime and were now the recognized rulers of Germany. The private property of private German citizens could not be.

The ukase was also, though not intended as such, a direct attack on both Swiss domestic law and Swiss sovereignty.

The Geneva newspaper *La Suisse* trumpeted: *We are being asked to comply with the provisions of a foreign military decree signed by four generals. Great as is our admiration for these Allied soldiers, we are not prepared to abdicate our sovereignty just to please them.* Speeches in the Nationalrat showed that the Swiss people felt that both Swiss honor and Swiss neutrality were at stake, just as they had been when the Nazis tried to crack Swiss banks.

Swiss jurists informed the Nationalrat to stand fast. They said no international tribunal would uphold the provisions of Public Law Number 5. And while no Allied government publicly admitted the fact at the time, both British and American jurists gave exactly the same opinion to their governments. It was no accident that the Swiss demanded, and the Allies refused, to place the matter before the newly formed World Court.

International law, like the Swiss Constitution, was codified before the age of total war and total government. The Hague Conventions clearly made private property rights predominant, a rule more often than not honored in the breach by all warring governments. Meanwhile, an article in the Swiss constitution made the confiscation of private property illegal, short of full and prior compensation, *for any reason.*

The Swiss showed themselves uncommitted to any defense of Nazi loot. A great part of the French gold reserves, looted from the French National Bank, had been transferred to Switzerland. The Swiss were willing to give these back. The some $9 million stashed away in Swiss banks by Reichmarshal Hermann Goering was also recoverable. The same applied to art objects and other private property stolen by the Nazis and sold through Switzerland. Goering had sent a number of paintings to an art dealer in Lausanne, who sold them. Without publicity, the Swiss police smoked these out, traced the paintings down, confiscated them, and returned them to the countries from which they had been taken. A number of Swiss citizens who had purchased stolen property suffered great loss, since they were not compensated.

Money or gold shipped into Switzerland by Nazi bigwigs as a hedge against their personal future was not the source of the dispute. The Swiss were not compelled under international law to return this, unless the connection between gold bullion owned by Goering or Goering's agents in Switzerland and gold looted in Poland or taken from the mouths of Auschwitz victims could be proved. But the Swiss were ready to hand over this kind of asset where it could be found. Actually, there was relatively little of this kind of German loot.

German policy had not been lenient toward letting gold escape into Switzerland. It was always treason under Nazi law for any German to sneak assets into Switzerland, and the German government only tried to do this in the last days of the war. In Nazi eyes, even among high officials, the transfer of money to the Confederation indicated a treasonous lack of faith in the thousand-year Reich. Few Nazis dared to try.

The real trouble centered around assets which the Swiss now claimed should be taken over by the Confederation in payment for goods shipped to Germany and never paid for, assets private citizens and bankers had smuggled into the cantons when they read the handwriting on the wall, and German property and money which had been held in Switzerland since before Hitler and never declared.

The Swiss also claimed that certain assets held by a "Swiss

corporation" under Swiss cantonal law were not German property, even though the principal beneficiary was a German national. Here international law upheld them.

The Swiss, who had defended these holdings against all kinds
of Nazi pressures and espionage, had no intention of submitting
to new American pressures. Certain of these holdings and the
manner of their transfer to Switzerland were illegal under the
laws of Allied nations, including the United States. But they were
perfectly valid under Swiss law, and here was where the question
of Swiss sovereignty was put at stake. As an independent nation,
Switzerland was not required to uphold either American corporate law or dominant American ideas of morality.

The Swiss government agreed in 1945 to seize all German
holdings, even private holdings, under American pressure. But
Bern insisted that any moneys so seized be used first to pay Swiss
banks and businesses for unpaid shipments to Germany during
the war. This compromise obviously satisfied the fear of Nazi resurgence argument. But the Allies rejected it—in August 1945 an
Allied commission had committed all German assets in Switzerland to be used for the rehabilitation of German victims.

The Swiss became stubborn. They considered they had made
enough concessions; they had already offered the Allies more than
they had made available either to Hitler or Napoleon. Traditionally, Switzerland was a refuge of money, any kind of money. By
empowering the Clearing Office to open bank boxes in certain
cases, they had already raised their hackles—and not just bankers'
hackles. The Swiss felt that one of their greatest industries,
banking, which was built upon the absolute confidence between
banker and foreign depositor, was imperiled. If the Swiss government gave in to American pressure in 1945, the next year it might
be British, French, or even Latin American pressures. The
world was filled with governments eager and demanding to see
what was in Swiss safety-deposit boxes.

Washington officials remained stubborn, too. In December
1945 eighteen Allied nations met in Paris to decide the question of
German reparations. A great deal more intelligence was brought to
the problem this time than had been done in 1919. The Paris conference agreed that any seized German assets were to be used
solely for general European rehabilitation, and a portion was even

set aside to assist German refugees expelled from eastern Europe. The eighteen nations—Russia did not participate—set up quotas for each country according to its damages and its needs. Under the agreement the US was to get nothing, but the United States, with Britain and France, was authorized to represent all the others in locating and liquidating German assets wherever they could be found. The American estimated totals of German assets in Switzerland were included in the commitments made at Paris.

The Swiss publicly protested the Paris meeting, arguing that under international law no nation had any claim to any German assets within Switzerland. They showed that Swiss claims against Germany amounted to five billion Swiss francs. These claims included both money owed for wartime sales and short-term loans made by Swiss banks to Germans prior to 1939—which had never been repaid.

In these circumstances, Washington kept the blacklist of Swiss firms in force, and retained its freeze on all Swiss assets in the United States. Both actions hurt Swiss commerce and banking badly. In October 1945 the blacklist was reduced from 1300 to 600 names, but it still included many Swiss firms whose only crime was that they had traded with Germany. Many of these companies went bankrupt, ruining Swiss businessmen and throwing several thousand Swiss citizens out of work.

The continuance of any kind of blacklist after the end of hostilities was contrary to international law, and the Swiss government considered this action punitive. It was obviously taken to make the Swiss see things Washington's way.

The Swiss government pointed out that the blacklist had been established by a Treasury decree in 1941. There had been no public hearings; Treasury evidence remained secret, and no Swiss firm had any means of rebuttal. Ironically, the continuance of the blacklist dissipated many of the assets the US was seeking to recover. German-owned Swiss firms, unable to do business, continued to pay employees out of capital until they went broke. After that, the question of their assets was academic.

The blocking of dollar accounts and Swiss gold reserves meanwhile not only hurt Swiss banking but actually delayed the recovery of Europe. Swiss capital which was prepared to be loaned to Allied nations was frozen in New York.

There were other forms of pressure. Albert Oeri, editor of the *Basler Nachrichten*, printed that American negotiators had threatened to cut off all wheat and fuel shipments to Switzerland. During 1945–1946 the US either occupied or dominated all of the territory surrounding the Confederation. Such a threat, if it was made, was neither idle nor unimportant. It was the same tactic Nazi Germany had used to pry some 5.3 billion francs worth of war goods out of Switzerland at bargain prices. Neither the Swiss nor the US government would confirm or refute the fact that such threats had been made. Oeri, a respected editor, had been threatened with assassination by the Nazis during the war because of his violently anti-Nazi stands.

By 1946 the Swiss government was aware that it would have to make some concessions. The United States was simply too powerful. But the one thing all Swiss hoped to avoid was any surrender of Swiss sovereignty or the Swiss principle of neutrality. In March 1946 Dr. Walter Stucki, Chief of the Swiss Foreign Office, flew secretly to Washington. Here he met with Randolph Paul, Special Assistant to President Truman, F. W. McCombe of the United Kingdom, and Paul Charguerand of France.

The Allied trio, with Paul dominating the conference, began by insisting that Switzerland hand over the entire estimated $750 million and further that an Allied commission be permitted to enter Switzerland to supervise the seizure and liquidation.

Stucki sat down to argue. Protracted negotiations began. None of these proceedings was known at the time to the American public.

But another struggle had developed, this time inside the American government itself. The Treasury Department had been allowed to handle the entire Swiss negotiations since 1940; Secretary Morgenthau had dominated American policy. Among President Truman's first acts, however, was the removal of former New Dealers from positions of power and influence in Washington. Truman increasingly got rid of the older crowd, and to a remarkable extent relied upon three main classes of Americans for his foreign policy: professional soldiers, diplomats, and international bankers. Truman's men were much more inclined to see shades of gray and not to take absolute moral positions in the world. By 1946 the question of a Nazi resurgence or a new armed Germany financed out of Switzerland, in light of the world situation and the deepening Cold War, was no longer relevant. The new American government was inclined to forget World War II and to begin worrying about something far more germane and dangerous—a possible World War III.

Treasury officials, carrying the battle against the Swiss, were neither diplomats nor pragmatists. They generally started from the premise that Swiss bank secrecy was immoral nonsense, and the Swiss shouldn't observe it. Swiss law made it impossible for the Treasury to get any real information, and this was a major irritant; domestically, T-men were not used to being blocked by law. Swiss neutrality angered Morgenthau and some of his people on the basis that anyone who was not against the Nazis tooth and claw must surely be for them. The Swiss determination to be neutral—in the true meaning of the word—was apparently not understood by Americans, who frequently remained uninvolved but were seldom neutral. Another thing which influenced Treasury policy was that a large number of agents and executives had made the Swiss-German asset investigation practically a life's work. It had become a sort of mission, coloring their judgment.

James Byrnes, the new Secretary of State, became concerned about the steady souring of Swiss-American relations during 1945 and 1946. Americans and Swiss had never had any quarrel with each other. Both were democratic peoples with long traditions of friendship. The normal American policy toward small European nations had always been one of sympathy and tolerance. State Department representatives who had gone through the war in Switzerland were aware of the deep anti-Nazi feelings of the Swiss, but also aware of the Swiss understanding of their sovereign, neutral position. Swiss sovereignty allowed the Swiss to have and interpret their own laws as they pleased, and State Department men so advised. Byrnes was told by his own people that the T-men did very well playing cops and robbers inside the United States, but that they had no understanding of international law or international politics and were making trouble.

A telling point was the fact that while the British and French governments had been given authority, along with Washington, to find and liquidate German assets, neither was putting the slightest pressure on the Swiss. The British had asked for, and got, a badly needed loan from Swiss banks. The French were accepting electric power, textiles, and chemicals from Switzerland —some from German-owned firms—and were not about to bully the Swiss. Both nations were happy to have Washington do all the work and get all the blame along with whatever assets were smoked out.

The United States was damaging its relations with a friendly power over an issue which in practical terms was no longer relevant and from which it stood to get not one red cent. This, Byrnes felt, was foolish. A surprisingly bitter underground power struggle between the State and Treasury officialdom was waged through Washington corridors. It resulted in standoff and compromise. Because of this, the US modified its position toward Dr. Stucki during March.

At the end of the month Stucki flew back to Bern. He went before the Nationalrat in executive session and stated that the Americans had at last agreed to certain concessions: proceeds of any German liquidation would be shared with the Swiss government, and the Swiss would be allowed to handle the matter in their own way. Swiss sovereignty would not be infringed.

Stucki said quite frankly that the United States still insisted on half the money found. It took the position that any losses taken by the Swiss for material aid furnished Nazi Germany during the war had to be absorbed by the Swiss. Stucki himself did not find the position unreasonable.

Finally he informed the Nationalrat that Swiss dollar accounts in the US would remain blocked until the Swiss accepted this compromise.

In his testimony it came out that the United States was to get nothing from the liquidation of German assets. This had not been widely known in Switzerland. Many Swiss had thought the US was simply out to grab these assets for itself. When Stucki's testimony was printed in Swiss papers, the fact that the German assets were to be used for general European rehabilitation impressed public opinion favorably. For the Swiss to surrender such assets for reparations would have been a violation of Swiss neutrality, and one which the Federal Council had been prepared to resist.

The Nationalrat authorized Stucki to return to Washington

and close the deal. Some Swiss papers announced that Bern was going to capitulate; there was still strong sentiment against any compromise at all.

On May 21, 1946, the US Department of State released certain broad details of what was called the Washington Agreements. First, the Swiss and American governments accepted two fundamentals: The United States was satisfied that no German assets in Switzerland would be used to finance a new German war, and further, the principle of a division of these assets was agreeable to both parties.

In the agreement, although the Swiss surrendered some German money, Swiss neutrality, sovereignty, and even bank secrecy were salvaged. It provided:

1. German holdings in Switzerland were to be identified and either liquidated or transferred to acceptable Swiss citizens. This work would be done by a purely Swiss agency.

2. Proceeds from such liquidations were to be divided equally between the Swiss and the Allies. The Allied share was to be used solely for rehabilitation, not reparations.

3. Private German nationals who suffered loss of assets were to be compensated by the Allies with German money, one half of which was to be provided from Swiss credit balances in Germany. The Swiss insisted that under their Constitution no private party could suffer confiscation.

4. The Allies were to accept payment of 250 million Swiss francs in lieu of restoration of German monetary gold deposited by the German authorities in Switzerland.

No Swiss government agency or official was allowed to enter a Swiss bank unless the banker reported that German assets were held. The census was voluntary. The German assets transferred or liquidated consisted for the most part of German-held companies where the ownership could be traced. Where a firm had "protective coloring" the Swiss followed their own law. If cantonal law said a company was Swiss, it was Swiss.

Major Swiss business and banking circles were in favor of concluding the agreement. Their major interest in 1946 was in freeing the large Swiss assets in London and New York and looking forward. While they did succumb to pressure, the Swiss never agreed in principle that the Allies had any right to demand or receive anything from German assets inside Switzerland. What was surrendered was given up under protest. The Nationalrat, making this clear, ratified the Washington Agreements May 25, 1946, by a vote of 142 to 29.

However, Swiss funds in New York were not immediately unfrozen, although this had been part of the agreement. Nor was the blacklist immediately removed. There was still strong pressure inside the American government to move against Sweden and Argentina, which reputedly held even more German assets than Switzerland. But the State Department knocked these ideas down. The United States was not in position to use against Sweden or Argentina the kind of pressures it had against the Swiss. And the State Department finally blasted the Treasury restrictions loose.

The question of payment of German citizens dragged on for some years. The Allies did not satisfy the Swiss in this respect, nor did the amount of money received from the liquidation of German assets satisfy the Allies. The entire matter was not finally settled until 1952. The Allies received a total of $60 million in all.

Both United States and Swiss banks cooperated in the recovery of Western Europe. Some authorities believe that Swiss banks put as much money into European rehabilitation—more than three billion dollars—as did the Marshall Plan. Since no official Swiss figures exist, no concrete statements can be made.

Most Americans understand that Swiss bank secrecy was breached in 1945–46, but they never knew the circumstances. The breach was handled in a way—voluntarily—that Swiss law stayed intact. And a fact few Americans know is that the Swiss share of seized German governmental and other assets was used to indemnify German citizens who lost firms, businesses, or property in Switzerland. The Swiss, like the Americans, kept nothing for themselves. *Eventually, the Swiss government repaid every franc it took from private assets or businesses to give the Allies.*

In this way the Nationalrat and the nation felt Swiss honor had been preserved.

Swiss banking was hardly damaged. After this act, there was more confidence in Swiss banks and in the Swiss nation by foreign depositors than there had ever been before. After World War II, more money than ever entered Switzerland.

Woodrow Wilson said in 1919, "In the next war there will be no neutrals." He was mistaken. In modern times, both Russians and Americans have made the same claim. The Swiss do not accept any such view. They have spent an enormous amount of money and effort on civil defense. They have burrowed into their Alps. If nuclear holocaust should sweep the earth, Swiss citizens firmly believe that at the end they would emerge intact and still neutral from their mountain fortress complete with Red Cross armbands and vast injections of hard Swiss cash to rebuild the world.

In the great squeeze play of 1946 both the US government and the Swiss people believed they were fighting for important principles. Twenty years afterward, it seemed the Swiss principles had better stood the test of time.

Blood Money

IN THE SUMMER of 1938 a Zurich cantonal lawyer named Kurt
Kägi made a short trip into Germany. He was met near Rosenheim
by Heinrich Blattman-Hollweg, the owner of an old and wealthy
German-Jewish publishing house, who had a small lakefront
estate in the region. Kägi and Blattman-Hollweg had had very little contact for years, though they had known each other during
student days at the University of Zurich, and once or twice Kägi
had handled small legal matters for the German's publishing trade
in the canton of Zurich. Kägi was thirty-four years old, and at that
time rather unsuccessful. It had virtually exhausted his family's
finances to put him through the University, and he had gone into
private practice at a very bad time.

He had been very happy to take the train to Germany on
Blattman-Hollweg's invitation. He hoped for a nice bit of business, perhaps even a retainer by the publishing firm to handle its
foreign legal matters. He was aware that Blattman-Hollweg's
house owned some attractive literary properties which were making good money in various parts of Europe and America.

When they were alone, the young, rather elegant German got
quickly to the point. He told Kägi that he felt Kägi was a man
who could be trusted, and that he desperately needed a capable
and trustworthy agent in Switzerland. Kägi spread his hands and
said he hoped he was a good lawyer. Blattman-Hollweg laughed
at this and said he did not need a lawyer, he needed a friend.

Very frankly, it was a matter of considerable moneys Blattman-Hollweg was accumulating in Switzerland, and he wanted someone to hold this for him.

Kurt Kägi suggested a good Swiss bank.

"My friend," Blattman-Hollweg told him, "it is impossible for any German, particularly one who is half-Jewish, to have dealings with a Swiss bank. But it is possible for you, a Swiss, to deal with a Swiss bank for me, and even to keep my name out of it."

Kägi had to agree this was possible.

Blattman-Hollweg quickly outlined a scheme he had contrived to get a large amount of money paid secretly into Switzerland. A Swiss bank was obviously the place for it, for the publisher wanted it invested, not just to stagnate in a vault. But he did not want the money to be connected with him or his name in any way. What he proposed, as both knew, was treason under German law, and there was a very real fear in Blattman-Hollweg's mind that somehow the German authorities might connect him with the money. "It is not only for me, " he said. "I want a legacy for my two children. Germany is going to war again," he added bitterly. "No one knows how it will turn out."

Kägi said, "I think it might be better if you took your family out of Germany altogether." Rather delicately, he mentioned the increasingly strident attacks by the Nazi leaders upon German Jews.

Blattman-Hollweg would not listen to this. He told Kägi that on his mother's side he was connected to the German nobility, and his father had been an officer in the Great War. His wife was Catholic, and his boy and girl only one-quarter Jewish by Nazi standards. He had an honored name in Germany, and certainly nothing could happen to him if he did not oppose the state. He argued with Kägi that the present wave of anti-Semitism must pass. The German Jewish community was talented; the Fatherland needed them, and after all, it was not possible to kill or put hundreds of thousands of citizens in jail. Kägi was forced to agree with the logic.

He also agreed to do whatever he could to assist Blattman-Hollweg in Switzerland. The German was generous as well as desperate about his money, and Kägi needed the fees agreed upon.

Kägi returned to Zurich. Shortly afterward, approximately

one million Swiss francs came into his hands—an enormous sum in 1938. Kägi was very careful. In the interests of his client he placed this money in at least a dozen banks throughout Switzerland, in his own name. A large deposit was made in the Bank at Wadenswil, a small town up the lake from Zurich.

Then, within a month after Kägi deposited Blattman-Hollweg's money, came *Kristall-nacht*. The Nazis launched their great pogroms, German-Jewish shops and businesses were wrecked, glass smashed, and Jewish owners carted off to concentration camps. Kägi never heard from Blattman-Hollweg again.

The war brought hard times for lawyers in Switzerland. Kägi's business did not prosper. Finally, he was called to the colors and spent three years as an officer in the Swiss Army. When the war ended in May 1945, Kägi found himself the father of three growing children, a complaining wife, and at the age of forty still without a practice which could support him.

Kägi was Swiss. It probably never occurred to him that he held assets now totaling half a million dollars in his own name, which no one could really prove weren't his. He took only the fees agreed upon with Blattman-Hollweg for handling the money, and as soon as he left the Army tried to make contact with his client in Germany. He did not really expect to find the publisher alive —but he did expect to find his heirs.

The search was completely unsuccessful.

Inquiries to American Military Government in Germany turned up nothing. The Blattman-Hollweg family was traced to a concentration camp, and there the trail ended. There was not even a record as to how the family died. But by the end of 1945 Kurt Kägi—and everyone else in the world—was well aware of what had happened.

Six million European Jews had died in Hitler's Europe. Most of them had died as entire families—men, women, and children. Kurt Kägi was the secret trustee of a rapidly growing fortune for which there were no traceable heirs.

There is no indication just when lawyer Kägi succumbed to temptation, or decided that charity began at home. But by 1950 Kägi was generally known to be a wealthy man. He moved large sums of money into Zurich, and invested heavily in real estate. What he did about Swiss taxes lies buried between him and the

Swiss government, and no outsider will ever know the details. He became a rich and respected man in Zurich, but a man certain ugly rumors followed all his life.

He told his oldest son something of the story of the family wealth, perhaps from conscience, perhaps from honesty, for Kurt Kägi was basically a very honest man. He never stole a rappen from anyone in his life. His sons gradually pieced out the whole story; one of them, at least, was greatly disillusioned and greatly disturbed. On a trip abroad he recounted the whole tale to companions, and the story spread.

But it was only a story. The Kägi riches were real. Kurt Kägi died of a heart attack in 1964, and his sons took over the family enterprises. By 1964 they were all a little older, and two of them had family responsibilities of their own.

Everything that happened in Hitler's Europe was long past, and few people worried about it any more.

The problem of the Jewish assets allegedly in Switzerland was always fraught with emotion. In 1946 the Swiss banks generally sent out several millions of dollars, much of it to the Western Hemisphere, to proven heirs of German or European Jewish families who had died in the Nazi holocaust. Later, a large amount of Swiss money went to the new State of Israel, whence much of it returned to Geneva to be deposited in Israeli-owned Swiss Other Banks.

There is no question that thousands of Jewish depositors in Swiss banks died between 1939 and 1945. There is also no question that these customers left millions of dollars worth of assets banked or invested in the Confederation. The Swiss banks and Swiss government claimed that all but about a million dollars of this money was repatriated or paid out to Jewish heirs by 1946. Jewish world organizations, and later the State of Israel, have claimed publicly that the Swiss figures are tragically false and misleading, and that at least $30 million in unclaimed Jewish money still remained in Switzerland in 1954.

During 1954 the government of Israel instituted international proceedings against Swiss banking, acting in behalf of "Jewish orphans and heirs" of Jewish families who had allegedly put money in Swiss banks and then vanished into Nazi gas ovens. The suit was accompanied by a biting propaganda campaign which was carried in newspapers all over the world.

The Israeli government specifically mentioned the figure of $30 million—which coincided with informed Swiss guesses of the total amount of unclaimed funds lying in all Swiss banks.

The great fear of the Israeli authorities, who were acting in the name of the world Jewish community, was that by 1965 the contested money would escheat to the banks in question. Under Swiss law, any deposit which remains untouched or dormant for twenty years, with no contact from its owner, reverts to the bank in which it is deposited.

The question of escheat is a legal matter poorly understood outside banking circles. All countries and most American states have some kind of banking escheat law. People everywhere put money in banks or safety-deposit boxes, then die without designated heirs—often without any known heirs or any instructions to the banks for disposal of the money. In most nations and states such money after an average of twenty years reverts to the state or government. Virtually every nation acquires a certain sum of money in this way each year.

In Switzerland, the money typically escheats to private banks rather than to government. This is in line with Swiss philosophy and Swiss law, and there is nothing immoral in it. But the fact that so many Swiss depositors do come to untidy or untimely ends in the modern world, from Rafael Leónidas Trujillo to wealthy European Jews in 1942, gives the Swiss problem a peculiar intensity.

Swiss banks always demand beneficiaries when deposits are made, but due to the nature of the modern world many beneficiaries die along with the depositors, particularly when there is war or revolution. Since Swiss banks are not required to report private money held on account or invested through stock exchanges for private parties, there is obviously no accurate figure on the amount of funds held in dormant or unclaimed accounts.

The $30 million figure, if correct, is small. More than $100 million is held in dead accounts in the American state of Texas alone—which is one state which does not have a regular escheat law. Texas banks, under Texas law, may not claim or take this money—but it is there for them to use, and they use it. For more than twenty years repeated attempts in the state legislature to allow the state to acquire this money by escheat have been blocked effectively by a powerful banking lobby. The Swiss situation is by no means unique.

The Israeli claims and pressure in 1954 brought an immediate, bitter reaction from both the Swiss government and the Swiss Banker's Association. Both insisted that every effort to locate Jewish heirs and assigns had been made during 1945–1946, and they did produce evidence that millions of dollars had been repatriated then. Further, the Swiss Banker's Association rejected the claim of the Israeli government that it could act in behalf of or as the "heir" to all slain Jews in wartime Europe. The Association, backed by the Swiss government, pointed out that this was exactly as if the British government claimed to represent Anglicans everywhere, or the Vatican insisted to be the physical heir and due the escheat of all Roman Catholics. On legal if not emotional grounds, the Israeli claim was actually tenuous.

However, many people agreed that Israel could advance a moral, if not legal, claim to the money. Jewish dormant assets were to be used for the benefit of Jewish refugees and Jewish causes everywhere, and this did have a definite emotional and moral appeal.

The moral appeal and the propaganda argument against heartless, profiteering Swiss bankers struck home. Few Swiss, including bankers and Nationalrat members, wanted to be accused of enriching themselves from the fortunes of the victims of horrible persecutions. But all proposed solutions for discovering the actual status of Jewish accounts in Switzerland ran counter to the whole fabric of Swiss opinion, banking practice, and law. It was unthinkable that any outside agency be given power to examine banks.

The controversy dragged on for years. Finally, in 1962, the Federal Council passed a law requiring all Swiss banks to reveal to a federal bureau all information about assets of "racially, politically, or religiously persecuted foreigners or stateless persons" which had remained dormant since World War II.

Under the language of this law, compliance was mandatory. But the determination of what was "persecuted" money was left strictly up to the banks. There was no provision for federal or outside examination; without overturning the Swiss banking code there could not be.

In 1964 the more than four hundred banks in Switzerland had registered only 1050 such accounts, with total assets of less than 10 million Swiss francs—about $2 million.

Israel, the Jewish World Congress, and other Jewish agencies immediately protested that this was a ridiculously low sum. If it were correct, the huge Jewish fortunes reputedly hidden in Zurich, Basel, and Geneva did not exist.

Beginning in 1965, dormant accounts not registered under the 1962 law began to escheat back to the banks, and the question rapidly became academic, although it would continue to occupy the press and courts for some years more. How many Swiss banks failed to report or gave themselves the benefit of the doubt will never be known. Unquestionably some did, because most Swiss bankers never accepted the validity of the Israeli claim or saw any reason why Swiss practice should be set aside in this one case.

The question of how many European Jewish fortunes or how much Jewish money was desposited in Swiss banks or entrusted to Swiss agents will never be determined to everyone's satisfaction. At the end of World War II a number of such banks and agents, including law firms, made strenuous efforts to seek out owners, heirs, or assigns. When no heirs could be found, it became a matter of conscience, in most cases, how the money was disposed. Informed Zurich gossip persistently lingered on several lawyers or law firms which became suspiciously affluent after 1945.

Swiss banks did profit from Jewish money, just as directly or indirectly Swiss bankers have profited from every persecution of modern times. If Protestant refugees from France gave a great impetus to modern banking in Switzerland, and aristocratic émigrés sustained it after 1789, people and capital fleeing from Nazism, Communism, and Socialism kept Swiss banking liquid and added to the Swiss banks' international importance. Much refugee capital never goes home, whether its owners escape or not, just as all through history a certain amount of buried gold and silver was never recovered.

But Swiss banks have been more useful to the victim than the persecutor. Each adamant defense of hidden money or refusal to cooperate with foreign authorities in its recovery has only added luster to Swiss banks where it counts—among people with money. Protection of foreign deposits assured that there would always be foreign deposits. And bank secrecy was like virginity. It could not be breached selectively and still kept intact, despite all the arguments in favor of breaching it from time to time.

The only possible way to prevent the complete disappearance of some kinds of money, like that of the Jewish victims of Hitler, into Swiss banks would be to permit Swiss federal intervention and control of banks as well as strict cooperation with other governments. But no Swiss government is likely to dare to make such proposals. To most Swiss citizens, this kind of cure would be more painful, more stupid, and infinitely more dangerous to their interests than any crime their banks could possibly commit.

SEVEN

Pecunia
Non Olet,
or Money
Has No Smell

DURING THE 1950s a dapper, balding, cigar-smoking Spaniard named Julio Muñoz—usually described in publications such as *The Wall Street Journal* as a "Spanish financier"—began to put together an elaborate financial network in Switzerland. Muñoz did not have a drop of Swiss banking blood in his veins, although he was imaginative, brilliant, and able to make important contacts with people with large amounts of money. Muñoz was a promoter at heart.

His main interest in Switzerland was the wonderful fiscal freedom and financial flexibility of the Confederation's laws. Because the Swiss permitted the institution of Other Banks—banks owned, controlled, and operated by and for foreign interests under Swiss banking codes—Muñoz was able to take advantage of the Swiss climate to the full. His specialty was luring Spanish and Spanish-American capital into Switzerland, using all the obvious advantages of Swiss banks, then using this money to finance his own soaring promotional schemes in many parts of Europe.

Muñoz acquired controlling stock interest in two Swiss banks, the Banque Genevoise de Commerce, or Geneva Commerce and Credit Bank, and the Swiss Savings and Credit Bank of St. Gallen. This sort of thing was by no means uncommon; it had become normal since World War II. The most spectacular growth in Swiss banking was in the area of Other Banks after 1945. Twenty-eight Other Banks were chartered in Geneva alone between 1945 and 1964. They were owned by Belgians, Swedes, French,

British, Italians, Americans, and (particularly) Middle Eastern interests. Geneva became the true financial center for the Levant. Israeli-owned banks also enjoyed a remarkable growth. The Swiss-Israel Trade Bank, Ltd., for example, opened branches in Zurich, London, and Manchester, and by 1964 its shares were traded on the Geneva Exchange. These Other Banks fascinated both the average Swiss citizen and the Swiss banker. But since they did no real business inside the Confederation—their capital came from outside, and their investments went abroad—they seemed to have no effect on either Swiss economy or the Swiss banking system, although they did have an increasing importance in the financial world at large.

The main reason most Other Banks set up shop in Switzerland was because it was the one centrally located place in the world where capital, currency, securities, and gold could be brought in or out completely without regulation or restriction. The Israeli banks, already bigger than the smallest of the Swiss Big Banks, were honest international financial centers. They were not in Geneva to conceal anything behind bank secrecy. But Julio Muñoz, taking advantage of the same free-and-easy codes, was an entirely different breed of cat. And although Muñoz's money came from outside, mostly Spain and Hispanic America, and was reinvested abroad, he was to do serious damage not to Swiss banking itself but to its worldwide image.

Muñoz garnered millions of dollars for his banks in Latin America, trading on the fear and insecurity which followed the Castroite revolution in Cuba. He made a point of contacting Spanish and Latin oligarchs and pointing out the advantages of having money in Switzerland. One of his biggest hauls came in 1962, when he convinced Ramfis Trujillo, the principal heir of the murdered dictator of Santo Domingo, Rafael Leónidas Trujillo, to put the family money in a Muñoz bank.

Muñoz had an advantage over the conservative, cautious, Protestant-ethic Swiss in procuring Latin money. He spoke the language; he had a cultural affinity with and deep understanding of the fears, ambitions, and hatreds of the Latin American mind. He and his agents deliberately sought out men like Trujillo; they deliberately worked for deposits of a kind which the older, eminently respectable Swiss-owned banks of Geneva pointedly declined. Rafael Trujillo had put some money in Swiss banks, as had Fulgencio Batista, whom Castro ousted in Cuba, and the Peróns of Argentina. But the majority of Swiss banks did not care for dictator money; the big private banks invariably turned it down. This was hardly a matter of legality—all dictator deposits were "legal"—but one of personal taste. By actual record Trujillo, Batista, Ubico of Guatemala, and the Somozas of Nicaragua always kept more money in New York, Miami, and New Orleans banks than in Switzerland. They also kept large sums packed in convenient suitcases. The Latin dictatorial mentality, always insecure, preferred cash in hand to cash in a distant bank.

No one ever complained about the Latin American deposits in North American banks, incidentally. The dictators, while not exactly loved in the United States, were still official allies. Most of them, including Batista of Cuba and Pérez Jiménez of Venezuela, received the American Legion of Merit from Washington, and local American bankers were glad to get their dough.

The dictators, cabinet ministers, and landed oligarchy of South America got most of the attention as Swiss depositors. Names like Perón, Trujillo, or the exiled Red boss of Guatemala, Jácobo Arbenz, who took up residence in Switzerland, made the papers. But an even more important bleeding of ready cash from undeveloped Latin America to men like Muñoz did not.

Long before the Castro revolt and the intrusion of Communist infiltration into Latin America there was always inflation, mismanagement, and political instability. But this uneasiness affected primarily the actual government leaders or the ruling classes. With the specter of Red revolution now hanging over the hemisphere, the pervading fear spread downward. Men with small amounts of money or property became as infected as the oligarchs. Men who had once felt it made no real difference who sat in the presidential palace, and life would go on, changed their minds after Castro. After what happened in Cuba, where the entire propertied middle class was destroyed, no one could be sure any more.

The average merchant and businessman in Latin America—anyone who could get his hands on foreign exchange—became fair game for men like Julio Muñoz. Between 1960 and 1964 Venezuela exported at least two thirds of its entire earned foreign exchange abroad to more stable regions. The amount of fright capital sent out in 1961 alone was $150 million, which was one important reason the nation's huge oil income provided no lasting social good. Venezuela was a prime Communist infiltration target.

Mexico, the most stable of Latin countries and a nation whose principal need was more capital, exported $125 million to foreign banks and investments in 1961. The amount jumped in 1962, and the trend was only stabilized when the ruling political party deliberately chose a known conservative for President in 1964.

In December 1962, the magazine *Business Week* reported that the flight of liquid assets from Latin America had risen from $5 billion to $15 billion. This enormous annual bleeding not only offset all the projected increase in gross national product but also swallowed Alliance for Progress and other foreign aid funds. It proved, or should have proved, that political stability had to come before economic reform, and that until it did any meaningful reform short of chaos was improbable.

A very large part of this Latin money went north to New York. Most of it continued to come from members of government, landowners, and the tiny but immensely rich capitalist groups. But a very high proportion of shopkeepers, small businessmen, and the like—almost everyone above the manual-laboring class—bought all the US dollars, Swiss francs, or gold he could find or afford. European mints and banks began a huge business striking gold medallions for bullion-hoarders, while the official mints of Chile, Peru, and Mexico continued striking gold coins on obsolete standards for the same people. All this foreign exchange or gold served no useful economic purpose. It went underground, or stayed hidden in North American safety-deposit boxes. Ironically, only that portion of it which reached Switzerland was apt to serve an economic interest, and then almost never in the country of its origin.

Beginning in 1961, the United States lost favor as the favorite keeping place for Latin cash. The reforms urged by the Kennedy administration angered the old South American oligarchic families who controlled most of the wealth. The pressure put on the few remaining dictatorships had the same effect on the strongmen. The case of Rolando Masferrer, the Batistiano "Tiger" of Cuba, who as a senator had kept a private army, also chilled Latin

American eagerness to invest any considerable sum of money in a US bank.

Masferrer was able to get both himself and a substantial amount of dollars to Florida at the end of the Castro revolution. Here he set himself up in luxury on a vast estate and continued to dabble in Cuban politics. But Masferrer's image was extremely bad. His attempts to subvert the Castro regime worried the US government. Legal claims were brought by Cubans against his fortune. Partly for political reasons, and partly through the normal processes of American justice, Masferrer's assets were impounded in his Miami banks. This prevented the ex-senator from creating international incidents trying to overthrow Castro—but it also effectively separated him from money that he thought was free and clear.

The Masferrer case taught Latin refugees and potential refugees (a large population) that the United States was not so "trustworthy" as Switzerland. Under Swiss bank secrecy, such an impoundment would have been impossible—it would have been impossible even for the Swiss government to establish whether Masferrer had any money or not. It was no wonder that the Trujillo family money, by 1962, was ripe for Julio Muñoz' blandishments.

As Muñoz could point out, if Rolando Masferrer had put his money in a Swiss bank, it could afterward have arrived anonymously and highly acceptably at any New York brokerage house, or could have gone profitably into European real estate. It was acceptable enough in Miami, of course, but much more vulnerable.

To handle the Trujillo money and the other fortunes passing into his hands Julio Muñoz soon found he had to expand. Control of two Swiss banks was not enough, because the money for the most part had to be invested outside Switzerland. Muñoz thought big. He was not interested in the normal procedures of a respectable Swiss bank, which managed money on account, or in trust, put it in conservative stocks or investments, and took only management fees. Muñoz was more ambitious.

He had visions of building a vast financial empire which would control banks, office properties, and real estate all over the European continent. He had ideas which contravened even the loose Swiss laws—because all Swiss banks operating under the banking codes were required to maintain strict liquidity-capital ratios.

These hampering restrictions irritated Muñoz, and he sought ways around them. He built a maze of holding companies to obscure his operations in both Panama and the principality of Liechtenstein, notorious corporate havens. He opened a bank in Rome and bought into banks in out-of-the-way places like Lebanon, Andorra in the Pyrenees, and the Duchy of Luxemburg.

His Trujillo and other Latin money flowed into his two Swiss banks, which remained small, because it flowed right out again into all kinds of speculative ventures. Many of his customers, including the Trujillos, felt safe. They thought they were dealing with a solid Swiss bank. Whatever kind of bad publicity Swiss banks received, no one ever questioned their good sense, honesty toward their clients, or sound conservative judgment with money. But they were putting their money into the hands of one of the most flamboyant speculators of all time, who had soon moved it about so thoroughly that even Ramfis Trujillo did not know what had become of it.

Some of this manipulation would have been needed in any case. Few respectable Europeans would have cared for Trujillo as a business or financial partner. But finally Muñoz went over the line: he borrowed heavily from the banks which he owned for his ventures.

The great European boom in real estate in 1961, 1962, and 1963 spiraled Muñoz' holdings ever upward. With any sober judgment, with the capital he controlled, Muñoz would have made millions. But he kept trying to stretch dimes into ten-dollar bills on the flimsiest kind of financial base, in violation of Swiss banking law.

In 1964 European real estate became stagnant. Prices fell. The boom collapsed. Muñoz owed money everywhere—some of it borrowed money—and his collateral was depreciating. He had reached the point most speculators eventually come to, because no true speculator ever knows when to stop.

Neither of Muñoz' two Swiss banks could stand audit by 1964, and Muñoz knew it. Somehow—this is not yet clear—Muñoz reached Max Hommell, the respected president of the Swiss Banking Commission, which regulated and audited all Swiss banks for the National Bank. Muñoz paid Hommell large amounts of money for his services as "a finance and tax advisor." This payment might have been acceptable if genuine—but highly significantly, Hommell failed to report the payments to his fellow members on the Banking Commission, and concealed all relationship with Muñoz.

He also concealed something else. In his official capacity as head of the Banking Commission Max Hommell, as the federal government later reported, "deliberately ignored the granting of large credits without proper guarantees by the Banque Genevoise de Commerce"—to Julio Muñoz himself.

His empire collapsing, Muñoz borrowed millions from his own banks and became their principal debtor, an illegal arrangement even in free-and-easy capitalistic Switzerland.

The money Muñoz borrowed was squandered like the other funds he had been entrusted. The Banque Genevoise de Commerce was not a bottomless well; in April 1965 it went dry. Out of cash, both it and the St. Gallen bank were forced to apply to the Banking Commission for a moratorium, or suspension of all payments. A few days later, Muñoz' Italian affiliate in Rome asked for the same favor from the Italian government. The banking moratorium was granted, but it attracted immediate attention. Max Hommell could not hold the lid on any longer.

Auditors descended on the Muñoz banks. And in the first week in June 1965 the scandal blew.

Hermann Hug, a close associate in Muñoz' schemes, whom Muñoz had made president of the St. Gallen bank and a director of the Rome bank, was arrested on charges of swindling.

Hermann Hug talked just enough. A few days later the Swiss police closed in on Julio Muñoz and jailed him on a similar charge. Muñoz immediately went free, but only on bail set at the enormous sum of $230,000. He still had enough foreign assets—and perhaps fearful friends—to raise this amount.

Hommell was summarily dismissed from the Banking Commission. It was quite probable, as an official communiqué stated, that he would eventually face criminal charges along with Muñoz and

Hug. If the Swiss government proved the sums given Hommell by Muñoz were a payoff, Hommell would go to jail. During the investigation and dismissal, Hommell himself maintained an icy silence, nor would any of his colleagues talk.

There had been Swiss banking scandals before, but nothing like this. This hit Swiss banking where it hurt. If the Banking Commission itself could be bought, something hitherto unthinkable, the damage to the Swiss name would not only be irreversible but fatal. Foreign depositors from unstable countries had long since lost faith in their own institutions and governments. The one thing the Swiss had maintained to the last was their own firm, if different, kind of integrity.

To try to ease the damage the government immediately appointed seventy-three-year-old Hans Streuli, a former finance minister and former President of the Confederation to Hommell's vacated post. Streuli had both the prestige and the power to clean the mess up quickly, though actually there was very little to sweep up. No real damage had been done to Swiss finances or Swiss banking itself. Muñoz had dealt with foreigners for foreigners and in foreign properties, using his Swiss banks only as convenient clearing houses. Only the image of Swiss banking—and this mostly because of Max Hommell—had been tarnished, and the real effects of this could not be quickly or easily assessed.

The Schweizerische Bankverein, or Swiss Bank Corporation, one of the Big Banks, requested and got permission to take over the Savings and Credit Bank of St. Gallen, liabilities and all, in an effort to save the name of Swiss banking, and above all, the $500 million a year in foreign money the banks drew in. Bern was ready to cooperate, because the foreign earnings of the bank industry almost equaled that of Switzerland's famed tourist trade. Any lasting tarnish would be a national disaster.

What happened, or would happen, to the Trujillo millions and the other fortunes Muñoz had lured from Spain and South America would probably never be revealed. Swiss banking secrecy would cover them. But sometimes there is a rough kind of justice in the world. Trujillo's and other Latin fortunes were extorted in the main, and no one really cared.

The Muñoz scandal was the first of its kind and an unusual case. It was not likely to be repeated, and in its way, it obscured a much more important facet of Swiss banking. Swiss banks take money from every part of the unstable, undeveloped world—the "poor nations" or "lower half"—but they rarely squander it or speculate with it. They invest it prudently and cautiously in the rich Atlantic world.

While old and honored banks like Pictet & Cie, which turned Trujillo's money down, and the respectable commercial institutions are reluctant to accept deposits from out-and-out tyrants or ruling classes which extort money by blood or terror, there are more than four hundred banks in Switzerland, and some of these will. Some Swiss banks are owned by Israelis, American investors, Arabs, and Asians. These Other Banks usually care very little where the money comes from, and even many genuinely Swiss banks are not overly fastidious.

No Swiss bank will knowingly accept stolen money, but the $15 million (often ballooned to a figure of $100 million) deposited by the Peróns of Argentina, the some $3 million stashed away by Fulgencio Batista—cannot be described as stolen money. In the days when they secured it, Colonel Perón and President Batista were the law in their respective countries. The fact that most dictators, like the infamous Rafael Leonidas Trujillo, used shotguns, armed thugs, military force, and nauseating tortures on many of their subjects to raise it does not change the fact. In point of law, Trujillo's money is as "legal" as the royal allowance that is paid by the socialist government of Great Britain to Elizabeth II.

Some strongmen merely put available revenues into their own pockets. Others, like Batista of Cuba and Juan Domingo Perón of Argentina, simply transferred government funds to their own account or manipulated official exchange in their favor. A few—such as Trujillo, whose control of Santo Domingo before his assassination in 1961 was complete—extorted money from everyone, businesses and private individuals alike, and "bought" control of important industries. Trujillo owned nearly everything of value on Santo Domingo, and assiduously milked the island dry for thirty years. But since for thirty years Trujillo and family were the Santo Domingan government, this was as "legal" as, for example, confiscatory taxation by an enlightened, democratic European or North American regime. Under any concept of international law any banker whatever is entirely within his rights in accepting it on deposit.

Significantly, the banks in Switzerland like Pictet or Bordier which turn their noses up at this kind of business vehemently defend the right of other bankers—who may need the money—to take it. And many of the banks which will not touch the "tainted" money of a Trujillo or Masferrer willingly accept deposits from people such as the late King Alexander of Yugoslavia, shot down in Marseille in 1934, King Farouk of Egypt, exiled in 1952 and dead of dissipation in 1964, or young Feisal of Iraq, murdered in a revolution in 1958. It is, after all, very difficult to draw a line. To some European minds any king or prince is inherently more respectable than a dictator, though both are equally autocratic.

And most of the crowned heads of Europe, Asia, and Africa in the twentieth century have placed money in Swiss banks, for basically the same reasons industrialists, widows, and capitalists do. If many rich men do not trust their native governments, many rulers hardly trust their own people. This century has been a time of revolution; tenure is uncertain, and few things are more pitiful than a royal or ruling family turned out without assets safely hidden beyond reach of a new and revolutionary regime. For this reason Feisal, Farouk, and Alexander all hid money in Switzerland as a hedge against the future. Neither Alexander nor Feisal lived to enjoy it, though fat Farouk lived royally to the ripe old age of thirty-eight, paying his Italian mistresses with Swiss funds to the end.

Such royal arrangements have to be secret. Few things are more politically unpalatable to poor subjects than the knowledge that a sovereign is stashing away gold in a Swiss bank; the news could hasten, if not bring, the revolution. But at times the secrecy has been so profound that it has brought complications in Swiss and international courts.

The governments of nations which have deposed kings or monarchs almost automatically try to get royal deposits back from Swiss banks, on the grounds that they represent "national" rather than personal wealth. The Egyptian government of Nasser claimed all of Farouk's property under this concept. Egypt was able to seize and sell those of Farouk's assets, including a coin collection, which he left behind. It had no chance at all in getting his Swiss deposits.

In the same way, the new government of Santo Domingo tried to locate and return Trujillo deposits in Switzerland—a hopeless task. This type of demand is a regular occurrence. Sometimes even the revolutionary tables turn a bit: Ben Bella, the strongman of newly independent Algeria, publicly accused Swiss banks of accepting and hiding $12 million that one of his own revolutionary leaders was supposed to have sneaked out of the country. Then Ben Bella himself was overturned, and his successor began to brood about what Ben Bella might have sequestered from the national treasury.

Whenever any money makes its way to Switzerland, it is usually lost forever to national treasuries.

Sometimes the loss involves another kind of claim or suit. Young King Peter of Yugoslavia was never able to recover any money from Swiss banks, or even to get a Swiss bank to admit it held any of his father Alexander's assets. King Alexander left no records; rulers never do. While Swiss banking practice is to demand a beneficiary from depositors in case of untimely demise, the rule has been known to be broken. Royalty, or very prominent men, with substantial deposits are not always pestered about small details. More likely, however, Alexander obscured his holdings very thoroughly in Switzerland, or even used an agent. Like the Romans who buried gold coin in ancient times, and to really keep the secret never told even their families—wives can be loose-tongued, and children can be tortured and have been by desperate regimes—some modern rulers kept their counsel very private. Some, like Louis XV of France, may not have cared what came after them. At any rate, some Swiss depositors carried any secrets they had to the grave. If the depositor left no specific instructions, the presentation of his bank book, or even his secret account number by a possible heir will get no cash. An heir can only open a bank vault with the consent of all heirs, and who is an heir may take years in court to answer. In the meantime, the Swiss Banker's Association has advised 320 member banks—all banks of any consequence in Switzerland—to maintain perfect silence. The rule "When in doubt keep quiet" applies in this situation.

King Alexander may not have had any Swiss deposits. Such deposits are often invented by gossip, and they are almost always exaggerated. But his son, ex-King Peter, living in Monaco, will never believe such deposits did not exist and hates Swiss banks to this day.

The relatives of King Feisal of Iraq complained of similar trouble after Feisal was murdered in 1958. They were positive the young king had money in Switzerland—but they couldn't prove it. A number of heirs of dictator Trujillo, assassinated in 1961, still have a suit pending in Swiss courts. These heirs, some legitimate, some illegitimate, and some alleged, claimed Swiss banks would not cooperate. Informed Geneva opinion also believes that a mixup occurred in the Perón deposits. The dictator's wife Evita handled most of the family financial and business arrangements, while the strongman ran the country. Evita made a trip to Geneva in the early 1950s, deposited about $15 million, then died unexpectedly. But Little Eva apparently failed to designate her husband as beneficiary for some of her deposits, and after she died Perón could only claim about one fifth of all of this money.

These continual claims by "bereaved" families have convinced some people that Swiss bankers are inherently crooked and that one of their favorite tricks is to accept money secretly from rulers with a notoriously short life expectancy, then get ownership of it through escheat. The surest refutation of this kind of charge is that few Swiss depositors seem worried. Men who actually deal with Swiss banks or put money in them know the banks demand a beneficiary in almost every case, and will faithfully carry out any instructions. What frequently happens is that some beneficiary—sometimes an unlikely one—is named, and gets the money—secretly, of course—from the bank. This beneficiary, in the case of a famous or notorious man, usually has the good sense to keep his mouth shut. Any leaking of the fact that he has inherited could get him in serious trouble. Ex-dictators still employ gunmen—the Trujillo family in exile notoriously so; governments get excited over taxes; and even a prince of the blood can be fearful of a great horde of indigent relations living off him after the goose which laid the golden egg is gone. The fact that Swiss banks are required by law to keep these transactions secret makes for interesting gossip and occasional wild charges—but it hardly hurts confidence in the banks.

If beneficiary arrangements are genuinely flawed or destroyed by circumstances, such as the same fate befalling both depositor and heirs at the same time, the money legally and properly does go to the bank, by escheat.

The days when any reputable Swiss bank will accept money on deposit from agents or third parties for someone it does not know have passed. An agent may easily deposit small sums, but no bank will take millions or hundreds of thousands of francs without a clear notion of where the money originates. The numbered or anonymous account does not mean the customer may be anonymous inside the bank. This kind of arrangement would not merely impair the normal banking function, it would make it impossible. Swiss bankers have tidy minds; they want no loose ends.

The banks are legally required to make a proper disposition of the funds of dead customers. The whole trouble comes from the fact that they are also legally required by Swiss courts to maintain bank secrecy beyond the grave. Who gets an assassinated dictator's money is nobody's business but the beneficiary's and the bank's.

What happens to dictator or strongman money while it is in a Swiss bank, however, is more important in the modern world than which bank accepts it or who becomes its eventual beneficiary. All of this money does not just sit in secret vaults—most of it is put to use.

The "national treasuries" which arrive regularly in Switzerland are a tremendous factor in Swiss banks' famous liquidity This money gives the Swiss banks their real importance in international finance. It is a position they could never achieve on purely Swiss deposits or small European savings accounts. Between 1956 and 1965 at least $500 million a year poured into Swiss banks from overseas. Much of this capital came in the form of gold rather than worthless paper printed with tyrant's portraits. It raised the per capita gold reserve held by the National Bank for each Swiss citizen to $465, five times the per capita gold held by the US

Federal Reserve for every American. While the US dollar had only token golden backing in 1965, the Swiss franc was backed by gold approximately 135 per cent. The Swiss franc became the hardest currency in the world. But the important thing was the fact that this flow gave Swiss banks the ability to invest and make large loans all over the world.

Without the money used by Swiss banks a great deal of the financing in the Atlantic world would be immensely more difficult. Swiss banks finance thousands of legitimate American and European corporations. They make highly significant loans to small nations.

Socialist Sweden's highly respectable Telefonaktiebolaget Ericsson would have found it more expensive to raise $10.5 million in expansion capital in 1959. The democratic governments of Holland, Denmark, and Great Britain would have had to pay higher interest for quick and needed loans in 1961 and 1962. If Swiss banks had not been liquid, they might not have found the money—or they might have had to put an additional drain on the United States.

Between 1959 and 1960 Swiss banks invested $94 million through the International Bank on worthwhile projects and loaned American private enterprise $48 million for European expansion. Many of the American corporations moving into the Common Market area get most of their financing through Swiss banks. The money is there and earmarked to go.

In 1962 the Bank for International Settlements in Basel, which tries to keep international finance and the reserve currencies of pound and dollar on an even keel, secured a quick $200 million for a shoring operation on the dollar. In 1964 American Treasury officials called on Swiss bankers to put up several hundred millions more in the $3 billion effort to save the British pound.

Since 1962 the amount of money annually loaned or invested abroad in the Atlantic world by Swiss banks has averaged nearly $500 million. Switzerland puts out all the money it takes in. Its per capita foreign export of $500 far exceeds both American investment and foreign aid overseas.

No one, respectable corporation or democratic government, ever asks where the money comes from. Swedish or German firms may be financed by South American blood money, the US dollar supported by smuggled Algerian gold. The Romans had a phrase for this: *Pecunia non olet*—Money has no smell. The fact is that once money has gone through the purifying process of a solid Swiss bank it has neither identity nor odor.

Swiss banks have become clearing houses for the passage of money from the unstable, undeveloped "third world" back into the relative freedom and stability of the industrial regions. Since 1960, as the situation in the poorer half of the world has generally worsened, the flow has accelerated. Even more significant, the return flow into these areas has virtually stopped.

Swiss banks, by financing Belgian corporations, dropped an investment of $120 million in the Congo when it became independent. They are no longer interested in loaning money in the ex-colonial or so-called "developing" world. The reason is simple: no bank can make a profit doing so. There is an intimate connection between political stability and financial development, and the Swiss are much more keenly aware of this than most American banks or government authorities.

In 1963 three of the Swiss Big Banks ran a sort of audit on their operations in the "third world" and discovered they were slowly losing their shirts. In Asia, Africa, and most of Latin America, Swiss banks not only could not operate profitably because of political and social restrictions; they could not even protect their investments. There were no profits to be made in countries devoid of industrial know-how, political stability, and financial discipline. Capital could be invested safely and profitably only in a basically sound capitalistic economy. Swiss capital was once important to the industrial (particularly chemical) development of Africa and South America. With the exception of Mexico, where there has been more than fifteen years of stable politics and government, Swiss investment has dried up.

Swiss bankers refused to be worried by any social implications in the fact that the rich nations get richer and the poor poorer. They are businessmen, not social workers. One of the favorite sayings of Dr. Alfred Schaefer, head of the giant Union Bank of Switzerland, is, "Nobody can be his brother's keeper."

The banker's job—and this is very hard to refute—is not to worry about the nature of the world but to protect his customers' money and make it grow.

Switzerland is by no stretch of the imagination a world power, or even involved in international politics. Yet Zurich's *Neue Zürcher Zeitung* is the best German-language newspaper and one of the two top political observers in the world. Because international banking in an age when governments try to control money is so interconnected with international politics Swiss bankers have to be both informed and astute. Swiss political analysis is completely apolitical in the ideological sense, and unsentimental. It is furnished by important newspapers like the *Neue Zürcher Zeitung* and the superb intelligence services maintained by all of the Big Banks. Swiss economic observers assess every US election, study the character and motivations of every British cabinet minister, weigh every De Gaulle speech, and advise their investment departments accordingly.

To some people this seems cold-blooded. But it is utterly necessary to the Swiss banking operation. Swiss bankers cannot afford to make many mistakes or do sentimental things with their money. If they did, their worldwide customers would take their money somewhere else. Premier Tshombe took his money to Geneva in 1963 precisely because he knew Swiss bankers would invest it in the safest and most profitable place and would under no circumstances return it to the Congo.

As a matter of record, it went to Wall Steet, for investment in US industry.

Certain elements of the world press and some governments, continually worried about what Swiss bank secrecy and practice conceals, have missed the point. The careful investors living in unstable nations, worried about their future, have not. Nor have the hundreds of European and American business firms and the dozen democratic governments of the Atlantic Community, who continually go to Swiss banks for money for honest purposes—and get it.

EIGHT

Les Rackets
Internationales,
or Who Needs
a Good
Swiss Bank?

FROM 1947 to 1957, a man called Pierre Du Val published a weekly investors newsletter, and the type of publication he issued was highly popular among new or small stock investors at the time. What none of Du Val's readers knew was that he was employed as an advisor to Lavan Trust and testified at Senate Committee hearings in New York that he worked indirectly for the Union Bank of Switzerland on instructions from Dr. Paul Hagenbach, president of Lavan Trust.

In 1955 while working for Hagenbach of Lavan Trust, Du Val ordered the purchase of a certain American stock for an American speculator whose name is not known. The stock was Cuneo Press, Inc., a perfectly respectable Chicago printing firm. Du Val received orders to buy 4000 shares of Cuneo at approximate price of 9.62½ with money sent him through the Union Bank. Almost simultaneously, Du Val wrote in his news letter about Cuneo Press and he advised everyone to buy at once.

Many of Du Val's readers had a bit of larceny in their souls and they dashed about snapping up all the Cuneo they could find. By September 14, 1957, five days after Du Val's "tip" was issued, Cuneo had gone to 14.50.

Du Val's American unrevealed client ordered him to sell the 4000 shares, and he did, on September 17. On a very simple operation, Du Val's client cleared $3.00 per share.

But the buy orders and the small furor over Cuneo attracted attention. The president of the firm told financial reporters he had no idea why the stock was advancing. Neither past, current, nor future profits justified it. Under the pressure of this news and the heavier selling pressure exerted by Du Val's unloading, Cuneo immediately fell back to 9. Several hundred people—who should have known better—suffered heavy losses.

Some promoters, speculators, and manipulators, and outright crooks were using Swiss banks as covers to operate inside the United States and swindle American citizens. An American stock promoter, for example, could place an entire issue of phony stock in the hands of a Swiss bank or Swiss trust handled by a Swiss bank. No Swiss bank could be subject to the jurisdiction of the US Securities and Exchange Commission. Therefore it did not have to submit a prospectus to the SEC, but it could sell the entire issue in the United States acting not as an underwriter but as an agent.

There were several Swiss banks willing to finance American speculators, legitimate or otherwise, on only 30 per cent margin. The European attitude toward stock sales and stock exchanges is different from the American. European banks and governments take the view that securities exchanges are for operators and no place for either the public or lambs. On the continent almost all stock purchasers operate through banks; the investors have a good idea of the risks entailed, and it is an entirely different kind of clientele.

Shoe clerks and car salesmen and people who know nothing about investment or finance do not get into the stock market, and no bank is interested in getting them in.

Dr. Paul Hagenbach, president of an outfit called Lavan Trust, used the Union Bank of Switzerland to handle sales transactions for him on some stocks. A consortium of Lavan Trust, Brandel Trust, and Sun Investment Establishment—all Swiss companies and all operating out of Swiss territory—sold stock in three American

corporations. The companies involved were Gulf Coast Leaseholds, Inc., Corpus Christi Refining Co., and Green Bay Mining
and Explorations, Ltd. Hagenbach's group, mostly Americans, put
these stocks on the market and by steady, small-volume buying
pushed the market up. Men were employed to help the
bandwagon along. The prices of the three companies' stocks
—all highly speculative, with low "book" values—rose enormously.

When Gulf Coast Leaseholds reached 14.50, Corpus Christi
Refining hit 4.00, and Green Bay stood at 12.50 a share, the Swiss
trusts unloaded. They cleared about $8 million, mostly out of the
pockets of New York investors. The three stocks immediately fell
to 1.75, 0.33, and no price respectively.

It was all very neat and, as it turned out, perfectly
safe.

The New York investors, too late, went to the police. An investigation by Louis Lefkowitz, the state attorney general, quickly
obtained evidence that both United States and New York laws
had been broken. But Lefkowitz, eager to prosecute, now ran up
against a stone wall. He couldn't bring a criminal action against a
foreign firm which, even though it took money from Americans,
had never even opened so much as an office on American soil.
Swiss corporations, headquartered in Switzerland, were beyond
American jurisdiction.

Lefkowitz complained to Washington, but the federal authorities only affirmed that there was nothing anyone could do. Meanwhile Washington, especially the Congress, had become concerned
with another kind of operation which was just hitting a peak in
the United States. This was the corporate raid, or proxy battle,
which by this time had begun to involve the three Swiss Big
Banks.

Thousands of shares of American companies had always been
owned through Swiss banks. These were held both by foreigners
and American citizens. However, the three Swiss banks operating on Wall Street—the Credit Bank, Union Bank, and Bank
Corporation—bought and sold in their own names. Under Swiss
bank secrecy, which applied to stock transactions on account as

well as to deposits, no bank ever revealed the actual beneficiary's name. Because of this long-established custom, insiders in Wall Street never paid much attention to what Swiss banks were doing in the market.

Leopold Silberstein, one of the more famous corporate raiders, like the Wolfson brothers of Florida or the Murchisons of Texas, hit upon the idea of using Swiss banks to buy up large chunks of the Fairbanks, Morse Company which he wanted to control. If he, or people known to be associated with him, had bought Fairbanks, Morse shares openly on the US market, the secret would have been exposed quickly, as the Wolfsons' abortive attempt to buy up controlling interest in Montgomery Ward was prematurely exposed in August 1954. But Silberstein's agents channeled money through Swiss banks, which bought the shares on order, and the plot only came to light after Silberstein staged his raid.

None of this was illegal. But the secrecy and cloak-and-dagger atmosphere surrounding it stirred up a hornet's nest in Washington, which still had uneasy memories about Swiss banks. Senators, and the chairman of the SEC, J. Sinclair Armstrong, expressed the fear that behind the cloak of Swiss bank secrecy Soviet, world Communist, or other subversive interests could buy up control of vital American defense industries. Armstrong was particularly upset because, as he said, it was possible for Americans to evade SEC rules as well as taxes through Swiss banks. He stated that more than two thirds of all American securities owned by foreigners were held in the names of the three Big Banks, anonymously, and there was deep concern in Washington who the actual owners might turn out to be.

Senate hearings were called to investigate the extent of Swiss influence, if any, in American financial affairs. SEC Chairman Armstrong repeated his fears and charges before the Senate Judiciary Committee on Banking and Currency. Senator Dennis Chavez (Democrat, N.M.) made a series of statements which revealed primarily his deep personal bias against most bankers, including the Swiss, and the committee chairman, Olin Johnston, even went so far as to notify the managing directors of the three

Big Banks of his intention to subpoena them if they ever set foot in the United States—something they were not now likely to do.

One fact which irritated Swiss opinion more than anything else was the assertion, stated or implied again and again by influential Americans, that Swiss banks would buy, sell, or do anything Communist interests wanted them to. As the Swiss angrily pointed out, Switzerland was one of the most anti-Communist nations on earth—even Socialists were in bad odor in the Confederation. While Americans might not know who the Swiss bank customers were, the Swiss bankers surely did. They considered charges that they could be manipulated by Soviet agents extremely unfair and slanderous, which they were.

But out of these hearings came a little light as well as noise. Several facts were presented which cooled Congress off considerably. One was that exactly one third of 1 per cent of all US industrial and rail securities were held by Swiss banks. This did represent a large amount of money, but it was a real indication that if the Russians had picked buying control of US industry as the way to subvert the United States they still had a long way to go. A Swiss newspaper blandly pointed out that it might be possible soon for the Communists to blow up the United States, but never to buy it. No Communist had that kind of money.

It was also revealed that under Article 14 of the Security and Exchange Act any owner, agent, or proxy holder attempting to vote more than 10 per cent of any American stock had to name the actual owner of the shares. There was no way around this clause, even for a secret Swiss bank. Further testimony showed that no Swiss bank, or all of them together, had ever come close to owning 10 per cent of the shares of any American defense industry.

The US Department of Defense got into the act and testified that even if Soviets should buy control of US defense industries this would get them exactly nowhere. The Department kept complete and detailed security information on each and every business firm and executive doing business with the government. One of the first things checked was the extent of foreign ownership, and all such checks had never shown a significant percentage of Swiss or any other overseas ownership in American industry. A secret security agency from the Pentagon testified it had never heard of any Swiss financial group which could represent a real danger to American defense industry. The American economy was just too big.

Finally, the powers of modern stockholders were much reduced. A mere stockholder, even a controlling stockholder in a defense corporation, was never permitted access to any secret work or production data in his own plants. Swiss banks might have their secrets—but the Department of Defense and American industry had their own.

Toward the close of the hearings, Senator Capehart of Indiana offered to introduce legislation to require anyone voting shares in corporate elections to reveal the actual ownership. But Armstrong protested this. Most large American brokerage houses such as Merrill Lynch and Bache & Company not only held securities but voted them for beneficiaries as holders of record. This was legal and the practice where the total shares owned did not exceed 10 per cent. Armstrong said to change this rule would work a hardship not only on American investment houses but the SEC itself. The issue was allowed to die.

But the hearings, acrimony, and extremely bad publicity taught the Swiss Banker's Association something. It took steps to keep its members from being used by American stock manipulators. It further made a hard-and-fast rule that all Swiss banks voting American shares in proxy fights would invariably vote for management unless specifically instructed otherwise. After 1957, no Swiss bank knowingly allowed itself to become involved in an American corporate proxy battle.

One problem, however, was that American operators would not always leave Swiss banks alone. In 1960, both the Chesapeake and Ohio and New York Central railroads became engaged in a struggle to gain control of another line, the Baltimore & Ohio. The B & O management had its troubles in 1960 and was anxious to merge with somebody. Both the competing railroads became interested in influencing the B & O's shareholders their way. Trying to find out who these shareholders were, Walter Tuohy of the Chesapeake and Ohio and New York Central Vice-president Walter Grant each discovered that between 20 and 40 per cent of the B & O's stock was held in the name of the three Big Swiss banks.

Each, at almost the same time, decided to strike a shrewd blow against the other. Tuohy, the Chesapeake's president, his secretary, and two minor vice-presidents of the line took a train from Cleveland to New York. There they boarded a transatlantic flight for Zurich.

One day later, July 26, 1960, Grant and Bates McKee, a partner in the financial firm of Bache & Co., flew secretly out of New York for the same destination. Like Tuohy, he thought he was unobserved, and like the Chesapeake president he carried a brief case full of arguments and offers for the stockholders of the B & O.

Both men knew the Swiss banks did not actually own the B & O stock, but they hoped they could convince the bank managers to advise the real owners to vote their way.

In Zurich the fun began.

Grant and McKee arrived at the airport at 8:30 A.M. July 27. They checked into the Hotel Storchen, then immediately phoned the Swiss Credit Bank for an appointment. The bank officer Grant talked to let slip that some Chesapeake and Ohio men had already arrived. Grant was immediately very upset; he demanded to know who, where, when, and why. Realizing what was happening, the bank official soothed Grant by telling him that the Chesapeake people had already left "for a vacation in the Alps."

At this moment, Tuohy and his party were actually in the Credit Bank making their pitch.

Grant became convinced that the rival corporation men were only low-ranking representatives and that his secret was safe. He made an appointment to see the Credit Bank officers, and later people in the Union Bank of Switzerland. After that, the next step was the Bank Corporation in Basel.

Now the officers of all three banks engaged in some delicate diplomacy. They got together and arranged a schedule which kept the two railroad executives from running into each other, or even realizing that the other was in town. It took careful timing, a series of phone calls, and tactful handling of important men— but the Swiss bankers enjoyed it hugely. In the next few days

Tuohy and Grant were sometimes inside the same bank, talking to different officials, and never knew it.

On July 30 Grant flew back to New York, telling McKee he was sure they had scored.

Walter Tuohy arrived back in Cleveland smiling and announced he was "well pleased" with his trip.

The Swiss bankers had promised each careful consideration. But after such consideration the managers of the three Big Banks, with their splendid intelligence services pooled, decided that the stockholders of the B & O would probably not agree to either merger. As it turned out, they were right.

The story of Grant's and Tuohy's wild goose chase got around, and since that time no top American executives have been eager to try personal influence on the Swiss banks.

Swiss banks do get involved, but only peripherally in some matters. In 1964 an American attorney in Texas was approached by a client who had owned a lucrative business in the Philippine Islands. The manager of this business had over the years embezzled a great deal of money, so much that the firm itself collapsed. Some of the firm's transactions had been cleared through a Swiss bank. There was nothing unusual in this, since a high percentage of all international businesses employ Swiss accounts for convenience in making payments without having to clear through currency restrictions or official national accounts. But in this case the Philippine manager of the business had deposited certain large checks to his own separate account.

The attorney, a bright young man, traced the case down reasonably well. But in the end he advised his client to take his losses and forget it. He had also uncovered evidence to show that any official international legal action, which would bring the United States government into the act, would also reveal certain things about the business to the Internal Revenue Service embarrassing or at least costly to his client.

The Swiss bank involved never suspected it had served in a swindle.

On July 18, 1958, the Ambassador of the United States to the Swiss Confederation, Mr. Henry J. Taylor, granted an interview to the president of United Press International, Frank Bartholomew. Bartholomew was looking for a sensational story, and he got one.

As Bartholomew reported in *The New York Times* and other large American papers, Taylor told him: "There has been a heavy increase in financial transactions in Bern in connection with the narcotics traffic from Communist China to the Western world" and "There is reason to believe that the Communists send out an average of $1,000,000 a week from Switzerland to spies, provocateurs, and contraband agents for their work in the Western democracies."

Ambassador Taylor blamed this state of affairs on the famed Swiss bank secrecy. Bank secrecy made any outside investigation impossible—but Taylor definitely hinted that Swiss banks connived at such trade. When the story was played up in the American press—provoking a New York *Journal-American* editorial against Swiss banks—the federal authorities at Bern lodged a strong protest with the US State Department.

On July 25, 1958, the State Department apologized. But the apology carefully omitted any reference to Mr. Taylor's allegations being untrue. Taylor himself stated he had been misquoted. In New York, Frank Bartholomew stated that what Mr. Taylor now said was "not in accord with the facts."

All this pointed up two things: the sweeping allegations continually made against Swiss banks and the unsavory connotations Swiss bank secrecy has in many American minds. Charges of assisting the narcotics, vice, and gunrunning rackets and aiding the Communist cause meanwhile deeply anger the Swiss people.

On inspection the charges do not quite cling. All kinds of rackets money does go through Swiss banks. But rackets money goes through banks in every part of the world, and the United States is no exception. Illegal international operations by their very nature have to seek disguises. At any given time, there are millions of dollars from North American heroin sales, or the numbers racket in New York, in perfectly respectable US national banks. Worse, as Congressional hearings in 1964 and 1965 revealed, there is evidence—though no case has been proved—that criminal organizations such as the shadowy Mafia have actually gained control of some US banks.

No bank can completely investigate every depositor—particularly if he operates through a perfectly genuine and respectable front.

It is extremely doubtful if any Swiss bank will knowingly serve as a clearing house for narcotics, rackets, or Communist cash. Switzerland may have bank secrecy, but crimes against property, commercial prostitution or white slavery, narcotics addiction or gambling rackets are virtually unknown.

Swiss banking is not orthodox by American standards, but the vast majority of Swiss banks are both legitimate and rather staid. Significantly, most scandals involving them revolve around foreigners. The whole idea that Swiss banks are easily open to criminal use is one that has been created in the American mind, and the principal reason is that US and Swiss law differ on what is "criminal." The ethic of the two countries meanwhile is almost the same.

The problem stems from the fact that in Switzerland fiscal, exchange, gold, and tax questions are not treated as crimes. Almost everywhere else money is not regarded as private property, and tax evasion is considered a crime against the state. Swiss freedom has ironically come to seem quite criminal in many eyes. But under international law the Swiss are under no obligation to make tax evasion criminal, or to help other nations catch their tax evaders. After all, the United States does not enforce Soviet notions of free speech on Russian citizens resident in America. The Swiss, like the Americans, simply extend their domestic freedoms to foreigners, whether their respective governments like it or not.

If this is immoral, Switzerland has still made the most of it.

Because the Swiss will not cooperate with other governments on fiscal matters, too many people, including some criminals, have jumped to the conclusion that Switzerland will not cooperate where swindling, fraud, dope peddling, counterfeiting, or Communist subversion is concerned. This is absolutely untrue. All these things are serious crimes in Switzerland, and are taken seriously.

For example, Swiss statutes against counterfeiting are the most rigid in the world. It is against the law to forge any note or coin, whether current or first issued by Julius Caesar. The Swiss look on counterfeiting as a crime against property and individuals, and therefore unlike the British, German, or American governments, enforce it against a forger of Roman as well as just Swiss coins. All most other governments are concerned about is that they themselves are not defrauded.

Switzerland does not belong to the United Nations, but it is not an island. It is a charter member of the International Criminal Police Organization, Interpol. Interpol, which operates out of the rue Valéry in Paris with an office of fifty men and women, is a little-known but powerful force fighting international crime. It can call on the national police forces of eighty-odd nations. To run afoul of Interpol, a criminal merely has to commit an international crime—one which spans or runs across the criminal codes of at least two nations. Interpol cannot investigate every international crime—but in 1964 there were 200,000 case files in its drawers.

Switzerland is a member of Interpol all the way. When the Interpol radio network calls, Bern acts. One spectacular international fraud case proves the point.

On April 16, 1954, the Kredietbank in Antwerp, Belgium, received a request from the Banco Nacional Ultramarino of Lisbon to open credit in the amount of $865,000 on behalf of the government of Portuguese Goa. The Portuguese bank asked that the money be credited to a Belgian shipping firm called Hantra. The credit was to be good through June 12, 1954, and it was for the purpose of financing a shipment of 8000 tons of Italian and Burmese rice to the seaport of Mormugao. Substantiating documents, such as bills of lading, insurance policies, and consular invoices, were to be mailed later.

The bank followed instructions. It was a perfectly legitimate request, the kind European mercantile banks handle daily.

Shortly afterward, the Kredietbank received instructions not from Hantra in Antwerp, but its branch office in Basel. These papers stated that the confirming documents would be sent the bank from a Colombo company called Modern Industries, Ltd. They further advised disposition of the Hantra credits as follows:

Slightly over $8000 was reserved for the firm of Outshoorn & Landau, for cargo insurance.

Another $6000 was authorized for Hantra itself, as fees.

A bloc of $669,860 was to be sent to the Banca Report,

Lugano, Switzerland, to the credit of one George Kaufman.

There was also nothing suspicious in all this. The amounts for fees and insurance seemed right, and international companies were always making disbursements through Switzerland because of currency and other restrictions.

Then, several days later, on May 21, 1954, a certain Herr von Hornung showed up at the Kredietbank. He introduced himself to Mijnheer Verbruggen, the managing director, as the head of Hantra's branch in Basel. He was handling the Lisbon–Goa rice deal. He gave Verbruggen letters confirming the transaction and an invoice showing the rice had been bought and shipped.

Now matters began to move with the intricate, exact timing all great financial frauds require. A messenger came to the bank with a consular invoice certifying the rice had left the port. It was signed by the Portuguese consul in Antwerp. The ship was *Trianon*, a Norwegian freighter owned by the Wilhelmsen company of Oslo. There was such a ship, and Verbruggen saw no reason to inspect the documents closely. The stamps and ribbons looked official.

While this was happening, a Belgian named Mayers, who operated an office for Marinex, a local shipping firm, procured an insurance policy from Outshoorn & Landau. Outshoorn was a respectable brokerage firm, and a genuine policy was written and delivered to the Kredietbank, which paid them with the credits established earlier by Lisbon. The bank now had all the necessary papers; the deal seemed consummated. Verbruggen airmailed the papers on to the government of Portuguese Goa and, following von Hornung's letter of instructions, transferred $669,860 to Banca Report in Lugano.

The money had hardly arrived when one George Kaufman arrived in Lugano from Italy and demanded $366,860, which he accepted in Swiss francs. The remaining $303,000 Herr Kaufman ordered transferred to the Hofmann Bank, Zurich, where it was to be placed to the drawing account of Herr André Klotz. This was done.

Now Herr Klotz made himself known to the satisfaction of Bank Hofmann, and the bank arranged with a large bullion trader in Zurich for a major transaction. The gold merchants were to hand over to anyone presenting an Italian thousand-lire note, serial number 6/85/18364, four cases of fine gold, worth about $300,000.

The same day an unknown caller showed the bill, collected the gold, and disappeared.

But back in Antwerp Mijnheer Verbruggen just now received a nasty shock. Banco Nacional Ultramarino wired from Lisbon, wanting to know which ship Hantra had placed the rice on and when it would arrive at Mormugao. The Kredietbank called the local agents for the freighter line in Antwerp and asked when *Trianon* would arrive. The Wilhelmsen Line's agents in Antwerp reported (1) *Trianon* did not carry rice, (2) Mormugao was not among the ship's ports of call.

Verbruggen insisted on calling Oslo long distance before he would accept the fact that the bank had been had. Neither Wilhelmsen nor the Antwerp branch of Hantra knew anything about the deal. Paling, Verbruggen sent a priority cable to Lugano, ordering the Report Bank to stop payment on the transferred credits.

He was exactly twenty-four hours too late. Kaufman had come and gone. All Verbruggen could do now was call the Antwerp police—who notified Interpol.

This was a case which eventually involved Portuguese, Ceylonese, Belgian, British, Swiss, and French police investigations, and it is one that is still talked about in commercial circles in Europe. The following facts are from Swiss investigative files.

The search began in Antwerp, by Belgian detectives. They quickly established certain facts: the papers furnished the Kredietbank—commercial invoices from Hantra, the consular invoices of Portugal—were forged. A party or parties unknown had stepped into the middle of a legitimate international deal and by clever timing made off with $669,000. The police had something to go on: the man named Mayers. They discovered he had talked to the Kredietbank about financing a commercial shipment out of the Basel branch of Hantra some time earlier. He had also handled the fraudulent insurance arrangements—needed to fool the bank—with Outshoorn & Landau. The police entered the offices of Marinex, arrested Mayers, and searched the place. In Marinex files they found correspondence from Hantra's Basel branch signed by G. von Hornung, branch manager.

Mayers screamed innocence. All he had done, he claimed, was to make his office and his services available to von Hornung, who had hired him. The insurance deal had been done at von Hornung's request. Mayer's story held up, while investigation showed that the Swiss, while in Antwerp, had placed phone calls to Paris, London, Lugano, Basel, and Olten, a town in Switzerland.

This was as far as the Belgian branch of Interpol could go. The case was turned over to the Swiss police at Bern. They went after G. von Hornung.

Von Hornung seemed to be a respectable businessman, in complete control of the Hantra Basel office. But the police gave him a bad time. Hornung could not answer all the questions sensibly, but they did not yet have enough to hold him. When the interrogation was over, Hornung was released under surveillance. He went home and committed suicide.

But von Hornung left behind a signed confession. According to him, he had been sucked into a trap he did not understand. In March 1954 he had received a letter from a firm in Ceylon called Modern Industries, Ltd. This company asked him to help in a deal which would get Modern Industries some badly needed Swiss francs. All they asked von Hornung to do was to allow himself, and his Basel Hantra branch, to be used as an intermediary. They would make it worth his while, and the home office need not be told.

Von Hornung knew the deal was illegal—currency restrictions and all that—but he claimed he never knew it was completely crooked.

The Basler went to Paris, where he met the top man in Modern Industries, Ltd.: a Ceylonese named Emile Savundranayagam. Savundranayagam laid out the steps von Hornung was to take, which included the forged shipping invoices from Hantra. He did not, however, handle the forged Portuguese consular documents. He returned to Basel with Dade, an Englishman who was Savundranayagam's aide. From there he proceeded on to Antwerp.

When the police questioned him, von Hornung realized what had happened and also that he was ruined. He took his life.

The Swiss police now turned to the question of Lugano and

George Kaufman. From the banks involved they got lines on Kaufman and the man called Klotz. They knew André Klotz—he had a reputation as a gold smuggler around the world. And they were sure that George Kaufman was actually a Swiss citizen named Fernand Geissman who had moved to Paris. They found that Kaufman, or Geissman, had approached Klotz in Lugano through the services of one Dr. Bera, an "adviser" to the Report Bank. Klotz' role was certain: he had eventually smuggled the gold from Zurich into France. A warrant was issued for Geissman, and sometime later he surrendered.

Geissman talked, but he seemed to confuse the trail even more. He said in Paris he had fallen in with two Yugoslavs called Miljusz and Sorz. Sorz had hired him to go to Lugano and collect some money at Report Bank under a false name. Geissman said Dr. Bera was in on the deal, or seemed to be: he had put Geissman in touch with Klotz, and had also vouched for "Kaufman's" identity at the bank.

After getting the money, Geissman claimed he had gone directly to Olten, Switzerland; here he gave 410,000 Swiss francs to a Herr Horn. From Olten he returned to Paris, where he gave Sorz the balance of the money.

The Swiss police went up to Olten, and looked up a lawyer named Horn. Horn indignantly denied any connection with Geissman under any name. He had been out of town on the date in question. His son, however, seemed to provide an answer. The younger Horn told police he had seen Geissman meet one of his father's clients, a Pole named Mniszek, in the family house. Doubtless Geissman took Mniszek for Horn. The police dropped the investigation of Herr Horn, but not until after they found out Mniszek had paid the lawyer two heavy fees, and Horn had told them the Pole was manager of Tewex in Paris, another shipping firm which had close connections with Hantra.

Bern wired Paris Interpol to run down Sorz, Miljusz, Mniszek (this put enormous strain on the Interpol phonetic alphabet) and to start looking for $300,000 in smuggled gold. Meanwhile, from von Hornung's information, Swiss police understood that Dade and Savundranayagam were now in England. They wired London.

British police took Savundranayagam into custody, and he was extradited to Antwerp, where the fraud had been committed.

Dade was released; there was nothing to connect him personally with the crime.

Savundranayagam was an interesting character. He had been an army officer in Ceylon, where he had made a fortune on "surplus sales" and military contracts. He formed Modern Industries, Ltd., the Ceylon firm, and subsequently set up his headquarters in London, from where he had planned the Kredietbank fraud.

Pickup orders crossed Europe on the three Slavs. French police acted on a Belgian warrant: Mniszek was apprehended trying to board a flight in Bordeaux. Sorz was arrested at an apartment in Montparnasse. The Swiss, Dr. Bera, who had disappeared from Lugano, was picked up by the Sûreté near Le Bourget. Miljusz disappeared—and so did almost all the money. The gold was never found.

Bera, Savundranayagam, Sorz, and Mniszek were tried in Belgium. The Ceylonese was found guilty, fined 40,000 Belgian francs, and got five years. Sorz and Mniszek were fined and given four years each. Dr. Bera was acquitted, but died within a short period of time.

The other men involved were not brought to trial. The Belgian courts considered them mere catspaws, not principals in the crime.

The convicted criminals, however, did not serve long in jail. They had money, and they retained the best and most expensive Belgian law firms. Some, including Savundranayagam, were able to get their sentences remitted, and received pardons.

When last heard of, Savundranayagam had reportedly set himself up as a businessman in London.

The narcotics trade, a dirty and deadly business, worries United States authorities greatly because it is almost wholly a Europe-to-America export. The files of Interpol, which devotes a major portion of its efforts to halting the narcotics trade, show some interesting things. One, incidentally, is that Interpol has no real quarrel with Swiss banks. Swiss financial freedom, bank secrecy, and free exchange of gold—used extensively in narcotics payments—are convenient to narcotics manufacturers and smugglers. But they could operate without them.

Opium, the basic commodity in narcotics trade, is grown in many places—Turkey, Africa, the Middle East, and most of all in or on the fringes of China. It is transported in very large quantities into Europe, because raw opium itself is not very valuable. In most of Asia it can be bought easily for about fifty dollars per pound. To make raw opium very valuable, it must be processed into refined products of greater potency and less weight, such as morphine and heroin. This processing is almost confined to Italy and France. For many years clandestine laboratories have operated in these countries. Also, the legal production of narcotics has generally far exceeded any possible legitimate medical use in Italy. Some of this regularly disappears into illicit narcotics channels. The trade is impossible to stop because the profits are immense.

A pound of opium made into morphine in a European lab is worth $360. Processed further into heroin, the real killer drug, the price becomes $1700. By the time heroin hits New York, the principal market, the 45,000 American addicts have bid the price up to a dollar per single grain. Narcotics processers and shippers clear millions. At least $300 million is spent on narcotics by Americans each year.

This money gives the highly organized narcotics rings real power. It makes the policing job difficult. Narcotics people have the money to bribe and the money to set up elaborate and costly fronts. Both Interpol and the US Bureau of Narcotics know that France and Italy are major transit points. In 1961 more than a thousand cases of Western European narcotics trafficking were revealed. In 1957 four tons of opium were seized. Some 250 narcotics smugglers were arrested. Eighty-three ocean-going vessels were involved. Seven illegal opium-processing laboratories were found and closed. In spite of all this, because there was so much money to be made, by 1964 the trade had vastly increased.

Bank secrecy has nothing whatever to do with this. Neither France, Italy, nor the United States has bank secrecy. Their police have full powers. If these nations cannot stop the trade, it is rather ridiculous to blame the Swiss. Narcotics money does flow through Swiss banks—behind respectable covers in each case—for the same reason General Motors, Caltex, and IBM money does. It is convenient, and worry-free, to use Swiss banks. An

Italian mafiosa combine sending heroin to the United States finds it as helpful to use a Swiss bank as an international clearing house as an American corporation to repatriate profits back to New York. The Swiss nation does abet international rackets in a minor way by its complete fiscal freedom. But to end fiscal freedom just to stop international rackets money would be to throw the baby out with the bath water, and the Swiss know it.

If suppliers, shippers, laboratories, and smugglers in China, Egypt, Lebanon, France, Italy, Mexico, and New York are paid out of Swiss banks, they could be and are also paid out of Hong Kong, Beirut, Rome, and US national banks. It is all part—a small part—of the international import-export trade.

The money milked from the American economy by other rackets, primarily gambling, is something else.

The American gambling and white slavery syndicates are homegrown and owned and operated by Americans. They have almost nothing to do with Europe, and consequently have no real use for a Swiss bank. The charge, continually printed in the North American press and widely believed by millions of people that many American gangsters, hoodlums, and other racketeers hide their money in Switzerland is false.

There are two reasons for this. One is the innate provincialism of the American gangster. A Mafia man may be of Sicilian extraction, but he is almost always anti-European in his outlook. Switzerland may have convenient banking laws, but they are outside his area of interest or sphere of operations. The charge that this kind of person does business with Swiss banks only brings rueful smiles to the faces of Swiss bankers—who will admit, privately, that they do sometimes let narcotics or Communist payoffs slip by them.

Most sophisticated investment men in the United States are aware that the big American rackets use what is known as the "Latin American loophole" for hiding and disposing of their money. If American racketeers sent their money to Switzerland it would have to be reinvested overseas, and most Swiss bankers would recommend that it be put back in Wall Street. This, naturally, hardly suits the racketeer mentality. The money could be simply stored in safe-deposit boxes, without interest—but American syndicalists are too smart, and too well-organized, for that. They have found safe and far more profitable ways.

Money gleaned from the numbers or racing rackets in New York, or from the gambling tables in Las Vegas is sent, in cash, to banks in South America. Panama, some of the Caribbean banana republics, and even Montevideo have convenient banking laws. Here banks either cooperate with or are bought by American syndicates. The South American moral codes, unfortunately, are not quite like that of the Swiss. United States agents have long been aware that illicit cash enters and leaves the US in many diplomatic pouches.

The money can then be "borrowed" back from the bank to finance legitimate and highly profitable business in the United States. Loans from Montevidean banks have financed more than one Las Vegas club, dairy farm, trucking business, and the like. The South American connection helps avoid US taxation, too, as well as covering any original odor attached to the money. It is as impossible for US government agents to investigate South American banks as it is for them to enter the Swiss.

Only when the Mafia or other organization pulls the same gambit with a US national or state bank does the operation become vulnerable. While no cases have yet been proved, investigations by Congress and the Internal Revenue Service indicated in 1964 that several American banks had been organized, bought, or capitalized by hoodlum money as a means of getting it back into the legitimate US economy.

Since organized illegal gambling drains several billion dollars a year from the American economy, giving it immense sums to operate with, this trade is as impossible to stop as the international narcotics racket. Money which reaches the seven-figure bracket automatically attains power, even a certain respectability. For one thing, the best legal talent in the country can be employed either openly or behind the scenes to set up almost foolproof financial deals.

The Communist connection with Swiss banks is as tenuous as that of the dope peddlers. There is no Communist movement in Switzerland, unlike some other Western European nations. But no country allows freer movement in or out, or is less a police state. Several million American and European tourists pass through the Confederation each year with minimum trouble and without customs inspection, and any Communist or Communist-front organization which wants to set up a bank account can. Of course, no such account is set up in the name of the Soviet Union or a local European Communist organization. But there are several dozen French, Italian, or Eastern European companies which serve the same purpose.

It is reputed that a certain number of Communist agents in Switzerland are neither citizens of Communist states nor Communists, and this is very likely. Like many spies, contact men, and other kinds of agent they are "businessmen" serving anyone who pays. Few, if any, of these men are native Swiss.

Again, Swiss accounts can serve as convenient clearing houses for payments from Moscow to local party organizations or agents anywhere in the world. A Swiss check can finance subversion in Africa or South America as easily as in Western Europe. Communist or any other kind of espionage is illegal in Switzerland, and is sharply limited by the Swiss security service. However, because of Switzerland's strategic position and neutrality, it is equally as hard to control as espionage in Vienna or Berlin, and again, as in the narcotics traffic, Switzerland and its banks are only way stations.

According to informed estimates, most Communist money passing through Switzerland does not go to pay spies, agents, or saboteurs. United States intelligence sources have guessed—there is no real way to get precise figures—that between $50 million and $100 million clears through Swiss banks each year. Most of this Soviet money—sometimes the result of Russian sales of gold on the open Zurich market—is used to finance Soviet or East European satellite purchases in the West. Since the Swiss don't care to handle Communist business, and because many of the purchases are of strategic materials which NATO nations are not allowed to export to the East, this trade also seeks protective coloration.

Actually, the rules banning the sale of certain strategic items to the USSR have always been full of holes. The contraband regulations were put in force on the insistence of the American government but never were favored by either European governments or businessmen. Except during hotter periods of the Cold

War European firms have generally wanted to develop the Eastern trade, and sell Russia machine tools, aircraft engines, or anything else the Soviet industrial plant required. The French and British governments, in 1964, even granted Moscow long-term credits for industrial purchases over Washington's strenuous objections.

Western industrialists and politicians want foreign exchange and full employment, and there are a number of very powerful interests favoring increased trade behind the Iron Curtain. The sale of American wheat to Russia in 1963 had the overwhelming approval of American businessmen, and this transaction further battered the few trading regulations on which European nations still stood firm.

While neither the United States nor the British government will openly issue an export license for certain strategic goods to go behind the Iron Curtain, there are ways around such controls. The same goods can be easily sold and exported to a Belgian firm or to one of several European companies acting as agents for so-called "neutral" nations (like Yugoslavia) which maintain regular trade connections with both East and West. Under this arrangement, goods arriving at Brussels can either be transshipped to a Yugoslav freighter—which then goes to Gydnia, Poland—or to Yugoslavia itself, for transshipment to Hungary and eventually the USSR.

Because of tight currency controls, the difficulty of convertibility between Communist and Western moneys, payment is most conveniently handled through a Swiss commercial bank. While Switzerland neither makes the materials nor authorizes their export, Swiss banks tend to receive the blame for the whole transaction.

Actually, the only effective way to control this trade would be to ban most trading between the United States and Europe and all of the neutral or uncommitted nations of the world, and this is not politically possible in peacetime. The US can no longer enforce a blacklist as it did during and after World War II.

Another frequent criticism of the Swiss is their participation in arms deals. Armaments are a federal monopoly in Switzerland. Bern neither makes weapons for export normally nor sells them to questionable parties. Other nations, such as France, Sweden,

Britain, and especially the United States, dominate the international arms trade, but many arms deals are closed in Switzerland. It is a convenient place for Algerian rebels and German arms-makers to meet, or for Angolan representatives to dicker for Czechoslovakian machine guns. Again, a check on a big Swiss bank is the simplest manner of handling payment. It even lends the transaction a certain respectability.

Ironically, the single biggest private arms dealer in the world is an American citizen, who lives in Monaco. He buys old or obsolescent European weapons, sometimes securing the whole supply of rifles or submachine guns of a smaller power such as Argentina or Finland when a model change is made. These guns can then be sold to a less-advanced nation in Africa or Asia which lacks the money to purchase the latest arms. This dealer operates openly, does nothing in violation of international law, and uses a good Swiss bank purely for reasons of discretion, taxation, and convenience. In all three, any Swiss bank offers a combination impossible to beat.

Regarding illicit trade and international rackets Swiss banks merely serve as clearing houses, and in doing so they merely reflect the state of a world which Switzerland itself never made. While American critics regularly and truthfully accuse Swiss banks of allowing themselves to be used by the Communist powers, the reverse of this coin is almost never broached: the Central Intelligence Agency, and British, French, and West German intelligence services all maintain Swiss bank accounts under careful covers. They use these to pay agents and informers and defectees all over the world as well as to finance their own operations.

British and American corporations use Swiss banks to handle all their difficult or intricate foreign payments. They channel overseas earnings back into Swiss banks to build convenient "outside" capital for foreign expansion or other perfectly legal operations. They do it to avoid currency controls, the bureaucratic regulation of central national banks, and publicity. They could use Hong Kong or Bahama or Beirut banks, but the Swiss are better bankers.

Complete inspection and control of all Swiss banks by Bern would not completely halt any of this trade. All international rackets and international espionage and subversion have adopted legitimate "fronts." It is increasingly harder to tell a Communist from a capitalist, or an IBM man from a paymaster for the Italian-American narcotics ring.

The US Department of Justice has waged a bitter fight against domestic American rackets for years. It is not winning, even by the Department's own score.

The US has nothing resembling bank secrecy, and any state or federal law agency can open any American bank. Warrants will be issued even for so-called fishing expeditions. But very little racketeer money has been found.

Phony stock is still sold in the United States every day, and Swiss banks have nothing to do with it.

Congressional hearings have revealed that in Pittsburgh, for example, IRS men regularly used electronic eavesdropping devices and wiretaps—illegal under American law—and still could not separate Mafia money from legitimate cash.

Some kinds of international rackets will probably go on forever even if Swiss banks should disappear.

Shysters and Sophisticates: The North American Trade

SOMETIME in June 1960, an obscure Middle Western attorney named Edgar M. Mendenhall turned a nice contingency deal for a client. He took the case against a contingency, but with a guarantee. The legal matters involved are not important, or unusual—but in the end Edgar Mendenhall became the owner of an Iowa apartment house, which he proceeded to liquidate quietly for $100,000 after all taxes were paid. The money crystallized a scheme he had in mind.

Mendenhall paid his taxes honestly, but he had a problem. Mendenhall was planning to divorce his wife, and he had no intention of having to split with her any of his newly made money. He had been sufficiently careful to keep her in complete ignorance of the $100,000 deal.

A lawyer, Edgar Mendenhall had a clear idea of what American courts would do to him on alimony and property settlements, because the only grounds he had for divorce was the fact he intended to remarry—this time a girl twenty years younger who was working in Des Moines. If his wife got most, or even half, of his money, all Mendenhall's dreams were out. He thought the problem through, and realized the only solution was to get his capital out of the country, or at least beyond the reach of any legal decree. His legal training informed him that if the money was safe he could easily avoid contempt of court proceedings, if necessary, by skipping the state or going to Mexico. A man who had never cared for the legal business anyway could do a lot on a hundred thousand dollars, especially if inspired by a young wife.

Everything Edgar Mendenhall had heard or read convinced him that a Swiss bank was the only place to put his cash. But this involved another problem: how did an American living in Iowa transfer his money to a Swiss bank?

Mendenhall made a few discreet queries, and discovered that Middle Western ignorance of Swiss banks was profound. He talked to a Des Moines banker whom he knew slightly, and delicately introduced the subject—without, however, indicating any personal interest. This banker told him that virtually the only Swiss banks which did any North American business were the Big Three—Credit Bank, Union Bank, and the Bank Corporation. These all had offices or branches in New York City: the Union Bank a Manhattan subsidiary, and the Credit Bank a branch at 25 Pine Street. Any American could do business with them in person, or by writing.

This was not exactly what Mendenhall was looking for. If possible, he wanted to put his money away in such a manner it could not be traced. The New York Swiss affiliates could transfer his $100,000 on to Switzerland, but the record of their Stateside transactions was of course available to American law.

Again concealing his personal interest by pretending it was for a client, Mendenhall queried another banker, one who had originally come from Chicago and who seemed both sophisticated and informed. Now, Mendenhall learned that a number of Swiss banks, both large commercial and private, had representatives scattered across the country. These men were generally not bankers, or connected with any bank, but investment men. They dealt with American investors who wanted to put, say, 10 per cent of their stock holdings outside Wall Street or the Big Board in Chicago.

Mendenhall got the name of one of these men and looked him up. This representative was a gray-haired, dignified American of about fifty-five who dealt in various sorts of investments, sometimes with very important people. He was on friendly terms with the Uihlein family of Wisconsin, the makers of Schlitz beer, who—though this was generally unknown—had millions of dollars in Canadian and other overseas investments, Schlitz being only one family enterprise.

This man received Mendenhall courteously. But the lawyer apparently convinced him that there was something shady about the business, and he showed no great eagerness to get his hands on Mendenhall's money. Rather ruefully, he also explained that one of his continuing problems was that the average American had an *idée fixe* that there was something crooked about Swiss banks, and that only crooks or hoodlums did business with them. It was rather the other way around, he also explained—generally, only the wealthiest and most sophisticated of American families, such as Uihleins, Reynolds (the tobacco people) or Whitneys saw the advantages of keeping some investments abroad.

The Americans most understanding of Swiss banks were people who were familiar with Europe, had spent some time there, or who were among that select group which kept a son or daughter in one of the superb Swiss preparatory schools.

Almost everyone else, unless he had a covert reason for trying to hide money, was suspicious of foreign banks.

Mendenhall showed some signs of annoyance because this Swiss bank representative did not jump to take his money, even after he made it clear he was talking about a six-figure sum. He left the man's office.

But he had learned more information. Swiss bank representatives traveled about, and from what had been said, they did quite a business in Mexico. Mendenhall decided to take a short trip south of the border.

His wife was surprised, but delighted, at the unexpected vacation. About a week after Mendenhall talked to the Middle Western representative, between the eighth and tenth of August 1960, they flew to Mexico City.

Here the lawyer felt he could operate more openly. Leaving his wife to shop alone, he entered the Banco Nacional de Mexico, S.A. Here he found a helpful executive who both spoke English and was intrigued by Mendenhall, mistaking him for some kind of *Yanqui* racketeer. At this time the lawyer still wore old-style suits, with broad lapels and flowered ties. The Mexican banker was quite helpful. He himself had nothing to do with Swiss banks, although he was very aware that a great deal of the Banco

Nacional's stock was sold and held through certain banks in Switzerland. He gave Mendenhall a couple of addresses and phone numbers.

A few hours afterward, Mendenhall entered the offices of a branch of a well-known large Swiss bank. He got an interview in a private office with a banker who was a Swiss citizen living in Mexico. He told the banker he wanted to put $100,000 in a Swiss bank, in Switzerland. He further stated bluntly that he had the money in cash. Mendenhall had converted the proceeds from the apartment building into large US notes at an out-of-town bank before he left.

The Swiss, who spoke perfect English, told Mendenhall politely he needed to have some idea where the money was coming from. In other words, Mendenhall would have to show it was not stolen funds. Mendenhall took what he considered a very small risk, and explained the whole story.

The Swiss was amused. There was just enough skullduggery, with a hint of sex in the background, to intrigue his very Protestant, puritanical mind. He listened, then informed Mendenhall that since so far as he could see no American or Swiss law had yet been broken, there was no reason why the bank could not accept the money. The fact that it obviously wouldn't be a joint account didn't bother the banker—almost all Swiss bankers, on principle, despise joint accounts as a ridiculous American invention. He even told Mendenhall that in the Confederation any Swiss male had the right to put his money in a bank account where no wife could get at it without his consent, even through the courts.

Mendenhall then asked for a numbered account. The banker explained that there was really no need for this—but if the customer insisted, he was entitled to it. He himself would attend to the details of transferring the dollar credits through the bank to Switzerland. To open a numbered account involved no trip to Switzerland; it could all be handled through the Mexican branch.

Papers were signed, and the deal went smoothly. The banker explained in detail various banking requirements: beneficiaries, and instructions on how the money should be used. Here for the first time the Iowa lawyer understood the Swiss banks were most interested in getting money to invest on account, like US brokerage houses. They did not care for plain deposits, but for money they could use to buy shares around the world, and hold for the customer's account.

The bank also demanded identification; they had to be sure that Edgar M. Mendenhall of Iowa was an actual person, and who he said he was.

Now, there was another complication, the banker explained. Since 1951 an agreement had been in effect between Switzerland and the United States on withholding taxes. The Swiss banks had to withhold 15 per cent of all dividends and interest on American citizens. If the money should be invested inside the US by the bank, then another 15 per cent would be withheld at the source, under American law. This meant that if Mendenhall's money came back to Wall Street he would be taxed a total of 30 per cent—which he could apply, of course, against his US income tax or get a refund if due by making the proper entry on his tax return.

Mendenhall did not like this at all, and he immediately specified that he did not want his money placed in American investments. He was also concerned about the 15 per cent Swiss banks withheld—how was this reported to the US authorities? The banker assured him that no special report was made; it was simply a matter of international agreement to cut down on income-tax cheating by investors in either country. The bank was obliged to collect the tax, but not required to report it or Mendenhall's money to the US Treasury. But, the banker added carefully, there was no arrangement on capital gains. If, through the bank's buying and selling stocks he made a capital gain, there was no tax and no report.

Whether he reported the gain or not was between Mendenhall, his conscience, and his government. The Swiss were not involved.

Mendenhall went into the question of simply depositing his money, without all the stock market folderol. The banker told him this could be done, but on this the bank would not pay interest, and further, it would charge him a kind of custodial fee for the service. This came about because there was a "gentleman's agreement" between Swiss banks that they would not invest foreign money in Switzerland, where there was already too much of it.

Mendenhall's $100,000 could be stashed safely in Switzerland, but he would have to pay for the privilege, which was different from any arrangement he had heard about. He didn't like this, either.

But it was a take-it-or-leave-it proposition. He instructed the bank to take his money on deposit, charge him, and await further instructions. They could charge fees against the account, while he arranged certain other details of his life.

Leaving his money, Edgar Mendenhall returned with his wife to Iowa, greatly relieved. In due time a decidedly bitter divorce contest came about. The lawyer played his cards carefully enough so that he was granted the divorce—but investigations by his wife's attorney uncovered the $100,000 apartment payment, traced down the check which had been given to Mendenhall, and even found out where and when he cashed it. Mendenhall had been able to fool his wife, but her lawyer was a different proposition. If Mrs. Mendenhall had been of a different nature, the divorce would have collapsed over the property settlement. But all the evidence tends to show that she was as glad to get rid of him as he was of her. She got the family house, the family car, and most of the money Mendenhall had in the local bank, and because her lawyer told her the kind of man she was up against, she did not hold out for alimony. Mendenhall's involved scheme worked. He got clear and free with $100,000.

But the girl he planned to marry changed her mind. His law practice was ruined over the divorce question. The IRS—which was never able to prove anything—made his life miserable. In 1964 he was living in Mexico, on checks drawn against his Swiss bank.

The American trade with Swiss banks breaks down into just four broad classes: sophisticates, shysters, overseas corporations, and their employees.

Americans who live in Switzerland, do business in Switzerland, or have some known connection with a Swiss bank are frequently approached, sometimes furtively, by people who want to know more about a numbered account. These are almost never the really big people, top industrialists or members of well-known American families such as Kennedy, Vanderbilt, or Dupont. These people know about Swiss banks as part of their general financial sophistication. Most of them have been to Switzerland, or lived there at one time. Many of them do keep Swiss accounts, for convenience or to finance children's education. About one third of the clientele of Switzerland's exclusive, snob—and very good—preparatory schools is from North America.

Very wealthy Americans, particularly those with assets of $10 million or more, have no particular need for any Swiss bank. They can hire the best investment talent at home. The number of really rich Americans who fear inflation, or revolution, or confiscation, is infinitesimal. Nor do the very rich have a real tax problem. Sullivan and Cromwell or any other topflight New York law firm specializing in estate, trust, or tax management can relieve them of this for a reasonable fee. Any family with large amounts of capital can avoid having income, and with it, the progressive income tax.

These North Americans may invest through a Swiss bank, or even own one, but only because it interests them. There is rarely much of anything for them to hide. There is such a thing as the American tax expatriate, but this is rarely the old-rich.

So much mystery and intrigue has surrounded Swiss banks since 1920 that most Americans who have never lived abroad instinctively regard them as useful only for shady characters. This, unfortunately, limits perfectly legitimate Swiss business in the United States. The suspicion is strongest in the interior and in the Southwest. A Swiss bank representative named H. W. Kremers, traveling Texas and Northern Mexico, in the early 1960s found it disappointingly difficult to interest substantial Southwesterners in Swiss investments. Many men Kremers approached on perfectly legal and potentially profitable business—investments in Mexican silver or German industry through a Swiss bank—shied away. They preferred to sink their money in dry holes or almost as risky cattle ranches.

Just as the reputation puts off legitimate investors, it tends actually to draw the shysters—the men who are looking for some way to avoid all legitimate taxation and think Swiss banks are the answer: the small-town doctor who has put together $25,000 or more in unreported cash, the lawyer who cannot declare a crooked payoff, someone who wants to hide money from wife or relatives or for some other reason wants to get it out of the country. There is also the speculator, who thinks he may take less than $100,000 and make a killing in European exchanges through Swiss banks.

If the money is not actually "hot" or stolen, any American who tries can eventually get it safely in a Swiss bank. Swiss banks check serial numbers of all American and other bills against lists furnished them by Interpol, but they are in business, after all, to take in money. They will take the American shyster's cash, charge him dearly for the privilege, and make a profit. Whether the American makes a profit is something else.

The American who wants to invest heavily in European stocks is welcome. Sometimes he can do very well; Americans who got into the European markets early in the 1940s usually made a killing. But in 1962 European exchanges collapsed, on Blue Monday, May 28. Wall Street fell, too, but it quickly came back. The European stocks were still on the floor in 1965. It was highly significant that after 1962 all Swiss banks tried to invest the bulk of their managed money in North America: in the 1960s it has been the best investment market. This means the American who goes to a Swiss bank is not apt to make any money he can't make on Wall Street.

For an American to invest in Wall Street through a Swiss bank is nonsense. This involves double commissions—the bank's and the American broker's—and to this Swiss banks add banking charges. A Swiss bank only makes sense for a very sophisticated investor who takes the long view, has a lot of money, and wants expert advice on completely foreign investments. The Swiss do have something to sell this man. Their knowledge of Mexican sombrero-making, Venezuelan emerald mines, or Japanese transit companies with shares on the world market is unsurpassed by anything which can be found in New York. The Swiss do make mistakes, but they do not like turbulence in accounts—constant moving in and out—and they understand long-term growth. Many a family has gotten very rich over a generation through its Swiss bank. But they seldom do it quickly.

The speculator who feels he can bounce around from one exchange to another and make a killing is a constant phenomenon. But no American can operate through Switzerland for razor-edge speculation on the London or New York market. Switzerland is six hours, or one trading day, behind Wall Street and the time lag kills him.

All these groups involve at most only a few thousand Americans. A larger group are Americans who have lived in Switzerland or Europe either with the armed forces or working for American corporations, made connections with Swiss banks for convenience, and when they return home leave some money behind. Sometimes they have learned to like or trust their banker, and often they do not want to disturb a long-term investment already begun. There is a great deal of this kind of American money in Switzerland.

But the really substantial American money comes from American corporations operating overseas.

Beginning about 1958, when most European currencies again were convertible, American firms, American industrial techniques, and American products started to flow into Europe like European ideas and capital once passed to the New World. American industry recognized the inherent value of the Common Market long before most European businesses did. The immense growth of the US economy between 1960 and 1965 accelerated the trend because there was more American money to invest. And the little-advertised but very real fact that American industry, like Swiss banks, generally stopped investing in the undeveloped or third world during 1960–1961 made even more money available. For example, while new US private investment in South America approached a billion dollars a year in the late 1950s, by 1962 it had dropped to virtually zero. Castro's revolution and the nationalistic trend in Brazil and Argentina was recognized in New York board rooms, too.

At first a few American firms tentatively entered Europe, mostly auto-makers, like Ford and Chrysler. But by 1964 almost one third of all European auto production was US-owned, and the annual rate of American investment in Europe topped $6 billion. The net assets owned in Europe by American firms had meanwhile grown to almost $90 billion.

A lot of this money poured through Switzerland's commercial banks.

Actually, American industry sold very few products in

Switzerland itself. About all the Swiss needed from the US was oil and petroleum products. But the Confederation quickly developed an immense importance to American business as a foreign headquarters, for five major reasons:

1. Switzerland was politically stable.
2. Switzerland was politically neutral.
3. Switzerland was centrally located in Europe, with superb air, rail, and wire communications everywhere.
4. Switzerland had hard money, complete business freedom —freer than in the United States—and no restrictions or control on the import or export of money. Currencies transfers did not even have to clear through a central bank.
5. Swiss corporate law was flexible and Swiss taxes low.

There were other considerations, too. Swiss economic and social conditions were more like the American than any other nation's. The post office was excellent and economical, the telephone system twenty years ahead of London's.

But more than anything else, Swiss business freedom drew companies like flies. The various governments, federal and local, welcomed corporations and made them feel at home. Import duties were based on weight, not value. For example, $20,000 in diamonds could be imported from the Orient for an import duty of only $12. Government authorities were never very greedy or tried to interfere.

Swiss neutrality offered immense, if more intangible, benefits. The Swiss had been neutral so long nobody hated them. This allowed Americans to sell products from an American-owned French factory under a Swiss label to Germans out of Basel or Zurich and to offer German patents, techniques, and engineering skills to French firms out of Basel or Geneva. Neither party would have considered buying what was offered direct. Further, many Jewish-owned businesses abroad salved their consciences about trading with the expanding West German market through a Swiss address. By 1964 there were more than 3500 American families living in the canton of Geneva alone, all doing business for American firms, and more arriving every day.

Swiss law was a thing of beauty to incoming American executives and attorneys eager to set up shop. It is the most pliable on earth, where company formation is concerned. And, in general, most cantonal laws offer exactly the same freedom to outside firms they do their own—there is no discrimination. Any foreign corporation can make a permanent establishment in Switzerland if it desires; it can organize a subsidiary company as an independent corporation, or it can simply incorporate its European headquarters as a holding company. There is some fragmentary antitrust legislation in Switzerland, but no one takes it seriously.

There are three main types of American operation: firms incorporated as "Swiss," branch offices of the main American company, or special holding companies for firms and branches all over Europe, Africa, and the Middle East. Holding companies can set up shop in certain cantons and pay no corporate taxes. Their only Swiss liability is a 3.5 per cent per mille federal capital tax. Technical, consulting, or control offices pay no tax at all. Any foreign corporation which does not intend to do business inside Switzerland but desires a Geneva or Zurich headquarters is allowed to negotiate tax questions on an individual basis, and the Swiss are always eminently reasonable. They like having foreign firms there.

All major Swiss banks are experts in and assist with company formation. Almost all include tax and legal advice in their regular banking services. It is almost impossible for American or other foreign firms operating out of Switzerland to get along without a good Swiss bank. Above all, it is a place to build and hold foreign reserves or to carry the credit of a European affiliate.

American Machine Foundry and Union Carbide were among the first US corporations to move into Switzerland. IBM, General Foods, Colgate-Palmolive-Peet (Zurich), Dupont and Caltex (Basel) came later. Other large firms centered on Geneva. A comprehensive listing is unnecessary; by 1965 almost every major American corporation had a Swiss connection. Even American mutual funds were moving in.

These four thousand American corporations, not the small number of American shysters and sophisticates, are the real customers of the Swiss banks and form the solid basis of the greenback trade.

How to
Avoid Taxes
by Really
Trying

DURING the months just after the war a New York businessman who shall be called Charles Ostrow served in a minor post in the American Military Government in Germany. There were several thousands of these American administrators, experts, and advisers sorting and picking the ruins of Nazi Germany. A few, like the carpetbaggers of the Reconstruction American South, were intent upon "liberating" more than the German people, but the vast majority were conscientious and honest. Ostrow was one of these.

Like many Americans in Germany, Ostrow discovered the peace, quiet, and hospitality of Switzerland. The Confederation was a minor sparkling jewel left untouched in the smoking ruins of Europe. The food and drink were good, the prices were cheap and honest, the Swiss people eminently friendly. Charles Ostrow took to spending his free time across the border where he could be free from the gloom and worries of the werewolf atmosphere of occupied Germany, and in the course of time he even opened an account at a Swiss bank.

Ostrow had always played the market in New York, but now his regular broker was far away. He found that in Switzerland only banks were members of the exchanges, and to invest in stocks and bonds you had to bank. With approximately a thousand dollars Ostrow opened an investment account with a respected Zurich bank. Ironically enough, he found his procurator (a Swiss bank title roughly corresponding to the American in-vestment counselor or customer's man) was pushing German industrial shares.

American over-all policy in occupied Germany was some-what confused, but in general it was based on not allowing Ger-man industry to come back. Swiss bankers were already betting that it would. Swiss investors, and the few Germans, Swedes, or other Europeans who had the cash, were already buying certain German shares, although most British and American investment people, otherwise intelligent, would not yet touch them with a ten-foot pole. The situation in West Germany was far from promising. But the real reason was that the war, and the scars it had left, were much too new.

Ostrow, intrigued, let himself be talked into putting his origi-nal investment in Daimler-Benz. He made good money, tax-free, in Europe, and he added regularly to his account. The extra money went into German auto shares.

When the occupation ended Ostrow went home and got a job in New Jersey. He left his European investment where it was. Ludwig Erhard, the German economics minister, had already be-gun his *Wirtschaftswunder*—economic miracle—and Daimler-Benz increased in value 5000 per cent. Ostrow's total holdings in his Swiss bank approached $250,000.

Ostrow was rich. But he had one problem. The bank had done some buying and selling for him; it had changed his portfolio about to achieve maximum capital gains. None of these Ostrow had ever bothered to report on his US income tax return. At first the oversight was accidental; Ostrow never thought about it. Later he became frightened at the thought of penalties and inter-est, and the concealment was deliberate.

Under US law he did not yet owe taxes on the bulk of his fortune, only on those parts he had turned as a capital gain. The matter could have been settled amicably, and not too expensively —but often, even with basically honest men, a little delinquency leads to more. Ostrow discovered that there was no way Internal Revenue could investigate his holdings. The bank made no re-port. So long as the money remained in Switzerland his secret was safe.

Ostrow was mainly worried about reporting past mistakes,

but in time he came to resent the 25 per cent the US government thought it was due. He had made the money through his own good sense; it had nothing to do with the US government or the American economy, and he convinced himself the government had no right to any of it. He discussed the matter briefly with a discreet accountant he knew in New York City, and this man explained the law. Ostrow said it wasn't fair. The accountant laughed and told him fairness had nothing to do with it—it happened to be the law.

Beginning in 1951 a tax-withholding agreement was concluded between the American government and Bern, and 15 per cent of the dividends from Ostrow's shares were withheld at the bank. This did not particularly bother him. His own tax level on his American salary was considerably higher, starting at 20 per cent. Even with 15 per cent withheld he was coming out ahead.

The Swiss bank, with his permission, transferred some of his shares again in 1959, and Ostrow's fund reached $300,000. That year he knowingly filed a fraudulent return, because he reported none of his immense capital gain. He felt completely safe, since the bank had assured him it made no report to Washington—in fact, it was specifically forbidden to by Swiss federal law.

The bilateral withholding agreement was made to cut down on cheating by Americans subject to US income taxes, but it had a definitely Swiss flavor. The Swiss would not have signed any other kind. To begin with, any dividends on US investments held by a Swiss bank were to be taxed, in the US, at 15 per cent. Since Ostrow's holdings were foreign, this did not apply. But if the holder of any income-bearing shares were subject to American taxes, then the bank was required to extract another 15 per cent in Switzerland. Since Ostrow had opened his account on his passport and was registered as an American citizen living in the States, this clause was enforced. Ostrow could have applied for a refund on this, if due, on his regular tax return, or the Swiss tax might have been applied for credit against his US tax if he had operated according to American law.

But it was written into the Swiss-American agreement (also similarly concluded with Holland, Germany, Great Britain, Austria, and Pakistan) that in no case would any Swiss bank furnish tax or fiscal information to any foreign government not available to Swiss authorities under Swiss law. Since Swiss federal and cantonal governments alike are permitted to get no financial information from a bank, Swiss bank secrecy was preserved. Washington would never learn Charles Ostrow's name.

The withholding tax agreement made tax evasion through Swiss banks unprofitable for Americans unless they were in an above-30-per-cent bracket. But it left the capital gains loophole wide open. Any American—or German or other foreigner— could buy and sell shares through a Swiss bank, make immense gains, and no tax man could ever prove a thing.

But by not reporting his profits, Charles Ostrow had committed criminal evasion. He was not home free.

He had a chance to use his money to buy into his own business. It was a tremendous opportunity, and he had the money. There was just one catch—he did not dare bring his money home. There was no way on God's earth he could explain where he got $300,000 if the IRS investigated, and Charles Ostrow was sure that sooner or later it would. Like many an "honest" man who commits a criminal act, he was far more frightened than a hardened criminal would have been. Ostrow had married in 1953; he had a family. He was a respected member of the Presbyterian Church in his city; he had standing, and he could not afford a mixup with the law.

He went back to his accountant friend and this time laid all his cards on the table. The accountant, who was an expert on tax avoidance but did not indulge in tax evasion, bluntly informed him that if he tried to bring his money back he could be in serious trouble. The Internal Revenue Service could collect back taxes, slap on a 50-per-cent penalty for criminal evasion, and charge back interest at 6 per cent on each dollar undeclared. They would end up with most of the money, whether or not they applied the law to the maximum and sent Charles Ostrow to jail.

Ostrow still has $300,000 in the bank. He is afraid to touch the money. He can't use it, spend it, or even dream about it. His accountant—the source of this story—does not believe he has even told his wife. He could write checks—in Europe—to finance a vacation or trip, but this is peanuts. He could retire abroad if he could convince his family to leave New Jersey; and this is what Charles Ostrow may eventually do, if his conscience doesn't get him first.

There is no way an American citizen or British subject living at home can evade taxes through a Swiss bank without breaking criminal statutes. This does tend to hold the practice down. The "Anglo-Saxon" governments do not approach the question of tax evasion with either reasonableness or good cheer.

The situation and ethic is quite different in different nations. In France or Italy the whole matter of income taxes is something of a game. Most Latin countries collect their essential revenues in the form of excise or indirect taxes on every product from boots to bread. These taxes—which fall heavier on the common consumer than they do the rich—keep the governments running. When it comes to income or corporate taxes, French and Italian businessmen keep double (or even triple) books, involved accounting systems, and all the money they can slip abroad in Switzerland. The Swiss know these deposits represent money from tax evasion and, in the case of French or Italians, do not care.

The French, from the eighteenth century to 1965, have been the largest depositors in Swiss banks. But the Italians, when the Italian "opening to the left" first placed withholding taxes on Italian dividends and in several other ways began to crack down on evasion, have come in strong. Italy, like France, has no tax agreement with the Swiss, although one is under negotiation.

The French and Italian governments know their rich men evade taxes; they expect them to try. Collecting taxes in the Latin nations has become a vast game of cops and robbers. It resembles hide and seek, or even collective bargaining. Each French businessman tries to prove his bankruptcy by his books; each government agent tries to establish the fact that he is rich. In France, taxes may be leveled on "appearances" or a show of wealth. This keeps many immensely wealthy Frenchmen living in a pinched way. There are few hard-or-fast rules, but some ameliorating customs. Hardly ever is anyone put in jail. Claims and counterclaims are usually compromised, for most European nations do not really consider tax evasion a true crime against the state.

Keeping money where the tax collector can never find it is a powerful urge to put money in Switzerland. Added to chronic political instability, the constant threat of a socialist or Communist regime, and endemic inflation, this pull is irresistible. It has become a habit. The fifty richest families in France—*Haute Société Protestante* like Christian Vieljeux (steamships at La Rochelle), Roland Peugeot (Paris autos), and Pierre Verne (*banques d'affaire*), industrialists like Michelin (tires), de Wendel (steel—the Comité des Forges), Dreyfus (textiles), or armsmakers like the Scheiders at Le Creusot—have a generations-old affair with Geneva and Basel banks. The Rothschilds, with their own banks, still find them useful from both sides of the border. French businessmen and industrialists, who have the most money, date their heavy deposits from Napoleonic times. Great French aristocrats who have kept some wealth, like the Marquis de Breteuil, began before 1789. A hundred years ago French parish priests advised each local provincial baron to put some money with the hated Calvinists in Geneva, where at least it would be safe. And safe from the tax collector it has remained, while it guaranteed the standing of Switzerland's oldest and most fastidious banks.

Any Geneva banker who might put a Batista or a Charles Ostrow through the mill would hardly dream of inquiring of a Douville-Maillefeux or Clouet des Pesruches if he has paid French taxes on his francs.

They will question an American or Briton more closely, and usually, on the advice of the Banker's Association, turn more than $50,000 in unexplained assets down. The US or British government is much more likely than the French to make an enormous stink.

West Germans—whose domestic taxes by American, British, or Scandinavian standards are quite bearable, stopping at around 50 per cent—also have gotten in the Swiss-bank act.

In 1950, when West Germany began to revive, German newspapers started carrying advertisements for Swiss lakefront property, primarily in the Italian-speaking canton of Ticino. Ticino was south of the Alps, sunny and Mediterranean, and until then it had never approached Vaud (Lausanne, Ouchy, Vevey) or Geneva in fashionableness. By Lake Geneva standards, prices around Lake Locarno were low. But in the next fifteen years

6000 German citizens bought land in Ticino. By 1965 almost a million German tourists passed through the canton on their way to Italy. The German language began to drive out the native Italian.

The Hamburg *Times*, a German weekly, carried an article on the Teutonic invasion. The *Times'* conclusions were that Germans buying in Ticino said they wanted a place in the sun, but what they were really looking for was a place to avoid taxes and enjoy the *dolce vita* on the shores of Lago Maggiore. Germans, newly rich, put a great deal of money in Ticino banks.

The head of the Union Bank of Switzerland once said, "Of course we presume that a large portion of our foreign customers are here for the purposes of tax evasion." He was merely being honest about a subject most Swiss bankers prefer to avoid. And Swiss banks, whose philosophy is decidedly that they are not their brothers' keepers, assist or at least acquiesce in most cases. Even tax authorities are not conventional in Switzerland; taxation is not a legal but an administrative matter, and if they can help a Frenchman, Swede, or German get away with something, Swiss bankers are only to themselves being true.

The flight of frightened capital from Europe to Switzerland in recent years has declined. The great era of transferring fortunes to Swiss control or to "Swiss" corporations is over; foreign governments have gotten more sophisticated and smarter on ways to prevent it. Sterling is not easily gotten out of England; all French electronic communication with Geneva is tapped or tape-recorded by the French authorities. At the same time, the need for getting money into Switzerland has lessened in most Europeans' minds, particularly after 1958.

Europe became again prosperous, and exceeded all prewar living standards in that year. Most West European moneys had stabilized and were freely convertible. Politics had also stabilized. The fear of war receded, and workers and socialists were no longer tranquilized on religion, antireligion, or irrational nationalism, but by the welfare state. The welfare state was one of the best things which ever happened to the European rich. It took most of the pressure off them.

With their very existence no longer in question, the magnates who once worried mostly about getting their money into Switzerland now are more concerned with employing it profitably at home. As soon as De Gaulle came to power in France, French money in Geneva started to trickle back to Paris. British and Swedish millionaires discovered they were not going out of business, but by making careful adjustments could live comfortably in the brave new European world. Taxation remained extremely high, confiscatory in Britain and Scandinavia, and even reaching a top of 50 per cent on income taxes in free-enterprise West Germany. But the European rich, old and new, had learned to avoid the income tax by judiciously avoiding income. Corporate taxes and capital gains levies are lower in Europe generally than in America—or more easily avoided. Swedish capital gains structures are reasonable, and that second Sweden, England, only imposed light taxes on capital gains in 1965. Taxation pays for the various welfare states, but even in socialist nations it falls most heavily on the relatively poor. Cigarettes, alcohol, and withholding on workers' pay packets pays for medicare. These kinds of taxes cannot damage the rich.

Meanwhile, the license, patent, real estate, insurance company, and investment-trust millionaire is an expanding breed, just as he is in the United States. The problem is not in making money, but in avoiding "income." Sometimes the ways are strenuous and complex, as with newer English investment-trust empires. Sometimes they are more simple. Ian Fleming, creator of James Bond, incorporated himself as an enterprise and sold the shares. He netted $2.8 million which could only be treated as a capital gain. The Beatles, in 1964, followed the same basic process. They sold themselves and future earnings as corporate gains, and undoubtedly will eventually net far more. It was much more tidy, and patriotic, than running off to a Swiss bank. For bringing vast amounts of American and other cash into England, and keeping it there, the Beatles were made Members of the Order of the British Empire in 1965.

But taxation is still a problem. Not everyone who gets money can arrange capital gains deals or take stock options like the heads of Krupp or General Motors, or like Ian Fleming convince a corporate combine that his future earnings will make a mint. Anyone in the Western world who earns a large, liquid income and has to take it in cash has a tax problem. Movie stars and successful writers, the new aristocracy of the century, have no real chance of equaling Howard Hughes, H. L. Hunts, Rockefellers, or Agnellis in bank accounts—unless they can obtain a Swiss residence permit.

Clever Swiss cantonal lawyers are still at work. A few years back one of them worked out a beauty of a scheme. Certain German, American, British, and other accountants have all tried to take credit for it, and many of them have charged money for showing it to their clients. The Swiss lawyer doesn't care; he served his canton and country well.

People with large, liquid incomes who are free to move around may establish residence in Switzerland. They need a villa and a residence permit, both easily gotten with money. Here, in a number of cantons, they are permitted to form personal corporations under their own or any other name they fancy. They need only a good Swiss lawyer, and one will be recommended by any Swiss bank. Once the corporate charter is granted, the next step is to have all income, whether from J. Arthur Rank, Hollywood, New York publishing royalties, American stock dividends, oil wells, or whatever, paid into it. For this purpose a corporate numbered account is opened at any Swiss bank.

Under present tax agreements and international law, such money departs the country of origin tax-free. It is earned by the Swiss corporation, and in most cases only Swiss taxes are due.

An interesting quirk of British law is that after the bitter lesson of 1776, no British subject domiciled abroad is taxed. Meanwhile, British income taxes have driven virtually every talented Briton—until the Fleming–Beatle inventions—overseas. Peter Ustinov, Noel Coward, Richard Burton, and Deborah Kerr have gone to Switzerland for good. They did not have to change citizenship to beat the British tax; nor, until the law was changed in 1962, did any American. Americans living abroad for eighteen months before 1962 paid no US income tax.

Orson Welles, Charlie Chaplin, William Holden, Mel Ferrer, Audrey Hepburn, and Irwin Shaw moved into various cantons, too. The favorite one was Vaud. Other names in the entertainment world who got a Swiss residence permit include Sophia Loren, Elizabeth Taylor, Yul Brynner, Georges Simenon, and the Italian star Valenti.

The reason was not Swiss climate, which is not particularly good. Swiss taxation of every kind is lower than that of any other civilized nation in the West. None of these stars had to change citizenship before 1962, or even live most of the year in Switzerland. All they needed was the vital residence permit.

They could move about, though this sometimes got them in trouble. The Americans and Britons had to be very careful about going home. In one situation Noel Coward, at Southampton, had to stay aboard his foreign ship. If he had stepped ashore on British soil, the game would have been up, and crushing British income taxes due.

Sophia Loren got in another kind of trouble. Few Italian or French stars need to move to Switzerland, except to be in the swim. French and Italian tax collectors lack the laws, skill, verve, and dogged determination of the Anglo-Saxons. Sophia Loren had another kind of problem which forced her to live in Ticino with husband Carlo Ponti: Italy refused to recognize his Mexican divorce. However, Sophia worked frequently in Hollywood, and she returned again in the spring of 1965. The state of California, like New York and many other American states, has its own income tax. It applies it, sensibly enough, to all income earned within California's borders, whatever the recipient's citizenship, and wherever he or she has moved to. Loren owed California $13,000 by its reckoning, and California agents were determined to collect.

Used to dealing with Italians, Loren laughed at them. She ignored the bills, but unfortunately checked into a Los Angeles hotel. The state tax men followed her to the hotel, got a warrant, opened the hotel safe, and seized Miss Loren's jewels. Unless she paid her tax, they threatened to sell them to satisfy the lien. Neither the lady's tears, foot-stompings, nor threats made them, unlike some European tax collectors, change their mind.

In the end, Miss Loren wrote a $13,000 check on her Swiss bank—in Ticino—in favor of the state of California to get the jewelry back.

If the tax expatriate stays abroad, however, he is safe.

Though there is no American or British tax on the moneys paid nonresident artists or movie stars, once in Switzerland the

Swiss taxes apply. Every Swiss canton has a corporate tax. But this would hardly get Elizabeth Taylor or Richard Burton upset. In their canton it leveled off at two tenths of 1 per cent. In 1962, if Miss Taylor earned $1 million—and she did—her Swiss corporate taxes came to exactly $2000.

$998,000 out of a million was home free.

Of course, Miss Taylor or William Holden or even writer Irwin Shaw had to have money for living expenses, which in Switzerland's sunshine coast can be quite high. For this purpose the bank holding the corporate funds usually set up a drawing account, somewhere between $5000 and $10,000 per month. On this money Swiss income taxes applied. But the Swiss tax, with a theoretical limit of 45 per cent, in practice did not progress beyond the first $5000, or 20,000 francs. And here—another beautiful thing—foreign residents who were not Swiss citizens could negotiate. With any luck at all they could settle for a small lump sum. If Elizabeth Taylor, on an income of a million paid more than $70,000 to $80,000 in all, she should change her Swiss bank and lawyer.

The 1962 American income tax would have been $870,000 less minor deductions. The then American rate reached a top of 90 per cent (since reduced to 70) and American IRS men do not like to negotiate.

No one had to be a movie star to enjoy this setup. A Belgian writer like Georges Simenon, author of the Maigret series, a director such as Anatole Litvak, or even a simple Swede who became heavyweight champion of the world could form a Swiss corporation and qualify. Ingemar Johansson, however, had to change his citizenship—something Yul Brynner did in 1965 and Elizabeth Taylor started to do; others may soon follow.

What caused this was President Kennedy's moves in 1962 to close this loophole. Under new legislation, only the first $25,000 earned by Americans living overseas became tax-free. This exemption was adequate to assure American executives living in Europe on legitimate business their villas and servants. It did put a crimp in the plans of Hollywood stars. In 1964–1965 a battery of Swiss lawyers were working on the problem, and the odds are they will find a way.

Otherwise, quite a few expatriate Americans may be forced to run up the Union Jack, take Panamanian citizenship, or something.

What is good for spectacular movie stars, retired California and New York business executives living on dividends, and Fritz Thyssen, grumpily sunning himself near Lugano among some 6000 other Germans, has become a bit too much of a good thing for the Swiss Confederation. Thousands of the rich flocking to Geneva, Vaud, and Ticino drove the price of real estate up. Needed Swiss productive capacity went into luxury apartments instead of middle-class housing, and villa acres on Lake Leman hit $250,000 in the first months of 1964. With all the foreign rich crowding in, the Swiss themselves were crowded out.

In 1960 the Swiss government put restrictions on the issuance of residence permits and the sale of property to outsiders. In 1964, these laws were tightened because they had not worked. In Geneva, where there were only 80,000 Genevois, foreigners already numbered 60,000. Ticino was being overrun, and Ticinese shopkeepers, to stay in business, had to take crash courses in German. It was made quite difficult to get a residence permit. Without one, no outsider can buy Swiss real estate. Conversely, the mere ownership of a Swiss home or land no longer carried the privilege of Swiss residence—a blow to thousands of Lebanese, Egyptians, and other Levantines who had invested in Switzerland as a hedge against a future need. In the Middle East since Nasser, the revolution has always been just around the corner. Many of the newer office buildings and "luxus" apartment houses erected in Geneva were owned by various brands of Arabs who were on the point of being shot at home and now would have to reside, like the late Farouk, in Italy.

The average Swiss tended to be angry over the invasion. It put little money in his pockets, drove the cost of living up, and often kept him in a substandard home. When villas reached $200,000 an acre in Geneva, many old Genevois families could no longer afford to live on their ancestral estates. They sold out— but this caused more resentment. No one, including the Swiss, wants to be owned by foreigners, whether they are Syrians, Germans, or Americans.

But the rich still come from everywhere—at Swiss rates, they

166 The Swiss Banks

can still save enough with land at $250,000 per acre to show a neat profit on a residence permit in one year. Eminently sensible Swiss law states that no one, unless a born Swiss, has an inherent right to live or work in the Confederation. The criterion for allowing more foreigners is simple and sane—are they good for the canton? If they are, they get in. If the permit would benefit the permittee more than it would the Swiss state—such as by saving his life—or he is a man of small substance merely trying to make a franc or two, he is apt to be refused.

Great leniency is also shown to all forms of business. Any bona-fide employee of an American corporation, or the corporation itself, gets a permit. Dupont, for example, wanting to build a new office headquarters, is welcomed. No Swiss is going to interfere with genuine enterprise.

An American citizen on any legitimate business has no trouble. It is a little harder for a German, because more Germans are trying to get in. It is even harder for Latin Americans or Arabs or other non-Europeans, because there is a certain snobbery in Switzerland, too.

Swiss banks, Swiss industry, and the Swiss government all like free-wheeling, free-spending, high-salaried American executives. They give them and their corporations all the benefits and liberal exemptions granted to native Swiss. An American corporation, furthermore, can go Swiss simply by having a predominantly Swiss board of directors while the actual shareholders remain American. Going "Swiss" qualifies any corporation for all the leniencies granted under Swiss tax law.

Not all the tax expatriates are people; some are corporations.

Each canton has its own tax and fiscal system, and since two thirds of all Swiss taxes are cantonal rather than federal, this is important. It tends to concentrate corporation in certain cantons, Zug, Vaud, and Zurich, too. Corporate taxes may reach a theoretical limit of 45 per cent—but they never do. The Swiss are not much interested in theoretical limits; 25 per cent—as opposed to the American standard tax of 47 per cent, until recently 52—is about as high as corporation taxes go. Again, any individual tax rate is reached by negotiation, and the Swiss prefer a small bird in the hand to two larger ones possibly snared. There is a Swiss internal revenue tax, and a tax on dividend profits. And if distributed, Washington and Bern have an agreement by which 30 per cent on corporate profits is withheld. If 95 per cent of a company's stock is held in the US by Americans, however, Bern refunds the corporation all but 5 per cent. Meanwhile, if the firm pays its Swiss tax, it may charge this against its US corporate tax, in the end paying only 17 per cent on all repatriated profits. All this seems complex, and is. But the main thing is that Swiss taxes are very, very light. Corporations end up paying less on more than almost any place else in the world.

The final point, and one of the nicest of all tax provisions, is that there is no tax in Switzerland on undistributed profits—and, unlike the US, there is no requirement that corporate profits ever be distributed. For businesses building capital, this is the sweetest thing of all.

No Swiss cantonal government likes to talk about taxes or tax deals. Swiss tax men admit they are not conventional, but they can become quite frosty if they are pressed for details. Deals are very private, like bank secrecy, but certain things are bound to leak out.

A Sheikh had heard from the former Aga Khan of the conveniences of Swiss residence. The Aga Khans—leaders of a Moslem religious sect, who among other things are paid their weight in gems and gold annually—have made Switzerland their playground for many years. The Sheikh had no tax problem, though he had oil and was paid regularly in newly minted British gold, since no Arab with any sense took paper. He was a bit tired of the blistering sun and 120° heat of the Persian Gulf.

Whether this sheikh came from Oman, Qatar, Muscat, or Bahrein is hardly important. What is important is that he arrived in Vaud—where they knew all about the Trucial sheikhdoms, and the exact value of the Gulf rupee issued for the British by the Reserve Bank of India—with his wives, a Swiss lawyer, a Swiss bank officer, and three blond German secretaries. Lawyer and banker made an appointment with certain cantonal authorities, old friends with whom business had been done before. The sheikh, a dark, shrewd, somewhat portly fellow, spoke perfect French and English. However, he let his Swiss friends do the talking.

There was, of course, no real trouble in arranging a residence permit for His Excellency, the Swiss being as fascinated with titles and every other form of royalty as that other democratic people, the Americans. But with residence came the question of taxes.

"His Excellency has a guaranteed income of five million Swiss francs," the lawyer stated. "He will arrange to have all of it paid into a local bank. He will further stipulate to spend no less than two million francs in the canton."

It is impossible for any Swiss not to respect money, and they also give the man behind it the respect that is his due. The cantonal people bowed. They had no doubt in the world that his excellency would spend two million francs. With a lake yacht, ten automobiles, an entourage and harem, this would be no trouble in Switzerland at all.

The lawyer went on, "In order to avoid all future complications, we should like a stipulation on taxes from the canton. Inasmuch as His Excellency will engage in no business in the canton, and his income comes from outside the Confederation, he is prepared to pay fifty thousand francs per annum, in lump sum."

One of the Swiss demurred politely. "That is a very small amount, *Excellence*."

"His Excellency is under no obligation or need to reside in Switzerland," the lawyer mentioned. "There is Monaco, Jamaica, Rome—"

The banker made his only comment. "By any balance sheet the canton cannot lose, gentlemen."

The authorities conferred briefly among themselves and agreed that what the banker said was true. Fifty thousand francs out of five million—ten thousand dollars out of a million—was not much, but it was money the canton would otherwise never see. Another royal residence would provide employment, but an extra million dollars in gold flowing into the banks would give Switzerland that much additional international importance. The deal was made.

Not long afterward, the Sheikh of Sharjah, Saqr bin Sultan al Qasimi, had difficulties with the British. Saqr bin Sultan let himself be talked into authorizing the issue of some silver five-rupee coins bearing the portrait of the late President of the

United States, John F. Kennedy, under his theoretical sovereign coinage rights. These coins were ordered from the French mint at Paris, and were to be sold in America and Europe to international numismatists. So-called coins like these were being struck in Swiss, French, and Italian mints every month and sold to collectors who paid enormous premiums. But the plan misfired. American coin dealers bought the issue, as was expected—but some of the coins, which were not supposed to be current in Sharjah, trickled into the Trucial States. The British—who had grown less than fond of Sheikh Saqr for other reasons—declared the unauthorized issue of coins "infringed on the liquidity of the Gulf rupee" and further usurped money prerogatives held by the British government since it assumed protection of the Trucial States in the year 1820. They deposed Saqr and they replaced him with his brother on June 30, 1965.

He will probably join the rest of his clan in Switzerland, but he will not be able to make any kind of tax deal with "John F. Kennedy rupees."

The little man who dreams of slipping away to Switzerland, or saving on taxes somehow through a Swiss bank, is fooling himself. Swiss authorities make no deals with unsubstantial people. The corollary that money brings the respect it deserves is that a lack of funds draws immediate disdain. Anyone is welcome to visit Switzerland. But the retired couple with meager funds who hope to set up a little business there, or the struggling novelist who thinks he can get a residence permit on the basis of possible future earnings are out of luck. Like Elizabeth Taylor or Irwin Shaw, they'd better make it first.

For the small man who has no fear of revolution or confiscation at home and nothing to hide, putting money in a Swiss bank is also foolish. Swiss banks no longer pay interest on foreign funds, and they have always paid at least one half of 1 per cent less on time deposits than US banks. Their custodial fees—set by agreement within the Cartel of Big Banks—are always above American banks' charges for managing money. Rent on bank boxes likewise has been pushed to record rates.

The "equalization tax" of 15 per cent, imposed by Washington in 1964 on all foreign loans and stock purchases made in the US as part of the program to slow American gold loss, can be avoided by buying securities directly through a Swiss bank. Washington still has found no way to tax Swiss banks, but this loophole is only useful for the big investor who knows what he is doing in purchasing shares abroad. The little man has no more business wandering lamblike down Borsenstrasse in Zurich than Wall Street, and risk capital—which is what Swiss banks are seeking—is exactly what the name implies.

The United States and other governments are well aware of the tax loopholes provided by the Swiss. But short of invading Switzerland and ending its sovereignty there is little they can do about it. The American IRS, again and again, as in the case of Texas promoter Billie Sol Estes' missing $7 million, have traced a probable trail to Geneva or Zurich banks. Here the trail ends abruptly. All it or the French Second Bureau can do is patiently hope the money will be someday brought home. Then national tax men can step in. Even reasonable evidence that money is in a Swiss bank does them no good in bringing action against certain nationals. In most democratic nations with honest judicial systems, guilt must be proven beyond the shadow of a doubt. This would require testimony or evidence from the Swiss banks themselves.

No one in a democratic country has ever been put in jail for having money in Swiss banks. Spain and other undemocratic nations provide a different story. In 1958 certain evidence came into the hands of the Franco regime that a number of prominent Spaniards had unreported funds in the Société de Banques Suisses. The evidence was genuine, but under American or British law as arbitrary as the evidence Hitler's agents had uncovered. The Spanish police got their hands on a bank agent's little black book which listed names, deposits, and account numbers. The result was an immense scandal both in Spain, where it was illegal to have Swiss bank accounts, and in Switzerland, where it was illegal to let the information out. The Spanish government confiscated assets of $2.9 million from the Spaniards involved and fined them $2.9 million more. With foreign exchange troubles, the Franco regime is quite bitter about Swiss banks.

One of the most ironic things about the Swiss tax haven, however, is that although a few Americans avoid the stock-purchase equalization tax or evade taxes on dividends or capital gains by dealing through Swiss banks, over-all the US government does not lose. No Washington tax man likes to talk about this. Washington prefers to try to keep the Swiss on some kind of moral defensive. But the fact is that since about 1959 at least $500,000 per year has been invested in the US stock market from Switzerland. Very little of this money originally comes from American citizens; it comes from Germans, Spaniards, Italians, Frenchmen, Syrians, South Americans, Arabs, and Scandinavians. On all dividends or interest paid on these investments in the United States the US government withholds 15 per cent.

Any foreigner from whom money is withheld can apply for, and get, a refund. But he must first prove that he has declared all the income on his American investment through his Swiss bank to his own government. He has to apply on certain official forms, which must be certified at home.

This means that 99 per cent of the dividends and interest money Washington withholds is not refunded and never will be.

The Internal Revenue Service is not at all unhappy over its arrangements with the Swiss.

On taxes everywhere, some rich men are fooling their governments, and some governments are fooling themselves. The Swiss system is unique. The Swiss handle domestic tax matters pragmatically—there is no tax ideology involved—reasonably, and invariably with good cheer. The Swiss governments get all the money they expect to get, and more than they need to run the kind of limited government Swiss prefer. The Swiss are unique, but not stupid. They have recognized man's nature with money for what it is, and found a means of profiting handsomely from it.

Elegance :
Der Privatbankier

ZURICH, where carved-stone lions still guard the swan-filled harbor and Zwingli still stands in bronze, Bible and sword in hand beside Gross-Munster, is a city of big banks. The Kreditanstalt, the Bankgesellschaft, Bankverein, Volksbank, and Bank Leu all have their main or a major office there. The massive four-storied, steel-windowed buildings dominate Bahnhofstrasse, the main street. Just off Bahnhofstrasse, on Börsenstrasse near the lake, where the banks trade *à la criée* on the City Exchange, the Swiss National Bank stores its immense stockpile of yellow gold.

Zurich has all the urban elegance of any great central European city, with its gardens, symphonies, and state theaters. But Zurich is also a city devoted to business, and as little devoted to nonsense as Dallas or Seattle. The native dialect is a variety of German, but almost everyone knows English, the language of modern international finance. English, like money itself, is the one tongue Scandinavians, Dutchmen, Germans, Swiss, English, and Americans all understand.

In Zurich the money changers are not just in the temple; Zurich itself is a temple of world finance, and the moneychangers form the priestly hierarchy.

Bahnhofstrasse, laid out in 1864, has nothing to be ashamed of beside London or New York. Like Bond Street and Fifth Avenue, its windows gleam with gems and diamond watches. From one end to the other, the long avenue drips with gold.

Zurich's banks along Bahnhofstrasse form one of the major

gold marts of the world. Each bank window shows, alongside its foreign-exchange rates and late stock prices, trays and trays of bullion bars and shining coins. Every form of capital is on display, but most people stop to see the gold.

Here the Egyptian regime of Nasser, hard-pinched, brings its meager gold reserves to trade for bread. The Russians regularly sell the produce of their Siberian mines through intermediaries, and the British government pays certain accounts in new sovereigns, of which more than ten million were minted in 1964. Germans, French, Arabs, Austrians, and Spaniards snap the offerings up. Only Americans, Russians, and citizens of certain sterling areas are not allowed to hold or trade in gold. Most Europeans still hoard it. Too many people since 1914 have learned the hard way that paper money is only what a government says it is, but nobody can either print or devalue gold. The big bars in bank windows are for bullion buyers. The coins of every age and country are available for the little man.

This gold trade is immense, and all coined gold brings a premium over the official $35-per-ounce bullion price. Swiss banks, operating on a free market, sell gold for less than others. The sovereigns of Elizabeth II, coined for export and officially worth $8.40, bring an average of $9.70 on the London Bourse. But in Switzerland they sell for only 41.60 francs. There is some variation, due to world crises and threats of war; but the Swiss price is generally lower, and people come from all over the world to buy. French napoleons (20-franc pieces) bring 36.90 Swiss francs; the US double eagle ($20) sells for 179.

The Swiss *Vreneli*—"little *fräulein*," or 20 francs—weighs the same as the napoleon, but it trades for 39.90 Swiss francs. People feel there is something special about Swiss gold. Strangely enough, image counts. The two-rand coins of South Africa, exactly equal to the British gold sovereign, sell for considerably less than the coins with the heads of British kings and queens. Germans nostalgically bid the price of *Reichsgold*—the pre-1914 German gold with heads of kings and Kaiser—up higher than the *Vreneli*. More sophisticated buyers try to find modern coinages with small mintings. The five-Pahlavi pieces of Iran or the limited rose-gold strikings of Peru, all coined on private account, may have numismatic value.

Until 1961, Americans could hold gold overseas. Many did, and kept it in Swiss banks. The law was changed, and after 1961 no American citizen is allowed to own or trade in gold anywhere, except for legitimate dental, numismatic, or jewelry purposes. Certain Swiss, however, have joined Canadians and others in offering Americans who want gold their services as agents. These men will buy gold and store it for Americans in Swiss or Canadian banks. This can be a hedge against inflation or devaluation of the dollar—but it is against the law.

There is a bank in Zurich which still has $400,000 in US $20 gold pieces belonging to a Texas group. The Americans involved have not made up their collective mind just what to do with their hoard. It is too late to bring it home, but they are reluctant to let it go. Until they do act, nothing can be proved.

Most people are aware there is a large and illegal gold trade around the world and think Swiss banks are intimately connected with it. Nothing could be farther from the truth. There is no gold smuggling in Switzerland, because bringing gold in or out is not against the law. Zurich is an open market.

Gold does figure prominently in such international rackets as narcotics, because it is acceptable everywhere and convenient for payoffs. But the gold-traffickers' major markets and their center of operations are in the Orient. Macao and Beirut are centers of gold exchange, and Pakistan and India are smuggler's paradises.

Most Orientals love gold both for its value and as jewelry, but Pakistan and India strictly regulate the ownership and sale of gold. Above all, these governments try to keep their foreign exchange from being spent on gold which then goes underground. But, unlike Americans, the people of the Indian subcontinent resist; they will buy, and bury, all the gold that is smuggled in.

Much gold sold in the East originates in Russia or China; the Russians sometimes switch their sales from London or Zurich to Beirut because the Eastern price is better. Beirut is the home of several large, well-organized gold-smuggling syndicates which take full advantage of Beirut's "bank secrecy." From Lebanon gold goes by sea and air, through all sorts of ingenious methods of smuggling, by way of Colombo, Bahrein, Teheran to Karachi, Calcutta, or Bombay.

Even after bribes, payoffs, and runner's expenses, this trade clears a handsome profit. A *tola* weight of fine gold, about 11.6 grams, which can be bought in Lebanon for around $13, sells for as much as $30 in India. Each year at least $5 million in gold, to be buried or used for jewelry, is slipped into India. This uses up much scarce Indian foreign exchange.

The penalty for running gold into Pakistan is death. But the desire is incurable, and the black-market price of gold in Asia is easily two and a half times the free rate in Zurich.

The Swiss themselves hoard little gold. Like Americans, whose money has remained reasonably sound over the years, they see no need to hoard. Swiss buy a few *Vreneli* and put them away, mostly for children's gifts. There is very little under-ground Swiss money. Such capital is much more profitably stored in banks.

This tendency of money to go into gold and underground elsewhere is one of the major arguments Swiss government officials make against ending Swiss bank secrecy. Swiss capital is usu-ally hard at work; even farmers in remote cantons keep their money in local banks. From the banks or loan associations it goes into commerce or industry, building Swiss prosperity. But the average Swiss is a very secretive sort. With his tendency to dis-trust all government and to deny it tax and other powers, almost all Swiss officialdom is convinced the average Swiss citizen would react to the end of bank secrecy by taking his money home. De-posits would be pulled out of banks. Many paper francs would be converted into gold and then buried in gardens, where no gov-ernment man could see. Swiss would probably start to hoard gold like any French peasant, and for the same reasons. The loss to the Swiss economy would be immense.

Buried gold, actually, is a great drag on some West European economies. De Gaulle likes to boast of France's new gold reserves of some $5 billion. But at least this much French gold is buried in private cellars or Geneva banks, where it does neither De Gaulle nor the French economy any good.

Germany is also rich in terms of new gold reserves. But West German authorities estimate that, burned by two wars and two occupations, Germans have stashed away $8 billion in secret and economically sterile holdings. In West Germany there exists a so-called bank secrecy—but any German with a badge or uniform can open any bank. It is no accident that millions of Germans pass through Zurich to buy gold coins, buying them at a cheaper price than at home.

This gold sale, however, like the currency exchange from which all big banks profit due to volume, is only the walk-in trade. The banks' real business takes place behind the geranium-boxed, barred windows on the upper floors. Men in dark, custom-tailored suits move through these offices and corridors. Most of them are multilingual and suave, shrewd-eyed and polite.

Some of the big bankers are sharks with sharks' smiles. But more are hard-working, God-fearing men, trying to make a franc in God's world as God has given them to see it. They are knowl-edgeable, and anything but provincial. Zurich has electronic com-munication everywhere, and bank desks are regularly littered with mail from the City of London and Brown Brothers, Harriman.

These men like their work. They generally arrive before eight and go home only after five. Zurich in the 1960s adopted the so-called English working hours, cutting down the former long lunch period, but banking hours and customs are still more Swiss than English.

As a group they have a deep respect for money and the idea of money, just as they all have a hatred for bureaucracy, espe-cially that in Bern. Their business is to create and husband cap-ital, and no government ever really assisted in that.

Most of the men in the Big Banks are aware their world image is very bad, but only a few of the younger bankers care. They shrug their image off. They do not expect outsiders to under-stand or love the financial mind. They liken themselves to dentists, unpopular but indispensible.

The Big Banks, with their fluorescent lighting, steel-and-glass doors, gray-uniformed porters, and power and intrigues and operations around the world are still nothing but large corporate enterprises. They resemble all such large corporations. The hierarchy which runs each Big Bank is not much different from the executive group of Prudential Insurance or General Motors. The lower ranks, however well paid such management may be, are really only corporate clerks. Bank managers are only cogs in the corporate wheel. In the vast corporation dehumanization is very far advanced.

Like most modern enterprise, big banking tends to be self-sustaining once it has grown big enough. The machinery runs itself. It is no longer necessary to push too many buttons; all that is needed is to keep the machinery oiled, and it will normally produce a profit. The banker himself becomes more and more faceless.

The private banker like Hans Vontobel of Zurich is a different breed.

A few years back, a nondescript Frenchman called at Bahnhofstrasse 3, J. Vontobel & Co., Bankiers. On the street, only a discreet metal plaque set in the building wall advertised the bank; no one would ever notice it unless he looked. The Frenchman knew where he was going, however; he entered the building, took the lift past the first floor, which was a small bank lobby looking like most small bank lobbies, and stopped at the executive offices up above. Here there was a small reception hall, a place for hats and coats, and a smiling *Fräulein* to help him if she could.

This Frenchman wanted to see Dr. Hans Vontobel, president and owner of the bank. Most callers did not strike so high; normally any officer or procurator would do. But Dr. Vontobel was not really hard to meet. He made it a practice to see personally as many customers as possible. The Frenchman, calling for the first time, was ushered into Vontobel's private office.

Another bank officer stood by. Not only could he speak French, but it was also Vontobel's practice to have all visitors meet at least two officers in the bank. This way, on return, they had both faces and names to seek out.

All important visitors automatically saw Vontobel, if only briefly. Otherwise, they would be waited upon by bank officials in a modern, soundproof room. Each customer, of course, has a room to himself. Swiss banks, and particularly private banks, never do business impersonally in open lobbies or at desks in large ground-floor rooms.

The French visitor introduced himself to Vontobel, a tall, gray-haired man elegant in boutonniere and black. He talked of this and that, and finally asked to open a very small account. He was in no way impressive. His suit was quite modest, the sort which could be tailored anywhere in Paris for $85 or $90. He made no pretense to wealth or importance. But Hans Vontobel, who inherited the bank from his father, had Zurich banker's blood. He knew his trade, and he knew his business. The Frenchman was treated to every courtesy.

A short time afterward, the new customer returned to the bank and again took up Dr. Vontobel's valuable time with two hours' discussion about his completely inconsequential investment. But Vontobel's ingrained courtesy, disciplined by his acute banking sense, held. He listened to the Frenchman patiently, because he knew his French just as he knew his Scandinavians and Germans. Every European approaches his Swiss banker in a different way.

The third visit proved the charm. The Frenchman now felt at home in the bank. He entered Vontobel's office and revealed his real problem. He held shares in an American steel company worth several million dollars on the market, and he wanted investment advice.

This Dr. Hans Vontobel and staff were most happy to provide.

The private banker is still a man of flesh and blood in an increasingly dehumanized corporate world. The private banks, even the biggest, such as Vontobel or J. Bär of Zurich, are of minimal importance in the financial structure of Switzerland itself. But to thousands of Europeans and others, a Swiss bank really means a private bank.

Thousands come to Vontobel, the bank *mit der persönlichen Atmosphäre*. Vontobel has numbered accounts, but the people who open them do not remain mere numbers. They are real people, to be recognized and catered to, just as Dr. Vontobel himself is no corporate clerk.

The private banker is the true entrepreneur of the banking world. His history goes back to the days when golden argosies sailed for the East and merchantmen went armed. Switzerland has become the last stronghold of the personal, private bank. England, with such famous names as Hambros, Warburg, or Lazards, has only seventeen. Switzerland still has sixty-one.

Most private banks did not open as true banks. They were once private mercantile houses, usually in the import-export trade. They were owned by the Dick Whittingtons and Morris Gimbels of an earlier age, the medieval *Patrizier*. Because of international trade they had to deal in international coin. They had to learn which coin was good, which debased, whose notes were payable in gold, and whose to discount from face. They placed goods across boundaries, often on credit. They had to know not only business but war and politics, and whom you could or could not trust. In the old days one bad guess, one misplaced trust, could ruin the wealthiest merchant, and today nothing much has changed.

Some Swiss private banks are very old. Rahn & Bodmer of Zurich began in 1750, Orelli in Thalberg in 1759. La Roche & Cie in Basel dates from 1787, A. Sarasin (whose door plaque states merely *S & Cie*) started in 1841. Geneva has almost a dozen eighteenth-century banks. The names themselves do not always tell the age. Swiss law does not permit the business use of a name unless somebody of that name still lives and operates. J. Vontobel & Company was once Haeberli, before Hans Vontobel's father bought the bank in 1924.

No private bank is incorporated. Each private banker is responsible to the extent of his private fortune, which, since no balance sheets are ever published, remains unknown. The only clue to the size of a private bank is the number of people it employs, the amounts of stock it buys, and the size of the loans it makes around the world. Most private-bank money comes from outside, and most leaves the Confederation. In Zurich, Julius Bär and J. Vontobel dominate the private banking world.

Hans Bär, Vontobel's rival and colleague, estimates that all Swiss private banks have resources of at least two billion Swiss francs. The largest, generally assumed to be Bär, Hentsch (Geneva), Vontobel, Pictet, and Lombard (both Geneva), represent private fortunes in the 200,000,000–300,000,000 franc class. This puts them in the top 3 per cent of all world banks. Private, in Switzerland, does not mean small.

And yet the private fortunes behind these banks mean very little, for their real importance lies in the amounts of private-account securities and currency they manage or control. Bär estimates this at more than two billion francs for each of the bigger houses, for a total of SF 20 billion in all.

It is impossible for all Swiss not to feel a deep respect, even awe, for men like the Bärs, Pictets, or Vontobels. They are merchant princes; when they make decisions they place their own, as well as customers', fortunes on the line. When a native Swiss talks to Vontobel, even on the phone, his back straightens and his voice becomes polite. Most Swiss respect any man who makes big money, just as they cannot help but despise people who make less than they do. It is not a caste system, but it is a class system— subtle, tenuous, but quite real. Dr. Vontobel is not only a banker but also an Army colonel. In Zurich, the *Patrizier* is still the *Patrizier*. Since the day of Alfred Escher nothing much has changed.

Few of Vontobel's customers are kings. But all of them like to feel they are treated like one. Moneyed Europeans prefer their own banker, just as they prefer their own lawyer or private physician. Bank relationships, once started, are usually for life. In the older banks, many European families have used the same bank for generations, and nothing could make them change.

No private bank may advertise, a peculiarity of Swiss law. But no private bank wants, or needs, to advertise. Open advertising would destroy the intimacy, and worse, create a lack of confidence. Moneyed customers do not like to think that a bank actually *needs* their trade.

Vontobel and other private-bank customers learn about the bank from *mund-zu-mund propaganda*—word-of-mouth advertising. No private banks wants *too* many customers, because it is a custom trade. Too many clients would destroy both private service and atmosphere. But word has no problem getting around. Hundreds of Vontobel customers come from Scandinavia as well as Germany. When they arrive in Zurich, they know where to go.

Vontobel's real problem is not getting money in, but putting it out again. Since 1964, foreign money may not be invested in Switzerland; it has to go back abroad. This means Vontobel, Bär, and all the other private banks must know politics, prices, and conditions across the world, just as the merchant who two hundred years ago sent his cargoes across the sea. In the late 1950s Vontobel pulled money out of Wall Street. After 1962 the bank went back in strong. They make their estimates and decisions, day by day.

Private-bank trade breaks down into two main classes: businessmen and ladies or others with private money to invest. The bank buys and sells shares on every major stock exchange in the

world, advises on international investment potential, manages
estates, handles current-account business, advises and helps form
corporations and trusts as the customer desires. With Bär and one
other Zurich bank, it pools capital to make huge loans across the
world. Vontobel's money stays in Europe, or goes to North
America or Japan.

Each investment is often tailored to the trade, just as Hans
Vontobel knows how to temper the wind to each customer.
French clients are unostentatious. After generations of hide and
seek with the tax man, they tend to poor-mouth it to the last.
Most Germans like to try to impress Dr. Vontobel with their
wealth and importance from the first. Either way, he smiles and
takes their cash.

Many of Vontobel's newer customers are Americans living in
Switzerland, and Vontobel likes the dollar trade. The bank,
which once used only German, has begun to print its investment
bulletins in English. *Mund-zu-mund propaganda* filters through
California now as well as Sweden. Vontobel demands a passport or
other identification from Americans wanting to deposit or invest,
gives them a numbered account without question if they want
one, and asks them for a signed statement their purpose is not to
evade taxes. The statement—though it angers some Swiss bankers if this is said—is more a sop to foreign criticism, or to their
consciences, than a working agreement. The statement may be
filed—but under Swiss banking law it cannot be used. No banker
would dream of making such a thing public, and no customer,
honest or not so honest, has anything to fear, either way, by sign-
ing it.

Anyone, actually, can open an investment account. Vontobel
will take the money as quickly as Merrill Lynch. There are private banks, the smaller ones, which will turn down anything less
than 20,000 francs, $5000. J. Vontobel & Co. will start with only a
thousand Swiss francs. The bank cannot make money on accounts of less than 10,000, but it has found that small accounts—
like the mysterious Frenchman's—tend to grow.

Most Americans, however, still do business with the three Big
Banks. It may be the very bigness which creates confidence.
More likely it is that many Americans have never heard of a pri-
vate bank. The fact that Vontobel, Bär, or Pictet are not in-

corporated bothers some. But private banks are subject to the same banking law and ferocious audits and must have the same capital-to-loan ratio and liquidity standing as the Kreditanstalt. Private banks must not only put up 5 million francs to secure and keep a charter, they must also show very respectable sums to trade on the Swiss exchanges. There are very few fly-by-nights. Between 1960 and 1965, a dozen American national banks failed or went into receivership; out of some four hundred the Swiss lost only two. If a private bank fails, its owner goes down with it. He has no limited liabilty or corporate sneak-hole which permits him to commit public folly and escape. Most Swiss private bankers do not think of themselves as builders of empires or entrepreneurs but as stewards of money, and this keeps them out of trouble as much as anything.

Vontobel, ironically, has become rich really by thinking small.

It is not necessary to make a personal appearance to bank at a private house or any Swiss bank. Accounts may be begun by mail, but here again there must be proper identification. Any unknown would-be client who sends money in, giving a post office box or some other incomplete address, will get it back by the fastest return mail. Vontobel has no time for mystery. Nor will they take more than $50,000 without being satisfied as to where and how the cash was earned. The bank has too many top-drawer, legitimate customers to spread its services among shysters.

Men like Hans Vontobel, Colonel and Doctor of Jurisprudence, own banks in Switzerland. But men such as Max Zaugg, who works as a procurator in Vontobel Bank, is more representative of the banker as a whole. The procurators keep the banks in business. Zaugg is typical: polite, unassuming, brilliant in his way, and unrich. He knows investments. He writes the daily stock column for the *Neue Zurcher Zeitung*, the world's most respected German daily, and does his best to keep up with everything happening everywhere in the political and financial world.

Unless he inherits a bank, a Swiss can enter banking in only two ways. He comes in as an apprentice, goes to night school, and in three years must pass a public banking examination. Then he goes on the regular payroll. Or, after twelve or thirteen years in school, he can secure a *Matura*— the equivalent of two year's American college—which allows him to work in any bank. If he has both *Matura* and money, he may enter one of the excellent Swiss universities. Here he can earn a doctorate in three and a half years. University training in Switzerland is private, and usually beyond the reach of the lower-middle or working class. Only 4.5 students per thousand population try for the Ph.D., which opens many doors.

There are limited executive-training programs, but only in the largest corporate banks—where the competition is both keen and cutthroat.

Most Swiss, if they are good enough, prefer to work with a small, or private, bank.

Bank procurators are well but hardly extravagantly paid. It is a social breach of the first order, akin to asking a casual acquaintance how many times per month he sleeps with his wife, to seek to find out how much money he makes. But patterns do prevail. A good procurator at a good bank probably earns between $8000 and $12,000 per year, with bonus. Swiss banks prefer to charge set management fees rather than percentages on each transaction, and their investment counselors are salaried, too. It reduces the urge to keep accounts churning—a very bad feature of the American stock investment system.

If the pay seems low compared to the money American customer's men make, the three-to-one differential between Swiss and American salaries must be taken into account. Again, the $20,000-to-$50,000 earnings of many American stock salesmen do not reflect their brains, but their personality, social contacts, or ability to close. The faceless men in Merrill Lynch or Bache & Co. who dig out the facts make no more than their colleagues among the Swiss.

Like most Swiss bankers, Zaugg spent time abroad. This not only gave him better insight, it qualified him for more pay. Employers prefer men who have gumption, or have widened their horizons. The peculiarity of the Swiss banker like Max Zaugg is that he can become immensely sophisticated abroad while remaining quite parochial at home—it is quite possible for a Zurcher to have a better understanding of London than he does of Zug. Also the Swiss, unaffected by any real ideology, uninterested in making the moral judgments so dear to most of the rest of mankind, can judge Mexican silver or Japanese rails on their profit-making merits and nothing else. It is primarily this ability which has made Max Zaugg and his bank so effective in the international financial world.

Zurich, and to a lesser extent Basel, trades with the German-speaking nations, Scandinavia, and the English-speaking world. Zurich is a city in which most American, German, and Swedish businessmen feel instinctively at home. But the heart of Swiss private banking lies to the south and west, in the tiny enclave of Geneva. The Republic and Canton of Geneva is all but surrounded by France. Officially Swiss only since 1814, Geneva might have been another Andorra or Liechtenstein except for two things: the Reformation in Switzerland and the Counter-Reformation in France.

When the power structure of the Republic of Geneva became Calvinist in the sixteenth century the foundations of Swiss international banking were laid. But the institution itself did not begin until Louis XIV of France revoked the Edict of Nantes in 1685. This drove French Protestants—Huguenots—underground or out of France. It also destroyed the burgeoning French banking industry, which was then an almost wholly Protestant affair.

Thousands of French Huguenots—the majority French gentry or highly skilled members of the urban middle class—fled to Geneva. France was the richest and most talented nation in Europe at that time, but it exported men and crafts it could not afford to lose, including the French banking community. In Geneva French refugees started the Swiss watchmaking industry; more important, these men assured that the real French banking network would ever afterward be controlled from beyond the borders of France.

Headquartered safely in neutral Geneva, the Protestant banking structure came back to Paris. By the eighteenth century a vast French-speaking financial network spread all over Europe. Hattinger, Mallet, Mirabaud, and De Rougemont operated in Paris. The banker Necker of Necker, Thelusson & Cie. struggled with the idiocies of Bourbon fiscal policies. Prévost was in London, Iselin in Denmark, Meuricoffre in Italy. Gallatin and Iselin made monetary history in the infant United States. This important structure was no longer really French, however. It was run by Frenchmen, but its heart was in Geneva. There a number of famous banking houses had begun: Lullin, Ferrier, Lombard, Odier, Hentsch, Bourdillon, Bonna, Pictet. Banks opened and closed, firms changed, but these names went on. Bankers tended to marry into banking families, just as families with sixteen quarterings sought their own kind out. French-Swiss fortunes grew.

Long before the French Revolution a large part of the French national income, as well as the French Exchequer, was administrated by the Swiss. The events of 1789 intensified the trend. Aristocratic wealth followed the former Protestants to Geneva; French clergy advised noble parishioners that money could be in no safer hands than those of the hated Calvinists. The Revolution and the Terror ended, but the newer Napoleonic industrial and mercantile fortunes continued what was already a national habit —going abroad. From 1789 through 1958 France had only brief periods of truly stable or responsible government, with the result that most rich Frenchmen kept at least part of their money in Geneva. The largest block of capital in Swiss banks was always French, and it was still French in 1965.

Geneva was from the first private-bank country. The feverish industrialization and capitalism which swept Germanic Switzerland and built Zurich passed it by. The gentlemen of Geneva stayed merchant princes, and just as the canton itself faced France on three sides, Geneva banks faced outward toward Europe, not inward to the Confederation. In the eighteenth century the importance of Geneva was to Europe as a whole, not Switzerland; by 1965 little had changed. The old banks, by and large, survived.

In 1931 the leading Geneva private banks (Ferrier, Lullin & Cie; Hentsch; Lombard, Odier & Cie; Pictet; Darier; Bordier; and Mirabaud Fils) formed the *Groupement des Banquiers Privés Genevois*. These seven banks together could pool funds and resources which enabled them to underwrite major foreign industries or bond issues. The *Groupement*, acting together, could and did rival the Big Banks in the foreign field.

German railroads, Norwegian nitrogen plants, Swedish telephone companies, and the Dutch and Danish government bond issues have been underwritten in Geneva. The *Groupement* provides the most liquid capital in the world. Interest rates are low, since money is plentiful. The discount rate of 2.75 per cent is the lowest anywhere, encouraging hundreds of major corporations and dozens of governments to come calling at Geneva. None of this lending money, of course, is genuinely Swiss. But emerging from Geneva banks it spends as well as any.

Between 1961 and 1965 Genevan private-bank holdings on Wall Street topped $3 billion. The *Groupement* operation was so successful that in 1961 Bär and Vontobel of Zurich joined two other banks, Rahn & Bodmer and Wegelin (St. Gallen), in what was called the *Groupement Zurichois*.

The Big Banks all have major offices in Geneva, which look exactly like what they are. There are also dozens of new banks, mostly Other Banks, which have sprouted up in Geneva like weeds. These banks, showing signs in Hebrew, Arabic, and English as well as the native French, find the extremely cosmopolitan atmosphere congenial. Their owners rarely live in Switzerland and rarely do business within the Confederation. Until 1965 they caused the Swiss no trouble and were tolerated.

The Big Banks and the chrome-and-glass-fronted Other Banks are scattered about the city. The heart of Genevan banking, the old private houses, are in an older part of town. These have no gaudy neon signs like the Other Banks. Most have no signs at all, only doorplates. Only the bars on the windows, in most cases, reveal what they are. The people who do business with them do not have to search. They know where they are.

One barred building fills a short block, at 6, rue Diday, Hôtel de la Banque. The brass plate reads *Pictet & Cie*.

There is greater security in a Geneva private bank than in the banks of Zurich. No one gets past the porter without an appointment, or at least convincing someone that he has legitimate business inside the bank. It is always sensible to phone ahead. There is secrecy, suspicion, and security in Zurich's or Basel's larger banks—but getting in is child's play compared to Geneva's. Genevan banks have been the targets for French, Middle Eastern, and Latin American government agents for generations, and are under continual pressure from German and American journalists. This has added to the natural French passion for financial discretion. In recent years there have been newer problems. Crimes against property were once almost unknown in Geneva—but with the advent of both the Jet Set and more than 60,000 raffish foreigners in the canton, things have changed.

In the 1960's there has been a series of bank robberies. There were no holdups *à l'Américaine*, with blazing guns and getaway cars. But banks had grown careless in transporting money from one house to another. It was usually carried in a satchel by an old pensioner, usually unarmed. On one occasion two brawny young men walked up alongside a bank messenger—whose habits they must have studied for weeks—knocked him down, grabbed his bag and made off with more than a million francs. The banks have tightened up.

Perhaps curiously, Genevan banks had been more concerned with protecting secrecy and guarding information than in securing the money itself, and the lapse cost at least one bank dearly.

The visitor who is known at Pictet, or who can say one of the magic names—Pictet, Gautier, Demole—is ushered in. Visitors come at odd hours, and appointments, for obvious reasons, are never made from France. And even some Arabs like to come by night.

There are no elevators in the Pictet bank. They would be as unthinkable as gray steel corridors, computers, or the whir of check-writing machines. A visitor ascends the stairs. As in Vontobel, there is no public "business area," but a reception room leading to private executive offices. The atmosphere of even the old banks in Zurich is modern. The atmosphere of Pictet, like that of most Geneva banks, is slightly shabby. There is period furniture, rubbed and old, and faded portraits on the wall. There is a certain carelessness about everything—but gradually a visitor realizes it is the kind of shabbiness only the very rich can afford. It is a form of elegance many Americans and most German customers do not really understand, which is one reason why both prefer Zurich.

In Pictet, Bordier, and Lombard there still remains something which is rapidly passing from the banking world—a personal charm, a way of doing business, a war against impersonal society which Zurchers in their hearts know they have lost.

Geneva still fights the malaise which in New York, Hamburg, or Basel has already won.

Blonde girls in fashionable sweaters take a visitor's coat. They help him off with it while others seek his business. These girls, with their gray-green central-European eyes and exquisite French, are quiet, charming, efficient. They have seen everything.

The faces which look down from the oil paintings on the walls are famous in Geneva and the financial world: De Candolles, Neckers, Pictets. The family resemblances, even across centuries, is strong. The faces more than anything else resemble those of a series of French bishops—the keen eyes, the firm, disciplined, yet tolerant mouths, the civilized half-smiles. Those faces also saw everything.

The offices are small, cluttered, somewhat faded. But this is not a modern temple of finance. This is a French Protestant bank situated in Switzerland, where men do business with each other as men. The air is leisurely but not relaxed. There is time to talk, but sooner or later a profit must be made.

In Pictet any language may be used, though the vast majority of the clientele use French. English is no problem; most banks have, like Pictets or Bordiers, sent sons to Harvard or the financial center of London. All the old banks are first and last family institutions. But the old families, being Calvinist, are still able to think impersonally. There is an immense sense of duty. Family is important, but it cannot take precedence over the bank. A place may be found for sons of no ability, but neither Pictet nor the others are completely closed enterprises. New blood comes in through marriage, merger, or purchase. In some of the old banks the names on the door are no longer in complete control.

But to the younger men moving into the upper hierarchy of the banks, such as Edouard Pictet, the motivation to hand something on to their children is strong. Duties as well as huge family fortunes are passed on. The Swiss banking families keep an umbilical around their offspring until late, sometimes the thirties or even forties. In Switzerland this is accepted. When Edouard Pictet was at the Harvard School of Business, one of the things he could not comprehend was the reluctance of American executives to enter their fathers' firms. To Pictet, this was unfathomable, as reprehensible as he would have found Elizabeth II's refusal to be Queen.

Pictet business is similar to Vontobel business, except it is French or Middle Eastern instead of Germanic. It is hardly any more gamy. French industrialists have bad livers, and countesses can be crotchety as well as ugly. Edouard Pictet, handling the limited American trade, has never met a gangster or a movie star, and his bank turned Trujillo's money down. The old banks are too solid, and have too much reputation, to do anything not in the best of taste.

The customers it accepts Pictet helps as only a good Swiss bank can. It charges them royally for the privilege, without complaint. They give it the large amounts of liquid capital which make the bank known all over the world.

After three years of De Gaulle's stability in France, Pictet began to experience a phenomenon common in Geneva—the gradual withdrawal of French funds. Frenchmen for the first time in generations began to have confidence in a strong French regime, and money went home to France. This money helped build the new hard franc and swell French prosperity. But not all of it did or will leave Geneva. French families and lawyers sensibly ask themselves, "After De Gaulle—what?" The answer still leaves much to be desired.

But just as the French cash was withdrawn, the 1958 Iraqi revolution, and the Nasser- and Communist-inspired troubles in the East shook a flood of Near and Middle Eastern money free. By 1961, capital was pouring into Geneva from Syria, Lebanon, Algeria, and other places where the French language and French cultural influence among the rich were strong. Piasters, lira, and dinars have easily filled the old French franc's place.

The restriction on investing foreign money in Switzerland did not bother Pictet and other Geneva banks. They always looked abroad, and this only closed a door they did not use.

But banking and the business world is changing, even in the heart of Europe. Labor costs go up; automation pressures come in. It is not really difficult to hand the bank down from generation to generation; Swiss inheritance taxes are based on consanguinity; a son pays less than a nephew, for example, and long-range provisions are always made. The real problem is to keep running an essentially eighteenth-century business with both grace and style.

Paternalism could go out, pensioners be cut down. Pictet certainly has more than enough money to bring IBM in. But automation and the newer way of doing things runs against Pictet's stock in trade.

Pictet's clients get handwritten statements when they call. They would frown or howl at impersonal symbols printed on a piece of paper. All Pictet documents are tailored to the customer's order: if a French lady desires her correspondence written by a quill pen in blue ink on red bond Pictet tries to oblige. After all, it is the customer who foots the bill.

Still, it is getting harder all the time to run a twentieth-century business, and an immense one, with quill and ink. The Banque Pictet will undoubtedly survive, but elegance may not.

With one bank for each 1300 people in 1964, more banks per capita than dentists, some authorities feel that Switzerland is "overbanked." But new banks open all the time. The influence of Other Banks across the world continues to grow, and more come in. Sometimes this upsets the Swiss: the American-owned Banque de Dépôts in Geneva once had to be restrained by the Banker's Association. It was carrying ads in American newspapers for numbered accounts.

In 1963 the First National City Bank of New York moved in. The entry of a major United States bank in Switzerland has provoked some serious discussion in Swiss circles. For instance, what happens in a case where US and Swiss law concerning a customer account contravene?

The Swiss branch in Geneva must refuse all information on American clients to Washington, under Swiss law. But what pressures might Washington then place on the home office in New York? So far the case is unresolved, but some Swiss do not like to think about it.

Beside the Other Banks, there seems to be room at the top for new private banks, too. One of these is Germann & Co., Basel, in 1964 just four years old.

Five million francs capital and a license from the Swiss Banking Commission really puts nobody in the banking business with a splash. New banks need new money, and Swiss banks find it. But they also need prime businesses to lend it to, and prime business is usually in the hands of older banks. Since under Swiss law private banks may not advertise—they cannot even place a notice in their windows stating they pay interest on savings accounts—they find getting started rather slow. Word-of-mouth propaganda is fine for banks like Pictet or Vontobel, They have been around a long time; they have thousands of customers, and they have made a few ripples on the pond. Germann & Co. faced certain problems.

The Banking Commission, on granting Germann's license, advised its directors to "look outside." In other words, Swiss authorities wanted them to get money and reinvest it abroad. But Germann, entering the feverish European financial and industrial world of 1960, was soon flooded with doubtful risks.

Germann's directors, with a certain ingenuity, determined to create new prime business. The spirit of old Alfred Escher was still alive. Germann helped organize and back a new Swiss charter airline; it provided money for expensive aircraft and equipment. Germann kept looking about for enterprising Swiss with new ideas for using money, and soon found them.

Frédéric Chapuisat, a Geneva-based director of the firm, summed up the bank's philosophy: "Businesses are made by men, not machines. We find the men. When we have found them, we find it much more easy to buy them the machines they need."

Like all Swiss banks in the 1960s, Germann stayed well within the Atlantic confines. Nowhere else could they find the men with the skill, ethic, and energy to start a capitalistic enterprise and make it tick. Without these, all the new tools in the world would not make a business profitable or repay the bank. Swiss bankers cannot take human needs, only human abilities, into account. If they did otherwise, they would soon be out of business and most of their customers broke. If many people hate bankers—and the directors of Germann & Co. find they are no exception—it may be because bankers must accord men only what they seem to deserve on balance and not one farthing more. Germann's initial enterprise, the airline, did well. They started others. By 1965 Germann was averaging an annual increase of 50 per cent in new depositors and prime loans. But it takes at least ten years to make a good Swiss bank, and it will take more than that before the old private banks accept Germann & Co. into their club.

The banking trade is therefore far from static. The recent industrial growth inside Switzerland between 1958 and 1965 was phenomenal. The Swiss boom made the more widely advertised German *Wirtschaftswunder* or French or Italian prosperity by comparison look sick. Swiss productivity in terms of population soared. New capital was created, and thus new banks were needed. They came into being in Basel, Geneva, and Zurich—but after 1963, the real catalyst was Italian-Swiss Lugano. By 1965 Lugano had at least a dozen brand-new banks.

Lugano had become a special case, and the reason was the political disintegration of Italy which started in 1963.

In the fall of that year, Italian customs on the Swiss border received an anonymous phone call: "Be alert at six o'clock. An American Cadillac with Italian plates will try to cross. It will be carrying smuggled gold!"

This sort of tip is not uncommon to border inspectors everywhere. By six, the customs men were quite alert and ready. And a pretentious, gaudy American Cadillac did come down the mountain road.

With a great show of briskness and efficiency the guards halted it and made the driver get out. There was only one man in the car, a tall, well-dressed Italian who said he was merely crossing the border to have dinner in Switzerland.

The border guards ordered him to take the Cadillac off the road, and immediately began a thorough search. They looked in the trunk. They examined the underside of the body. They pulled off the wheels and checked them one by one. They opened the upholstery and picked the fabric apart. They found nothing.

After a few minutes of this, the Italian started to put up a terrible screech. He shouted that he was the *Commendatore* G—a title given him by Mussolini—and he was being subjected to indignity. He got red in the face and threatened political retribution on the customs agents. He called them names as only an angry Italian can.

The guards became thoroughly angry, too. They shouted back, and began to get nasty themselves. They were certain they were onto something, and the protests only made them more determined. They took parts of the Cadillac engine apart, checking the cylinders to make sure they were only steel. They pried pieces out of the tonneau itself, to make sure it was not platinum in disguise.

Then, the final insult, they searched the Commendatore himself. They made him strip in the customs house, and probed his shoes and clothing inch by inch. They made him bend over and probed his rectum to see if he had concealed diamonds inside. All through this, the Commendatore threatened them with fates worse than death.

Two full hours of this kind of search turned up exactly nothing. Both car and driver were clean. Now dark-faced and muttering among themselves, the guards began to think someone had set them up—tried to make fools of them. They apologized and agreed to let their victim go. But he was now in a violent rage and demanded a telephone.

In the end, a minor official arrived at the border station; there was more passing of insults and shouted recriminations. It was now very embarrassing for the official—who in turn became officious and extremely sarcastic with the guards. He chewed them out for ten minutes straight.

With a final insult, the Commendatore got in his Cadillac and roared off.

Three days later the same car and driver passed this way again. The Commendatore braked, smiled nastily at the same guards, and inquired if they wanted to search again.

Stiff-faced, the guards said, "Pass, Signor!"

The Commendatore called them cretins, and sped away. He drove on into Switzerland, and an hour later pulled up in front of a Lugano bank. Scattered throughout the Cadillac, carelessly crammed into several suitcases, was approximately a million dollars worth of gold. The bank was happy to help him lug it in.

Zurich is a northern city, Geneva an eighteenth-century bit of France. Lugano, between snow-covered Alps and deep blue Italian lakes, is in the sun. There are palm trees, cacti, and a carefully cultivated Mediterranean look. To some Californians it looks like home. Lugano is small, some 30,000 people. It has considerable light industry; Lugano makes 80 per cent of Schaefer's pens. It is spotless, Swiss, but with huge Italianate arcades. Lugano looks like Italy should look but doesn't. And it has more than thirty banks.

In 1964 and 1965, new ones were springing up almost every day.

Basel and Zurich are industrial and commercial, Geneva has the *elegance* of earlier times. Lugano is something new. It is gamy, feverish, new-rich, and in the new-rich European way, *molto snob*.

Money, and only money, counts. A bank procurator who enjoyed keeping score counted sixteen new Ferraris (at an average of $20,000 each) parked on Lugano streets. This is where the new aristocracy—the new industrialists, the new millionaires, the newer film stars—comes. They are most welcome, so long as they bring cash.

This is where Sophia Loren, Katharine Valente, Fritz Thyssen, and a horde of lesser lights have fled. There are 6000 German propertyholders in the canton and almost as many European actors, most of whose names no one has ever heard. Of the whole group, only Maria Schell and Ursula Andress are truly Swiss. The German winter brings them from the north, and the Italian tax collector drives them from the south.

In 1963, the Italian government, beset by inflation, cracked down on taxes. Withholding taxes on dividends and interest were clamped on for the first time. At the same time, there was the "opening to the left," the net result of which was to frighten most Italian businessmen to death. Italian economic and political troubles—in a basically prosperous economy—were inextricably mixed. Modern capitalism came late in Italy—it did not really begin, with a truly national market, until after World War II. Italian industrialists, many of whom had been running local family businesses, made billions of lire. Overnight, thousands of them became new-rich.

One prominent Swiss banker, who has made a fortune in Italy, has called the new industrialists—not the old, established families in Milan—the stupidest businessmen in the world.

The new wealth went into the *dolce vita*, not new industries. The opening of the national market, with new prosperity, was something few Italian businesses understood. New metal-working plants often lacked toilet facilities for the help, or even places for the workmen to wash up. Modern English or American cost accounting was virtually unknown. Making money, many Italian businessmen began to spend it like it was the national sport. Italy, in good financial shape in 1959, by 1963 was $1.2 billion in the hole. Italy spent more abroad than it even tried to take in. Businesses borrowed weekly from banks when they needed money, and kept no records; the tax collector had to be confused. When business inevitably slacked off—and banks refused to make free-wheeling loans—trouble arrived.

Meanwhile, little of this wealth trickled down. The Italian workers saw conspicuous consumption on every hand but enjoyed none of it. It was not an accident that northern Italy—the supposedly prosperous half—still maintained the largest Communist Party in the Western world. And in Italy, workers had the vote. The huge leftist parties, as unwilling as the industrialist to live for tomorrow, forced the basically conservative Christian Democrat Party to try to accommodate with the left. A minority, the ruling party had to make concessions, and suddenly Italian businessmen who had helped make the condition began to say, "My God, we've got a Communist government. We must get all our money out!"

Some manufacturers tried to punish their workers by cutting down on employment. Most took whatever money they had free and ran. In 1963 alone, more than $4 billion left Italy for Lugano.

But Lugano banks, more than happy to receive it, hardly knew what to do with such a golden flood. Some of it went on to Wall Street—in 1964, one New York investment house got one third its total money from Swiss Lugano alone. Most of the money was shoveled back into Italy, and it kept the basic Italian boom from complete collapse. But since Switzerland and Italy had no tax conventions, the money was reinvested in the Italian economy tax-free.

Italian businessmen quit doing business with local banks. They went to Lugano with their currency, gold, and assets, often smuggled. The Lugano bankers issued overdrafts back to them in Italy. It was and is a crazy system. But Lugano and its burgeoning banks got rich. Italy between 1963 and 1965 had no really effective government, but the economy ran; life, for the wealthy, stayed quite sweet. Happiness was a drawing account on a new Swiss bank.

There were old banks in Lugano—the Banca della Svizzera Italiana, a Swiss branch of the Banco di Roma (operating under Swiss law), and offices of all the Swiss Big Banks. These were all first-rate. They all got business. But there was more than enough for newcomers, too.

The new banks came in from other parts of the Confederation and brought their top people with them. The bankclerks, porters, cashiers, and secretaries are Ticinese. Higher management is something else. Many of the newer Lugano private banks—Banca del Gottardo, del Sempione, Commerciale de Lugano, perched like hungry falcons, facing south—are owned by outside interests. The manager of the brand-new Banca Commerciale is called Basler; the head of Banca del Gottardo's name is Condereau. Italian-Ticinese names are hard to find.

The 80 per cent of the banks' trade which comes from Italy arrives with a nervous and conspiratorial air. Some of this is merely Italian play-acting; some of it is real. The portly, nervous, excitable customers who throng the red-carpeted, chandeliered, and Spanish-furnished executive suites of Banca Commerciale are not only concerned with Communists. They are determined to avoid Italian taxes, every one.

Many of the Swiss bankers handling the Italian trade in Lugano are slightly contemptuous of it. They feel the Italian new-rich have no social conscience. This does not, however, prevent the banks from treating lire assets with proper respect. No Swiss is quite prepared to sneer at money.

Despite this conspiratorial air in the private banks, there is a laxness in Lugano which would be unthinkable in Zurich or Geneva banks. Anyone can walk inside the new Banca Commerciale or Gottardo and take stairs or elevator directly to the executive suites. It is even possible to wander around inside without finding a porter or secretary. Not only the moral atmosphere of Lugano, but even the efficiency, is Italianate and relaxed. No one can talk very long to a Lugano banker, particularly in the newer private banks, without getting a strong impression that anything goes.

The newer banks all look to the Banca del Gottardo, which itself is only a few years old. Gottardo is Lugano's outstanding success. Gottardo is private, and therefore publishes no records or balance sheets. This not only adds to customer secrecy, it also helps the bank itself with Ticinese taxes. The Ticino tax authorities have never been conventional, which means also that no bank can afford to be. Banks, like foreign residents, try to make their own deals, and most of them succeed.

Gottardo in 1964 reached capital and resources of 240 million Swiss francs and managed another $350 million in private stocks and bonds. These are estimated figures, but close enough. Gottardo in 1964 had only 80 employees, which meant a bank employee—deposit ratio of about three million Swiss francs. For this reason alone Gottardo is a shining example to other banks.

Just as Vontobel and Pictet tailor their services to their trade, Gottardo understands its milieu. Its people wheel and deal. They are very up-to-date. They care nothing for tradition, because their European new-rich custom has no tradition. But Gottardo provides handsome Italian-Swiss *procuratori*, urbane French-speaking directors, and men with a sharp sense of sports-car values as part of their services. They also have officers with impeccable German, and even a financial adviser or two whose name may be Italian but who wears a flannel blazer and smokes a Bond Street pipe. Gottardo's clientele includes retired Californians, German industrialists, and tax-evading Italian film stars. Most of them thinking doing business with the bank is itself *molto snob*.

Among Banca de Gottardo's services is criticism of American and German banking and investment practices. Gottardo's people tell their customers that the American and German systems, in which the investment firms get commissions from each buy and sell order, is made for gullible clients. The urge of the banks or brokers to keep accounts churning is too great, and it is seldom to the customer's advantage. Gottardo, like many Swiss banks, charges one flat fee, and tries to set the customer up for life. Gottardo men also say flatly that the Dow-Jones stock theory is full of holes—and quite a few Americans on Wall Street agree. Gottardo keeps no ticker tapes, for fear of the deadly mesmerization which might result. And there is some evidence that the Wall Street ticker tapes, the constant reporting of rises and falls, does produce irresistible urges to buy or sell. Gottardo prefers to deal with people with substantial funds and to work with them for the long run. A typical Gottardo customer in 1965 was advised as follows:

With five million Swiss francs on account, Gottardo had him put two million in safe bonds as a hedge against the market. Then, with European exchanges still depressed and Wall Street behaving quite erratically, the bank had him hold the other three million in gold. Like all major Swiss banks, Gottardo buys and sells bullion. The bank is never afraid to tell substantial customers to wait. And frequently, though by waiting a little interest or dividends may be lost, the gain in eventual capital appreciation is immense.

Swiss banks can operate this way while Merrill Lynch cannot, because Swiss banks begin by getting the money, *then* start their investment advice. The customer does not have to be lured into a Swiss bank—he brings his money in of his own volition. And banks like Gottardo can be relaxed once the customer is inside. They provide one-stop service. They can sell him anything he likes. If he does not want securities or gold, they can offer advice on, and sell, either real estate or investment trusts. A large Swiss bank offers under one roof services Americans would have to consult at least six different firms to get.

Last but hardly least, Gottardo offers its good customers complete tax advice, completely free. Once inside, it is not likely that Gottardo customers will ever want to escape.

The fact that so many Gottardo customers buy and hold gold is symbolic of the uncertainty which hangs over all Lugano's feverish prosperity. There is real fear of a collapse in Italy. There is a constant, underlying worry that the United States will engage in war in the Far East (the acute fear of a European conflict is almost nil) or, through labor pressures or cheap-money policies, get in the same kind of financial trouble as Britain. All these things would inevitably devalue the dollar, on which most international finance is based. Despite all the supposed sophistication, the highflown financial talk, of Gottardo and many Swiss customers, gold itself remains the one thing Swiss, Americans, English, Indians, Germans, Chinese, Italians, Arabs, and even Russians all understand and mutually respect.

Gottardo recognizes customer psychology and makes a nice profit from its bullion trade. With stable government slowly crumbling in Italy, with tax evasion by Italian businessmen a major Italian sport, and with Lugano conveniently close above the border, all Ticinese banks seem to have acquired a certain smell. But at Gottardo and many others, it was the sweet odor of success.

MIGROS: The Voice of Dissent

JUST AFTER World War I a young Zurich importer named Gottlieb Duttweiler was ruined by the financial chaos into which Europe fell. Like many Swiss—10 per cent of the population goes abroad—Duttweiler decided to widen his horizons. He went farther than most; he became a coffee planter in Brazil. But here again he failed. The great coffee glut of the 1920s broke the wholesale commodity price, and after working his heart out uselessly in the tropics for several years, Duttweiler returned to Zurich.

The first time he bought a cup of coffee he was horrified. They were burning coffee beans in South America—but in Europe the retail prices rose.

The reason was basically simple: the Swiss coffee cartel was at work.

Duttweiler, who had very little understanding of the basis of import-export prices, was driven to make a study. He found that even if coffee was worthless in Brazil, it would still be relatively dear in Europe. There were transport costs, and the inevitable middlemen, who had to live. Each hand which advanced coffee on its way added to the price. This Duttweiler understood. But what he could not understand was why, despite wide fluctuations in the worldwide costs, coffee prices in Switzerland never changed—in fact, on a depressed market, they sometimes rose.

Duttweiler soon found that a cartel or coffee "trust" controlled the entry of every bean by agreements and conventions.

This gave the cartel the power to set retail prices at and to its pleasure. Duttweiler discovered also that what applied to coffee was true for almost every other commodity in Switzerland. There was a chocolate trust, which set all retail prices—and manufacturers' costs and policies as well. Cartels controlled the making and sales of textiles, metal products, and the import of basic foods. There was even a strong convention which controlled builder's prices and cement. Government in Switzerland was not highly centralized, but business was. Pharmaceuticals were regulated by boardrooms from idea to patent to drugstore sale. Any unauthorized change in prices or practices was forbidden by agreement; the cut-rate sale was unknown. Even Swiss labor was taken into cartel agreements: manufacturers and teamsters signed conventions as to how trucks and lorries should be loaded and when deliveries should be made.

Prices, Duttweiler discovered, were always set to guarantee the least efficient producer a decent profit, which meant that all others received a "rent." The more efficient producers certainly did not mind, nor did Swiss labor, whose jobs were protected, too.

Going a step father, this cartel system at the top resulted in the fragmentation of retail outlets into thousands of small shops, each with a controlled or protected price and profit level. It had certain undeniable social advantages—stability and the fact that thousands of Swiss were self-employed—but the delivery and sale of groceries in Zurich had not changed essentially since the Middle Ages.

There were still no chain stores, and every shopkeeper had to buy, and therefore sell, at exactly the same price. Anyone who got out of line, or refused to acquiesce in the system, soon found his sources of supply cut off. The system affected so many industrialists, workers, and retailers—all of whom had a stake in it— that it had a firm grip on the Nationalrat in Bern. Most Swiss felt that to change it would drastically damage the basis of Swiss commercial life.

The only one who suffered was the consumer—and the consumer, in Switzerland, had no voice.

Gottlieb Duttweiler was not the first Swiss to see the inequities in the system, or to preach the virtues of free trade. But

Duttweiler was not just another "Manchester liberal" or theoretician. He was a failed businessman who was still an empire-builder at heart.

Duttweiler was a Swiss radical, but he was a radical more in the mold of the American West than of the socialist intellectual. Dutti Duttweiler, in fact, hated Socialists and Communists as much as any Swiss. But out of his personal experiences he came to hate the cartel system more.

Duttweiler saw that the average Swiss housewife had to go to a variety of shops—greengrocers, butchers, bakers, tobacconists, candy stores, and spaghetti shops—on her daily marketing chores. It took all morning to buy, and worse, each little store bought only in limited quantities, which even without cartels would have meant a higher retail price.

The idea of big stores, high volume, and big profits from small markups on rapid turnover was not unknown, but it was rigidly suppressed. Duttweiler saw a way to put himself back in business in Zurich, and at the same time do something for the average Swiss. His scheme was nothing new. Woolworth, Hartford, J. C. Penney, and others had used it successfully in America, and at the same time changed the fabric of American life. In August 1925, Duttweiler began something Zurich had never seen. With a fleet of five decrepit automobiles, he started a door-to-door delivery service selling seven common articles.

Duttweiler began with foods the poorer people bought, like spaghetti, sugar, macaroni. He concentrated on workers' neighborhoods, and he undersold the local stores on every block.

The move was an instant success. The Swiss are an intensely frugal people; old loyalties to shopkeepers cracked under the opportunity to save a franc. Few Duttweiler customers had any interest in breaking the cartels. They wanted to save a few rappen day by day.

But Duttweiler, of course, ran into an immediate buzz saw. The cartels moved to shut him off and freeze him out. All wholesalers in Zurich were forbidden to sell to him. Importers were told to cut him off.

Duttweiler, more than once almost down and out, fought back. If wholesalers refused to sell to him, he expanded and opened his own wholesale store. When Swiss importers declined to supply him with sugar, spaghetti, and salt, he obtained his own importer's license. The Swiss cartels did embrace Europe, but they could not command the world. Duttweiler, with immense energy, putting together a devoted band of associates and supported always by the eagerness of the public to buy, bit by bit forged his own mercantile chain. If he had to go to China to buy tea, he made his own connections there. He grew too big for the economic boycott (permitted under Swiss law) to work. The cartels boycotted him, but could not bring him, like the scattered small retailers, to his knees.

His organization, which he called MIGROS—from the words "half-wholesale"—grew. MIGROS soon established small but genuine chain stores on the American model, where a housewife could engage in one-stop shopping. And Duttweiler, a keen businessman as well as dreamer, did things which put MIGROS on firm ground.

The most rigid quality control was enforced. Lower prices in MIGROS did not mean inherently shoddy goods. Duttweiler, after the little people, did not try to sell the finest products. But he retailed a reasonably good product at a more than reasonable price. His image with the public grew. Thousands of Swiss began to understand his fight with the cartels and to realize that he was independent of everyone except the customer. No price was fixed; the customer was king.

The constant harassment from the entire Swiss mercantile structure ironically was the one thing which made MIGROS grow. Pressured by the trusts, no Swiss newspaper would carry MIGROS ads or list the weekend specials. Duttweiler organized his own paper, called *Die Tat*. It called for fair prices, fair standards, and fair play. Later, MIGROS went into publishing and formed a book and record club. Duttweiler was interested now in providing reasonable insurance for his growing throngs of customers. He tried to make a marketing connection with a large insurance company in Geneva. Here again the interlocking directorates which dominated all Swiss mercantile life defeated him. Insurance avenues, as well as regular wholesale channels, were closed to the pariah of Swiss economic life. But Duttweiler was not stopped for long. MIGROS organized its own insurance company.

By 1941 Duttweiler's chain of stores and sideline companies

had become so large he was forced to form his own holding company to control them all. It was called MIGROS Trust. MIGROS no longer sold only groceries, books, and insurance; groceries were still the backbone of the business, but MIGROS had become a retail empire selling many things, from bicycle tires to chains.

MIGROS stores were still small and cramped and antique by North American standards. MIGROS was no Sears, Roebuck, or even an A. & P. But by 1964 MIGROS accounted for 15 per cent of the turnover of all Swiss food, and between 8 and 10 per cent of the entire Swiss retail trade.

MIGROS, growing, needed financing. But the Big Banks in Switzerland are cartelized, too. It was inevitable that MIGROS, now a mercantile giant, should open its own bank. This bank, organized in Zurich in 1958 with only two full-time employees, became Switzerland's most unorthodox financial institution.

For one thing, MIGROS Bank cared nothing for prestige. The Zurich branch, which by 1964 had thirty-two employees, began openly stark and small. When it opened its first branch, in Winterthur, this office started with one man. No commercial bank in Switzerland, where foreigners have to be impressed, would have dared to do the same.

MIGROS Bank is the only mercantile bank in Switzerland which has no interest in foreign cash. Duttweiler opened it for the Swiss, and above all, MIGROS' growing family of devoted customers.

MIGROS failed to become a member of the Swiss Banker's Association. It refused to join the club. Only MIGROS stayed open Saturday morning in downtown Zurich and did business each weekday from eight to five. And finally, only MIGROS paid Swiss citizens interest on bonds beginning with six years.

The whole MIGROS system is a sort of giant cooperative, and MIGROS Bank fits in with the rest. All MIGROS club members, all MIGROS customers, are automatically entitled to every courtesy at MIGROS Bank. The bank started with a built-in, loyal clientele. At the end of its first seven years in business, it had 60,000 Swiss families on its deposit books and was capitalized at 200,000 francs. The Kreditanstalt began with less.

Anyone can bank at MIGROS. The bank offers all services. It is even equipped to take in foreign money and reinvest it abroad.

But Herr Wechsler, its managing director, had a positive aversion to doing this. Under his direction MIGROS is a *Swiss* bank, and 98 per cent of its customers are Swiss. Naturally, considering its origins, MIGROS draws few large accounts. The people who bank in Zurich at Seidengasse 12 are mostly working, or small-burger types.

MIGROS feels frankly that the interests of MIGROS members and the MIGROS organization come first. But the MIGROS directorate itself makes sure the bank follows the standard MIGROS practice: the bank gets MIGROS business and makes MIGROS loans only if it can handle both at lower or better terms than the rest.

Forming the bank made MIGROS Trust independent of the Big Banks. This made Duttweiler's organization freer to wheel and deal; it now had its own built-in system of finance. But equally important was the idea of offering Swiss citizens regular banking services at a reasonable price.

Director Wechsler, typical of the average MIGROS executive, takes a very dim view of the practices of the large Swiss banks. To him they have made the average little Swiss the forgotten man of Swiss finance. MIGROS offers the little man both investment and management advice, free. It is not concerned with company formation or high finance except within the MIGROS Trust itself. The bank loans out money as cheaply as it can—and Wechsler makes a great point of trying to offer little customers the same privileges the big banks give only the wealthy few.

MIGROS Bank in seven years established a fine reputation for fair dealing, something even the Big Bank directors admit. Obviously, MIGROS is not exactly beloved in Swiss banking circles. MIGROS has tried to maintain normal, friendly relations with other banks, but it has not had complete success. To begin with, MIGROS took 50 million francs in Swiss deposits away from the other banks. For another, as Dr. Schaefer, head of the Union Bank, told Wechsler, "We are quite aware that you are going to be damned big competition." And all this suits Wechsler and the MIGROS people fine.

Duttweiler always attacked the cartelization of the Big Banks, which compete with each other, but only with standard policies, charges, and interest rates. The sense of competition among the directorates of the Big Banks is far from keen. To most of these gentlemen, who also sit on insurance and industrial boards, open competition between Swiss banks is something which might get out of hand. Quite understandably the Kreditanstalt, the largest, seems to like the idea of competition least of all.

Conversely, relations between MIGROS and the state-owned banks, the cantonal banks, are excellent. Both banks are organized primarily to serve the Swiss people, and they do not get in each other's way.

The very fact that MIGROS will inevitably get bigger had become a minor worry to Paul Wechsler by 1964. MIGROS would eventually open branches in all Swiss cities, following the MIGROS stores pattern. The bank would become rich. Wechsler broods about the obvious dangers here. The Volksbank, or People's Bank, of Bern started in 1869 as a bank for the little man. It grew, and became just another cartelized Big Bank.

The great influx of foreign money into Switzerland, lured by the big commercial banks, hurt MIGROS and slowed its inevitable growth. This came about indirectly. The foreign money, too much of which was invested inside the Confederation, overheated the economy and pushed real estate and other prices up; in January 1964 Bern required MIGROS and other banks to place at least 40 per cent of all their investments outside. In 1964 MIGROS collected 30 million francs from Swiss, but had to reinvest 12 million abroad. The bank's quota for domestic investment—SF 18,-000,000—was completely exhausted within nine months. This was a considerable hardship for MIGROS and all other banks doing business with Swiss primarily with Swiss money.

This heightened MIGROS' disenchantment with the Swiss banks' love affair with foreign money. Wechsler has made his feelings plain. "This taking of foreign money was always a mistake. The Big Banks were founded, and grew, on foreign capital, not Swiss funds. From the first, their vision was wrong. It was focused outside, not inside the Confederation. For too many years there was no control over the Swiss banks—and all the banks, except the cantonal, were responsible for the situation which developed in 1960–1964. The commercial banks just could not bring themselves to stop accepting foreign money when it was thrust at them, and it was too easy and convenient simply to invest it right in the country. No wonder the economy overheated—and the bureaucrats in Bern, some of whom are of course owned by the Big Banks, were much too late in noticing the turn things were taking. The regulations which came in 1964 were five years too late."

Through Herr Wechsler, and through most of the executives of MIGROS Trust runs a tenuous disagreement with the arguments and standards of Swiss economic life. Unlike most Swiss businessmen, they have a certain hankering for more government control. This is understandable, since with Duttweiler most of them have had to battle the peculiar form of Swiss capitalism all their business life. Wechsler and the others are mostly rather young; they are sincerely democratic, but many of their ideas, like Duttweiler's, coincide with the notions of other youngish men in Washington or London. The idea of federal intervention in the economy in certain cases—for the general welfare—has a definite appeal.

They fully understand the Swiss repugnance toward any kind of governmental control, and even share it. But unlike most Swiss, MIGROS men are problem-oriented. They are not much interested in precedent or custom. Wechsler, for example, is the kind of man who thinks the problems of the economy, if solvable, should be solved without too much regard to the past or even the Constitution. Wechsler can sense a New Frontier in the world, and wants to bring it into Switzerland.

This does make a sort of split personality among the MIGROS crowd. For example, they are no real admirers of the autocratic De Gaulle. Yet they admire, almost wistfully, the way De Gaulle autocratically stabilized and regulated the French economy and state.

MIGROS men tend to feel the Confederation itself an anomaly in the modern world. Twenty-five sovereign cantons, which Bern can cajole but not really pressure, strikes them as being as medieval as the Swiss marketing and distribution systems. The government and certain of its policies also strike the heads of MIGROS Trust as illogical. The unconventional tax setup irritates them, because it in no way favors the average Swiss. The facts that real estate shares bear no taxes unless bought through a bank and that corporations or wealthy individuals can deal directly with cantonal governments or Bern—even making deals and paying taxes directly in some cases—bothers them almost as much as conventions and cartels. The fact that there is no national bank bookkeeping system in Switzerland, as there is in France, Germany, or the USA, to Wechsler is absurd. Bank secrecy or no bank secrecy, the fact is that France knows exactly how much foreign money is invested in its economy or on deposit at any time, and until 1964 Switzerland did not. It is, as the Swiss real estate inflation of the 1960s proved, a situation which can get out of hand.

Though no one among the MIGROS men will quite say it, what they really want is for Switzerland to stop thinking small and become a nation-state.

Some of this is merely modern intellectual thought, from which the Swiss are by no means immune. The rest can be traced back to Gottlieb Duttweiler himself. Duttweiler was a reformer at heart, another Zwingli in disguise. To put his "radical" business ideas before the Swiss people, he went into politics in 1935. He was elected to the Nationalrat from Zurich, and he formed his own political party, the Independents. He could not make a working agreement or feel at home in any established party—all of these would have as quickly touched the economic shibboleths of cartels and control as they would have overturned Swiss freedom of religion.

The cigar-puffing men who laughed at Dutti Duttweiler in Bern were probably right in this. In Switzerland certain kinds of economics and religion are not too far removed, and politicians know it. But Duttweiler the Independent fought an uphill battle trying to get some of his ideas put into law in Bern.

He was something of a Franklin or Theodore Roosevelt, but unlike the Roosevelts Duttweiler was naïve. He never understood the conservatism of men, or how the gears of power mesh. He was too independent for his party's good. He did not, unlike Roosevelt or Kennedy, know how to make a deal. It can hardly be questioned that he honestly believed in "service for the small people," as he said, or that he hated the economic royalists. His problem was he did not know how to attack them. As a politician Duttweiler failed.

The best he could do was build an empire, honestly, not in but in defiance of the Swiss system. In this alone he had a profound, and growing, influence on Swiss life. There was something almost American and very un-Swiss about Dutti Duttweiler, although few of his countrymen, even his admirers, saw it. Two things he said stand out:

One was that the Swiss should cease being *"Eine Nation von Watch-und-Cheese-makers, Hotelportiers, und Bankiers."* The other was "Think big!"

These ideas are quite subversive in Switzerland. The whole sweet Swiss success has always depended on the Swiss continuing to be watch-und-cheese-makers, hotel porters, and bankers— and nothing else. The Swiss are a confederation of five million people, split into twenty-five historic states, four thousand communities with an immensely strong tradition of local rule, four languages, and two major religions. They do not have the basis of a nation-state. A unitary system in Switzerland would bring a greater mess than Belgium's, setting Swiss on Swiss. And being a tiny nation, thinking big could only get Switzerland eventually into serious trouble.

The monopolists and cartel executives in their paneled suites were probably right about that "damned Duttweiler," but for the wrong reasons. He was thinking of Switzerland as a nation when actually it is a business.

But Duttweiler and his MIGROS had over-all good results. One was an impact on the system; MIGROS forced Swiss merchants to change their ways. Few Swiss stores went out of business due to MIGROS, but all improved. Small retailers followed MIGROS' lead, and formed their own sort of union, *Konsumvereins*. These groupings can mass their funds and buy in quantity, which brings each individual store's prices down. In other stores, to hold both the price line and the trade, services have vastly improved. Since Duttweiler, retailers who charge more have to offer something in return. The big and growing independent Swiss department stores now sell Nestlé's chocolate ten rappen below the chocolate cartel's established price.

MIGROS bank is still small, but someday it may change the complexion of Swiss banking. It may make more Swiss bankers realize that, after all, in Switzerland the Swiss should come first.

But one completely ironic fact remains. MIGROS has become a vast and influential octopus in Swiss economic life. Gottlieb Duttweiler set out to break the trusts and cartels. When he died in 1962, he had instead made the biggest cartel of them all.

Interhandel

IN THE summer of 1943 a European refugee living in New York received a telephone call from a highly respected law firm. An interview with a partner was arranged. When refugee and lawyer met, the law firm revealed that it had been approached by a Swiss bank and empowered to offer a large sum in American dollars in an Argentinian account, at the time still transferable to New York. In return the law firm, acting for the bank, wanted an assignment of certain securities; the total assets of a Swiss holding company which was also a personal corporation, and of which the refugee owned all the stock. The securities themselves were in a bank in Lausanne. The American law firm was representing a Swiss bank's legal branch, which in turn was acting for certain people high in the German Nazi government. All this came in the middle of a vast and bitter war.

The refugee, who had fled from the Nazis, was badly frightened. He had believed that only he and his Swiss bank knew of his secret holdings. The stocks in Lausanne represented control of an industry in a German-occupied nation, and the refugee was afraid his bank had talked. This was not the case. What had happened was that when the Nazis had overrun the refugee's country they had entered his former office, seized his safe, and with it his private papers. This put them on a certain trail. A little investigation by the Gestapo revealed that the refugee's immense European holdings had been legally transferred before the war to Swiss control. The Nazis had the physical property, but there was no way certain individuals in high Nazidom could acquire its "legal" ownership, which they were determined to do.

Many people are not aware that both the German government and some of its ranking individuals had a policy of acquiring significant European properties in occupied Europe by forced or other quasi-legal sales. The Germans politely named a price, usually in valueless paper currencies. If the property-owners were thinking men or women, they accepted with thanks. Otherwise they sometimes simply disappeared. In this particular case, where both the owner and the legal papers were beyond Nazi control, the Germans could seize and operate but not legally confiscate the estate. There was only one thing Reichsmarshal Goering could do, and that was buy. And this he sought to do, through a Swiss bank.

This kind of deal would stand up under international law and, the Germans thought, beyond the war no matter who might win.

The circumstances, the offer, and the deal—which shocked the refugee, who turned it down—could only have revolved around Swiss banks. In the later uproar in America and England over Nazi assets in Switzerland, one thing was often forgotten. Switzerland "protected" hundreds of millions in foreign assets from German grabs. Much of this money or property had not been transferred to Swiss corporations expressly to foil the Nazis. It had been done prior to 1939, and by some of the most prominent, and for that matter patriotic, names in Europe, who loved the land of their birth but could never trust its shifting governments where their money was concerned. When assets were placed where France, Holland, the Weimar Republic, Austrian socialists, or Polish dictators could not get them, they became "safe" from Nazis, too.

And in the middle of a hideous ideological, global war Swiss banks performed the miraculous function of removing all national taint from money. Once in a Swiss bank, it was a purely useful, everywhere-acceptable international medium of exchange between men who failed to hate each other and understood each other perfectly, even while their respective governments tried to remove one another from the earth. For example, in 1943 no American law firm would treat with any Nazi agency, nor could any German openly make direct contact with anyone in the United States. Here Switzerland served. Its people were so neutral and so generally respected internationally that both sides could deal "with" them with a clear conscience. Swiss banks not only offered a priceless haven for rich men determined to protect their fortunes from the vicissitudes of war, inflation, and confiscation. They were the last refuge of the corporation with long-standing international affiliations, which between 1939 and 1945 might be broken up due to a purely temporary unfortunate misunderstanding, in this case the war.

This whole question of prewar agreements between men who were anticipated national enemies is a very ticklish one. Few things make some people more upset, particularly those who really believe in "total" or "holy" war. It has always been disillusioning, and even a little frightening, to many people in America or Britain to find that some of their own citizens regarded the world wars as mere power struggles between hostile governments in which they at heart had no part. If it is any comfort, the same thing enraged the true Nazis, where Germans were concerned, even more. The question is delicate because the great international corporations and the men who run them are on the whole anything but disreputable. The men involved are pillars of their communities who in some instances saw nothing wrong in having close or even intimate connections with their colleagues in nations with which their own was, or soon would be, at war. War, after all, had nothing to do with the making of aspirin, except to give the Bayer people in 1917, and again in 1941, an enormous headache.

The first big international corporations came about because the men smart enough to assume management of large national concerns in Europe or America soon realized that an agreement to live and let live, plus a guaranteed high price, was preferable to international trade wars, price-cutting, and the other unpleasantness involved. The first European cartels were purely national. But by 1850 they had started to spread over national boundaries. This was the normal, natural growth of Western capitalism, and top managers soon understood that if cartelization was appealing at home, it worked equally well abroad. International conventions and price-fixing cartels between European and American business firms in the late nineteenth century became commonplace, though not public.

Cartelization in the industrial world was reinforced by the

close connection between industry and the applied sciences. During the formative years of Western industrialism Germany was the undisputed center of scientific experiment in both metallurgy and chemistry. German patents became vital to these industries in other countries, and to exploit and profit from these licenses and patents many international corporations were formed. The idea of the Atlantic Community was grasped by industrial managers long before it was shared by populations or politicians. Corporations were made with Germans, Britons, Dutchmen, Frenchmen, and Americans on their boards, to meet the requirements of expanding world trade. At the same time there was a crosslicensing of new patents taken everywhere, which had worldwide importance. Many of these new patents were German. This meant that Germans had to be taken into international corporations and into all agreements to slice up the world chemical or metallurgical markets.

These businesses were global in nature long before Europeans began to use the word. The numbers of men and corporations involved was always small. Their total economic power, however, was often immense.

The executives involved were rarely ever possessed of political sense. The arrangements they made with each other—to allow a German patent to be used in England, or to fix a "fair" return on sales in France—were never made for political reasons or to exert political influence, as a whole generation of critics later claimed. Most writers and other complainers about international corporations never sat on any board, owned a thousand shares of any stock, or understood the profit-making process. The international deals were made to ease international trade. Like purely national cartels, they did of course also restrict trade. And unfortunately every national government, in turn, tried to use both the businesses and the licenses to national advantage, often very much against the corporation executive's desires.

The charges of lack of "patriotism" often hurled at the international cartel officers were in many cases true. What began to happen in some huge international corporations, almost without anyone realizing it, was that corporate heads and executives were acquiring a dual citizenship: a man might travel on a German, British, or American passport, but he was also a true citizen of a small and select international business community which really had no national citizenship. They had become "organization men" of institutions which in reality owed no national allegiances.

This was extremely disturbing to some critics of international business. But on examination it is not easy to understand why the same men who preach the solidarity of laboring men or religions across national boundaries are often driven to rage by evidence of business or industrial solidarity. If many priests, common men, humanitarians, and poets could maintain a certain sympathy and understanding across the trenches, why not industrialists?

World War I was not a holy war, although the governments involved all chose to fight it as such. It was merely a struggle for predominance in Europe, and therefore the world, and fifty years later most historians recognized it as such. Men who took a longer view, and tried to maintain business connections through 1914–1918, were not wholly immoral, though by all national laws they committed treason at the time.

World War I, however, took the world business community by surprise. Most international corporation heads, who read and approved Sir Norman Angell's *The Great Illusion*, never believed it would happen. And what happened to the international cartels during 1914–1918 (most were destroyed) made it entirely clear to the men who had to reconstitute them in 1919 that some modification must be made. After 1918, international cartel agreements always dealt at considerable length with the problem of war. The problem was to find some way to survive, come strutting Kaiser, French chauvinism, Bolshevik high water, or Nazi hell.

Businessmen on international levels themselves created none of these world problems, but they were determined to survive them. All during the 1920s high-powered and highly paid brains were devoted to the problem of how to maintain the international business community even though war should intervene. The men involved may have been immoral. However, if they let the corporation become the be-all and end-all of human existence, it is reasonably certain that the be-all and end-all is not the modern parochial nation-state.

The only sensible answer to the problem seemed to be Switzerland. Switzerland was neutral, and the neutrality was established and recognized by all possible European belligerents. Furthermore, the Swiss' complete freedom in cartel and holding-company law and freedom from financial restrictions was made for international business. Switzerland was not, then, just a refuge for single rich men; it welcomed internationally owned corporations, investment trusts, multiple-contract agreements, and patent pools as readily as it did liquid cash.

Switzerland, after World War I, drew international pools and cartels like water pouring down a sluice. The men whose destiny it was to try to save firms whose stockholders might be spread across a dozen mutually hostile nations looked to the far future. Management on top levels is nothing more than prediction. Management must have long vision or perish; and international business management almost everywhere foresaw the inevitability of another European war even while the politicians were saying at Locarno it could never happen.

One reason these men knew was that many of them, in their own countries, were privy to secret armament deals or contingency plans and knew the thinking on high political levels, much of which was never made public. The irony and agony of some of these cartel managers was that they were only interested in trade and profits, but as war turned increasingly total their enterprises became increasingly vital to the munitions of war. By the 1930s most large industrial companies were producing directly or indirectly for war. Most of them at that time had no other source of profit. But at the same time, all cartel executives were desperately afraid of the effects of a global war upon their businesses.

The real attitudes of the largest corporate industrialists have not been thoroughly enough explored. These tend to be organization men, members of a "state within a state." As a matter of fact, many European industrial empires were in being long before the nations in which they reside took their modern form. Krupp, for example, made cannon for Napoleon, for the House of Habsburg, for the Hohenzollerns, and for Hitler—that is, for whichever power happened to be ascendant in Central Europe. While some people looked on the Krupp family works as a great conspiracy, Krupp executives have long looked on the outer world in the same light. Their purpose in life is to make steel and find markets for it, nothing else.

When Alfred von Bohlen, the head of Krupp, was led off to jail by the Americans in 1945, he was asked about the future. He merely said, "I hope to make steel again." The Third Reich went the way of the first two—but in the fullness of time Krupp made steel again.

After Calvin loosed his far-reaching and depersonalizing ethic upon the world, enterprise itself, whether in science or industry or government, transcended man. And all giant enterprises, whether they make steel or patent drugs or rule peoples or forge nuclear bombs, tend to be amoral. Enterprise is like a sword. It does not make war. It is, however, very useful to those who do.

About 1929, with the winds of fear again blowing about Europe, cartel executives began strenuous efforts to realign European and American company structures so that if war came the component parts of international corporations might still function. If the various parts could each survive across the flame and hatreds of war, there was always the possibility that the sum could one day be reassembled.

The best North Atlantic legal firms, with offices in London, Paris, Berlin, Amsterdam, and New York, were paid to study the problem. These firms had contacts or colleagues in Basel, Lausanne, Fribourg, and Zurich. They got together. It was quite simple to plan a succession of "Swiss" corporations to inherit licenses, assets, patents owned by certain international cartels. This was to muddy the track and to confuse all possible investigating governments. The transactions themselves were incredibly complex. Usually the intermediary trustees had no clear idea where the assets were coming from. The directors of the final corporation holding patents or assets normally had no real notion of who the actual beneficiaries were. These men, often prominent businessmen or bankers, took their fees, got some excellent stock deals in the process, and were content to keep quiet.

By 1939 Switzerland had itself become one giant cartel of international interests of every kind: patent empires, licensing pools, mutual funds, supranational holding companies, insurance firms. Most of these businesses were perfectly respectable. The only interest of their managers was that their British, French, German, Dutch, and American stockholders should continue to draw dividends even while they were fighting each other. Swiss insurance companies, for example, have always been international in scope. Most were capitalized with British funds, while customers and shareholders were scattered across all belligerent countries.

Figures available in Bern showed that in 1939 Switzerland was the registered home of 2278 international corporations, with an admitted capital of SF 3,925,855,000. This admitted capital was misleading—it was only the tip of an iceberg. Balance sheets were usually manipulated; vast sums were transferred just before publication so as not to get governments at home upset. Two hundred sixty firms fled into Switzerland during the seven months preceding September 1939. In all, there were 214 banks with purely international connections, 38 insurance firms held from overseas, and 2026 holding companies, trusts, and personal corporations in Switzerland whose majority stockholders were not Swiss.

Between 1939 and 1945 these companies experienced varying fates. Some failed, others were destroyed by war. Many proved the wisdom and forethought of their managers by living to do business another day. It is impossible to examine all these operations at length. But one case has received much attention. In its way it shows both all that is good and most of what is bad about Switzerland, Swiss corporate law, and Switzerland's secret banks.

This is the case of the Société Internationale pour Participations Industrielles at Commerciales, S.A., commonly called Interhandel.

In the years just before 1914 two men, one a Swiss citizen, the other a German with an uncanny financial knack, worked for the Metallgesellschaft A.G. in Frankfurt, Germany. The German, Hermann Schmitz, was at the start of a fantastic career. The Swiss, Eduard Greutert of Basel, was making important contacts.

In 1920 Greutert returned to Basel. With capital almost wholly provided by his former employer, Metallgesellschaft A.G., he opened a private bank called Greutert & Cie. The opening of this bank and the beginning of Eduard Greutert as a "banker" reflected the great move of German industrial assets and German foreign exchange out of the Weimar Republic to Switzerland. Greutert was only one among many, but he was somewhat different from most Swiss bankers in that he was from the first wholly German-owned.

Two things were driving German firms with international business to make Switzerland a base of operations. One was fear and distrust of the German government, which could not control inflation, Communists, or the new right-wing parties. The other was the disastrous German image which came out of World War I. Nationalist or anti-German sentiment was strong in most parts of the world. This made it prudent for German cartels to conceal their foreign dealings and to mask their ownership of American and European firms through Swiss corporations.

Greutert & Cie. for several years handled only Metall A.G. business. The bank had no other purpose or mission than to serve as a drop-box and international cover for Metallgesellschaft, a big nonferrous metals firm.

Sometime between 1920 and 1924, however, Eduard Greutert made contact with his old co-worker, Hermann Schmitz. Schmitz was now head of a large German dyestuff firm, Badische Anilin. Badische Anilin began to do business with Greutert, and now Greutert & Cie. hit the big time.

In 1925 Hermann Schmitz put together a vast industrial empire through the merger of the six largest German chemical and dye companies—Bayer, Griesheim-Elecktron, Weiler-ter-Meer, Agfa, Badische Anilin, and Hoechst. The new giant was called Internationale Gesellschaft Farbenindustrie A.G. (International Dye Industries, Incorporated), or I. G. Farben. I. G. Farben continued to buy out or merge with other firms in this line until by 1929 it was producing almost all German dyes and chemical products, photographic supplies, nitrogen, pharmaceuticals, rayons, and synthetics. Farben also bought foreign companies; by 1939 it was indisputably the largest chemical concern in the world.

Farben was the corporate "state within a state" *par excellence*. Without it Germany would have been as hard put to wage World War II as the United States would have been hampered by not having Dupont or General Motors.

Hermann Schmitz, the organizing genius behind Farben,

began to channel Farben business through Greutert. Later, Farben bought out Metall A.G.'s interest in his bank, a relationship which was to have worldwide consequence. Schmitz' motives were complex. There was the distrust of the Weimar Republic felt by all German industrialists; Schmitz became an early Nazi supporter and eventually a Hitler Reichstag deputy and *Geheimrat* (Secret Councilor). But Schmitz, knowing Nazi monetary and foreign-exchange policies, wanted to keep both money and business abroad. Further, after Hitler came to power, the German image worsened even more, and it became more and more essential, until the war made it mandatory, that Farben mask its international subsidiaries and profit-making ventures. I. G. Farben was immensely successful, but it got a very bad name.

Schmitz' financial dealings were even more complex. Some of them will probably never be known in their entirety. Eduard Greutert and his bank, and a large number of "desk-drawer" corporations formed through Greutert's services, became Schmitz' agents. Schmitz, who can only be described as a financial wizard, made a weird and wonderful financial structure in Basel involving a dozen corporations and sixty-five accounts in Greutert Bank. Each account was in a different name. Some were for the paper corporations, and some were in the names of corporation groups or syndicates—the European term is *consortia*. These corporations and consortia were owned by each other, in a never-ending circle, and by Greutert and Farben executives. Their directors were normally Farben men in Germany and Greutert employees in Switzerland.

This maze became known as the "Greutert-Sturzenegger Circle," from the names of the two principal Swiss involved in it.

One reason these dealings are so hard to follow is shown by a typical example: one of the Circles's companies was capitalized with SF 100,000. But this corporation invariably held assets of SF 10,000,000 until the day before its annual balance sheet was published. Then the assets were moved, and a few days later came back again. With a dozen corporations and sixty-five accounts, the Schmitz-Greutert team had room to maneuver.

Greutert bought and sold securities and whole companies, formed and unformed new corporations, made loans, extended credit, and performed all kinds of operations in the name of each corporation or consortium. Generally transactions were completed without such normal procedures as orders of guaranty or documents of purchase. Herr Greutert and Herr Schmitz understood each other. Eduard Greutert was once described in an official German document as a "man of confidence of I. G. Farben."

The Greutert-Sturzenegger Circle, all within the inner sanctum of Swiss bank privacy, concealed Farben ownership and interests in these world firms: Parta-Bayer (French chemical sales companies); Parta-Chehamij-Mapro (a Dutch corporation with operations in England, the Netherlands, Belgium, Sweden); Romanil (Bucharest); Athanil (Greece); Budanil (Hungary); Defa (Arnhem, Netherlands); Norsk Hydro (Norway); and Trafford Chemical Company (England). There was also Winnica, a supposedly French-owned Polish firm which the Nazi occupation later destroyed, and several Latin American chemical holding companies. These firms were not small business. They were major corporations, and their prestige lay in the fact that they had access to all-important German licenses and patents. Until 1939, German chemical know-how was generally the best in the world, from dye products through photography. These patents and licenses gave I. G. Farben power.

In addition, Greutert and his Circle held control of about 60 per cent of the Deutsche Laenderbank, one of Berlin's biggest, for I. G. Farben interests.

And among the worldwide Farben holdings were certain corporations which every American will recognize: The Bayer Co. of New York, makers of aspirin and other products; General Aniline Works; and Winthrop Chemical Co. Another was Agfa Ansco Corporation, important in the photographic field. These companies had long been German-owned; Bayer had been seized by the US in World War I, then returned. They came to Farben with the giant merger Schmitz conceived and executed.

By 1928, Schmitz had decided to organize these German-American companies into one big holding company or complex. A Swiss corporation was founded, called Internationale Gesellschaft fur Chemische Unternehmungen A.G., or I. G. Chemie. The original capital was 20,000,000 francs. This was another Farben-Greutert desk-drawer company; its sole purpose was to hold controlling interest in Basel of Farben enterprises abroad. A Swiss Compensation Office report stated succinctly in 1945, when German assets were investigated in Switzerland: "It is beyond all doubt that I. G. Chemie was brought into being by I. G. Farben."

I. G. Chemie was legally a Swiss corporation, but its records had one interesting proviso. Farben pledged that shareholders of I. G. Chemie stock would receive dividends equal to those payable on Farben shares. In return, Farben was to have an option to buy any or all Chemie stock on call, at book value. Also, interestingly enough, I. G. Chemie's capital structure was arranged so that voting power was always owned by Farben members of the board or by executives of Greutert Bank. Hermann Schmitz was chairman of the board. Two other members were Albert Gadow, Schmitz' brother-in-law, and a German citizen named Roesch. A majority of the board was always Swiss by citizenship—which meant, so far as control was concerned, exactly nothing.

The actual ownership of I. G. Chemie was blended into the notorious Circle until it became just another Greutert-Sturzenegger holding company. In this Circle only three companies had individual stockholders, a total of just eleven men. Of these eleven, as a US Department of Justice court brief detailed, the biggest stockowners were Hans Sturzenegger (who took over the bank when Greutert died in 1939, E. Greutert & Cie. then becoming H. Sturzenegger & Cie.) and five longtime employees and pensioners of the bank. The remaining five were all close personal friends of Eduard Greutert.

With this ownership, I. G. Chemie of Basel eventually came into control of 89 per cent of Farben's German-American companies' stock. Schmitz himself arranged the details. A Delaware company was organized in early 1929 called American I. G. Chemical Corporation; the name was later changed to General Aniline and Film. Nowhere was Farben's name involved on the record as a stockholder in this firm.

But Schmitz contracted with the National City Bank that he "would cause" General Aniline and Film Corporation (hereafter called GAF) to be organized with a capital of three million no-par common "A" shares and three million par-$1 common "B" shares. He would then cause the holdings in German-held companies such as General Aniline Works and Agfa Ansco to be transferred to GAF, plus $10 million in cash. He guaranteed the principal and interest on $30 million in debentures, which upon such guarantee were snapped up by the National City Bank. In consideration there were to be issued to I. G. Farben "or some other company affiliated with Farben" 400,000 shares of common "A" stock of GAF and the whole issue of "B" stock.

This deal was signed between I. G. Farben and the National City Bank on April 24, 1929. With the charter of GAF that same year, 400,000 shares of GAF "A" stock and the entire issue of common "B" stock was placed in Greutert's hands. Here the trail grows muddy. Greutert Bank transferred many of these shares to various GAF officers, Farben officers, and Farben-connected men

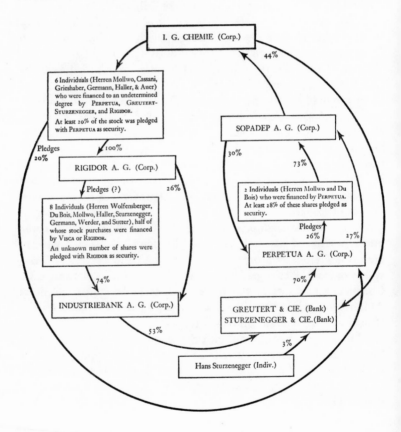

in the US, kept large amounts itself in its desk drawers, and put the rest through various Swiss and Netherlands companies. Later, questioned by the Swiss government, Greutert admitted to have been acting for the I. G. Consortium, a syndicate which represented Farben assets. For several years the stock of GAF changed hands with bewildering rapidity through "intricate transfers to and from Greutert, consortia accounts on Greutert's books, and various subsidiaries, both Swiss and Dutch." As a US government investigation revealed, many of these arrangements cast "grave doubt upon the genuineness and sincerity of the transfers." The time came when I. G. Chemie claimed 89 per cent of the ownership and control of General Aniline and Film—but how this was accomplished and the "exact chain of title to the shares," as the American Attorney General reported later, "will be known only if and when Chemie complies with the order ... for the production of the Sturzenegger records.

This of course Sturzenegger Bank will never do. After the war, the Swiss federal government even seized the records for the express purpose of preventing this from happening. Such disclosure would be a violation of Swiss banking law.

Another interesting thing is that in most of these transfers no fair value was ever paid for the shares so moved. For example, in 1928 I. G. Farben "sold" its interest in Winthrop Chemical Co., including 1928 dividends, to Greutert for a supposed book value of $300,000. The dividends declared soon afterward came to $869,000.

More than 50,000 shares of General Aniline's stock was sold to Greutert so far below the market that Farben's accounting office, not in on the deal, queried Herr Schmitz as to what was going on. The accountants feared they would not be able "to get such deals past the German tax authorities" as a loss.

Restive Farben officers and executives were assured that the "loss might be considered a reserve for which Herr Greutert is liable."

Farben was, in fact, merely transferring money from one pocket to another.

The above Winthrop stock sold to Greutert was resold by Greutert to General Aniline for $250,000 in April 1929. The 1929 dividend on this stock alone was more than $800,000. This kind of thing went on for years, and resulted in more than one investigation by the US Securities and Exchange Commission in the 1930s.

GAF was never anything more than a holding company for Farben's various American companies. The first meeting of the GAF board in 1929 was indicative of what the company was and how it would be run. There were ten members of the board: Schmitz himself, Bosch, and Greif, all Farben men; Metz, Weiss, and Kutroff, executives of American companies selling Farben products; and four prominent American industrialists and bankers: Mitchell, Ford, Warburg, and Teagle of Standard Oil. These last four men all became directors of GAF because of business connections with Farben. Farben in one instance gained a large block of Standard Oil stock by selling certain patents to the US firm; these shares were later sold to the American subsidiary, GAF, at some $4.5 million under current market value. The American GAF directors in some cases had large blocks of GAF stock registered in their names. According to their later testimony, none of them "knew anything about the beneficial, or actual, ownership" of AIG or GAF stock.

This was possible. Many prominent directors lend their names to the boards of companies they know very little about. And it would have taken a clairvoyant to discover all the ins and outs of the Schmitz-Greutert bank transactions.

But more significant than this board membership was the fact that the board made Hermann Schmitz, chairman of I. G. Farben, president of GAF from 1929 through 1936, then elected his brother Dietrich to the job through 1941, at which time the post became too hot for any German citizen.

Also significant was the fact that the board of General Aniline voted to loan the $10 million cash once paid by Greutert for some GAF stock to the Deutsche Laenderbank in Berlin.

In all this the Greutert-Sturzenegger combine and holding company, I. G. Chemie of Basel, had no real management function. Greutert was Farben's errand boy and convenient cloak. Greutert took Farben's orders, kept Farben's foreign deposits, managed its securities and foreign loans, and most of all, cloaked Farben's interests in and dealings with chemical firms abroad. Greutert even handled Farben's mail—sending it with a Swiss postage stamp to Japan by way of Timbuktu. When war broke out in 1939, I. G. Farben advised its foreign correspondents to send all mail and money due to Greutert & Cie., Basel, and for God's sake not to mention Farben's name.

In 1939–1940 it became even more necessary to conceal German assets overseas. German companies and the German government worked together to unload, license, or cloak everything possible. For these transactions, once war began, Farben and other German concerns had to have the approval of the Reichswirtschaftsministerium (German ministry of Economics).

On May 15, 1940, a letter from I. G. Farben to the Ministry stated that Farben had earlier established "trading strong points" in America. These were listed as General Aniline Works and Agfa Corporation, subsidiaries of American I. G. Chemical Corporation, merged into General Aniline and Film Corporation. Farben assured the ministry that while it wanted to prevent vital licenses or know-how from falling into unfriendly American hands, a "weak point" of GAF, which might lead to seizure, was that it was owned by I.G. Chemie, a Swiss firm which too many people knew was tied to I. G. Farben.

Farben proposed to reduce the danger in this way:

1. GAF was to be "somewhat more Americanized" by giving it back one million "B" shares of the three million held by I. G. Chemie in Basel.

2. I. G. Chemie was to be "de-Germanized" by (a) cancellation of the famous dividend-guarantee agreement between it and I. G. Farben, (b) the 28 per cent of I. G. Chemie stock owned by German citizens was to be reduced to 15 per cent, and (c) Geheimrat Schmitz was to resign as I. G. Chemie chairman.

3. I. G. Farben patents used on license by GAF were to be "sold" to the "American" firm in lump for $500,000. By this device, Farben hoped they would not be seized as German property.

The letter ended *Heil Hitler*, signed Henze by order of Kruger.

The Reichsministerium approved. Later, I. G. Farben in another letter informed the Ministerium: "The whole transactions have been worked out."

Unfortunately for I. G. Farben, the whole record of this correspondence fell into American hands when Germany surrendered in 1945. Ninety-three and a half per cent of the shares of GAF had been seized in 1942–1943 as suspected German assets. The evidence found in Germany in 1945 was to result in the US government keeping control of General Aniline and Film for twenty years.

In 1945 the Swiss government investigated I. G. Chemie to determine its Nazi connections, decided and reported that Chemie was "Farben-organized," and in the Washington Agreements of 1946 Chemie's American assets were specifically excluded —though later some Swiss officials disputed the point. Meanwhile, in 1945, I. G. Chemie tried to brighten its image by removing Albert Gamow and other German citizens from its board of directors and by changing its name to French: Société Internationale pour Participations Industrielles et Commerciales S.A. In German-speaking Basel, however, this translated into International Industrie und Handelsbeteiligungen A.G., or Interhandel, the name by which it became better known.

The Greutert-Sturzenegger Circle retained control.

In 1948, a suit was filed by certain minority stockholders of Interhandel against the Attorney General of the United States, as successor to the wartime Alien Property Custodian, and the US Treasury, for the return of 89 per cent of GAF, of a value of $100 million plus $1.8 million seized in cash in 1942. Interhandel, through its American attorneys, first filed an administrative claim, which was denied. The suit was then pressed in the United States District Court for the District of Columbia.

The Swiss claim was based on the argument that Interhandel was a Swiss corporation, that it was not nor had it been an enemy of the United States, and that it owned the shares in question. The US government's rebuttal was that Interhandel was the result of a conspiracy or common plan between the private bank of H. Sturzenegger, Basel, formerly E. Greutert & Cie., and I. G. Farbenindustrie of Germany and others "to conceal, camouflage, and cloak the ownership, control, and domination by I. G. Farben of properties and interests in many countries of the world, including the U. S. . . ."

At issue was whether Interhandel was an enemy or enemy-tainted under US law, whether Interhandel actually owned the shares, and whether Interhandel participated in a conspiracy with the Sturzenegger banking firm in Basel and I. G. Farben of Germany in the interest of I. G. Farben.

The suit, like all such torturous international legal proceedings, went very slowly. In 1949, both parties "moved for discovery" of the documents in each other's possession as provided by US law. The court so ordered. But while Interhandel's lawyers got and photostated 20,000 Department of Justice records under this order, Interhandel itself produced no Sturzenegger files. The federal government of Switzerland, acting under the Bank Secrecy and Economic Espionage Laws of 1934, froze the Sturzenegger bank accounts. Thus the heart of the evidence which would show who actually had owned, and still owned, Interhandel in the major interest, or if there was a conspiracy, was not produced. But the Swiss action was repeatedly affirmed by the Swiss ministries ordering it, and the matter was taken before the Swiss Nationalrat and upheld in an acrimonious vote.

Some Interhandel papers were produced, but these were attacked by Department of Justice lawyers. Interhandel offered 41,000 documents—but this was 9829 short of the documents numbered by the Swiss Compensation Office in 1945 when it had checked I. G. Chemie—the numbers of which had been turned over to the US during the Washington Agreements. Challenged, Interhandel lawyers then came up with 5000 more, which they claimed had only recently been found. They also produced a set of books—which the US attorneys quickly proved were doctored.

Evidence showed that eight of the eleven volumes of Interhandel books were actually purchased in Switzerland long after the purported dates of their entries.

And there was no question but that these books were a different set from those examined by the Swiss Compensation Office —which was of course not allowed to testify in an American court. Interhandel admitted as much.

The Swiss newspaper *Basler Nachrichten* quoted officers of Interhandel as saying that the firm's books had "always been kept in a preliminary version." A "final" version was "specially" prepared for the American government. As a matter of fact, as it was privately admitted out of court, one of Eduard Greutert's most appealing stocks-in-trade was that he kept very loose books.

After lengthy procedures lasting until 1953, the Interhandel suit was dismissed with prejudice by the District Court on the grounds that Interhandel had refused full disclosure and had shown itself unable to comply with fundamental rules of US jurisprudence. Under these rules the facts must be fully developed and revealed, and the facts obviously included the Greutert-Sturzenegger bank records.

The court ruled that the fact that Interhandel was prevented from disclosing the bank papers under Swiss law was irrelevant— "due process would be denied if a foreign government were to be allowed to frustrate the procedures established in the courts of the United States." The court noted carefully, however, that it was not sitting in judgment of Swiss bank secrecy laws.

The next higher US court, the Court of Appeals in Washington, D.C., upheld the ruling. Interhandel took the case on to the US Supreme Court. This court refused to review, but sent the case back to the District Court. In June 1955 the District Court granted Interhandel an extension of time in which to produce the records. They were still not forthcoming, and the case was dismissed. The dismissal was appealed.

By now Interhandel's suit had international implications. The Swiss government had become deeply involved and concerned. There were certain side issues: the minority stockholders, in whose name the suit was filed, quite probably had not known or cared who controlled the old I. G. Chemie; they had paid their money, and they had a point. Secondly, the whole unmasking of the Greutert-Farben-Interhandel mess, and the refusal of a powerful government to respect what were, in international law, "legal" Swiss rights hit the Swiss banking industry where it hurt. Under Swiss law, a Swiss corporation was a Swiss corporation no matter who the stockholders were. In some ways the whole usefulness of Switzerland as an international cartel haven was at stake. Worse, bank secrecy was again getting a bad name.

Interhandel was cleaned up even more. Powerful and fully respectable Swiss citizens became interested. Interhandel stock was sold, and the older, more odorus Greutert-Sturzenegger Circle men replaced on the board. Charles de Loes, past president of the Swiss Banker's Association, was elected chairman, and the general manager of each of the three Big Banks was appointed to the

board. About 25 per cent of Interhandel stock was now registered in the name of the Union Bank, whose manager, Dr. Alfred
Schaefer, was a man of known integrity. He later followed De
Loes to the chair. The Swiss felt that this must immediately establish full confidence in Interhandel in the USA.

It did not, because there was still no revelation of who owned,
or had owned, Interhandel stock. The Big Banks had excellent
names, but they were still only acting as agents. Union Bank held
no stock in its own interest. The Swiss government was satisfied,
but the Swiss government was neutral and more easily satisfied
than the government of the United States. For one thing, none of
the Farben–I. G. Chemie deals had been illegal under Confederation law.

The whole Swiss nation felt outrage in 1958 when a US Senator, Olin Johnston of South Carolina, stated if the three Big
Bankers ever visited the United States, he would subpoena them
and put them on the stand—and if they did not talk, and talk
plain, Interhandel's hope of ever getting back control of GAF
was quite remote.

Meanwhile, the US State Department, concerned with Swiss
relations, issued a bulletin: "United States courts are known for
their independence and readiness to do justice ... whether the
suitor is an alien or whether the United States government is the
party against whom complaint is brought. These courts have a
continuing preoccupation to maintain the principles both of American constitutional law and of international law that property may
not be taken from citizen or alien without due process of law and
that for every taking claimed to be illegal there must be full
remedy."

Whatever the moral problem, the legal problem was simply a
clash of Swiss and US law. One required full disclosure, the other
specifically prevented it. And both nations, with sovereignty at
stake, remained rigid in their attitudes.

The US now considered the case closed. The Department of
Justice refused an official Swiss federal offer to arbitrate, basing
its refusal on the fact that full remedy was available in US courts
provided Interhandel complied with US law, and on a lengthy
legal document purporting to show that neither the Washington
Agreements nor the Swiss-American Arbitration Treaty of 1931
applied.

But the Swiss government was not willing to let the matter rest. It stated in a note to the US: "The fact that considerable assets of the Société Internationale pour Participations Industrielles et Commerciales S.A., hereinafter called 'Interhandel,' which were vested in 1942 and 1943, have to this date not been returned to their rightful owners, is a cause of great concern to the Government of Switzerland. Indeed all attempts of the Swiss owners to obtain the return of their property have so far remained unsuccessful.... The Federal Council, in principle... finds it impossible to acquiesce in such a situation....

"Since, over a long period of time, differences of opinion have existed between the Governments of Switzerland and the United States...the Swiss Government now finds itself compelled to submit the matter to settlement by international proceedings."

The Swiss took the case to the International Court of Justice at the Hague, The Netherlands. But meanwhile the appeal from dismissal was still pending in the US, and the Supreme Court remanded the case once again to the District Court for further proceedings. One reason for this action was that US attorneys so advised—the US government had no desire to argue Interhandel before the World Court; the US might lose its case here. On purely international law, which tends to hold private citizens' rights pre-eminent no matter what their nationality, the US had a bad case. On the grounds that action was still pending inside the US, the World Court dismissed the Swiss application until such time as American domestic remedies were exhausted, as US representatives argued they must. The case now dragged on for years, never coming to trial. Finally, it ended up before a special master appointed by the District Court.

When Robert F. Kennedy became Attorney General of the United States in 1961, among the problems he inherited was Interhandel. The government was still controlling General Aniline and Film. This was an unnatural role for the Department of Justice, as Kennedy admitted. And while the Department had tried to interfere as little as possible with GAF's operations—the company had never ceased to operate since the war, under fully American management—government ownership had had an inhibiting effect. GAF inevitably became something of a political football. The awarding of its annual advertising account had come to be regarded as a political plum. GAF management, unlike other management, had no freedom to oppose government when necessary. GAF had prospered, but as most American industrialists and bankers said privately, it had operated at nowhere near its real potential.

Meanwhile, the Interhandel suit was the second oldest proceeding still pending in the Department of Justice. A whole generation of lawyers had been tied up with it, and absolutely no progress had been made on either side. Kennedy, who was a man given to decisive action, saw immediately that ten more years would probably not produce a real decision. There was, in fact, no clear-cut solution.

US law authorized the government to sell GAF—but the Sales Act had never been tested at law, and Kennedy was aware that any attempt to sell GAF would bring on a court test of the constitutionality of the Sales Act. This could take another three years. Meanwhile, some sixty interventors, both foreign and American, had gotten into the act. The case, costing the government millions, could last the century out.

There were a number of pressures on Kennedy to end the matter. Some came from American businessmen, anxious to get the US out of the chemical business; some from Congress, for various reasons. There were some Americans who hoped to profit. There were others worried about Swiss-American relations. Robert Kennedy decided to find a way to settle Interhandel once and for all, outside the courts. Since he enjoyed a power and prestige no other US Attorney General had ever had—because his brother was in the Presidency Robert Kennedy was in effect the Executive Vice-President of the United States—he was able to succeed.

It is only fair to say that the decision to settle, and the settlement, was made over great opposition within the Departments of Justice and Treasury and by prominent members of both political parties who had been involved with the case. But Kennedy had another asset. The war was long over, and the time had come when few people knew or cared about I. G. Farben and its Nazi-connected dealings.

What Kennedy proposed in 1962 was to offer General Aniline and Film Corporation for sale to the highest bidder among American investment and underwriting houses. The successful bidder would then be required to offer the stock at public sale. Since Interhandel only claimed 89 per cent of the shares of GAF, the US was to receive 11 per cent of the sales price automatically. In addition, Interhandel would pay the US $24 million out of its share to settle back-tax claims and to redeem shares the government had accepted in lieu of dividends. Further, a small percentage of the US share was to be set aside to cover interventors' claims, if and when successful.

The remainder of the proceeds of the sale would be split between the US government—which would pay its share into the War Claims Fund to settle war claims of American citizens against former enemies—and Interhandel stockholders.

The arrangement was approved by the District Court and by the stockholders of Interhandel, now headed by Dr. Schaefer of the Union Bank of Switzerland, on March 3, 1963.

An American advisory committee under Donald C. Cook, president of American Electric Power Company and a friend of President Johnson, took the sale under study and made recommendations concerning the terms of sale. These were that no more than 15 per cent of GAF shares be sold to foreign nationals, and not more than 3 per cent to citizens of any one foreign country; that institutional investors be limited to 50,000 shares; and that no one individual be allowed to buy more than 1000 shares out of the total of 11 million to be offered. GAF would become a widely held public company.

Only underwriters who were members of the National Association of Securities Dealers and registered with the SEC were allowed to bid.

The sale, by sealed bid, was held in March 1965; it was the biggest competitive auction in Wall Street history. A 225-firm underwriting syndicate headed by First Boston Corporation and Blyth & Company, 14 Wall Street, nosed out Lehmann Brothers' bid by $13.5 million. The bid price for each share of GAF was $29.476.

The total sales price came to $329,141,926.49, a sum beyond the wildest dreams of the Department of Justice. And the underwriters, reoffering the shares at $30.60, were assured a cool profit of $12.5 million in underwriting fees and commissions. They would make far more than this, however, since the price of GAF immediately began to rise. The public, sure that General Aniline would double its growth rate with government removed from its management, crowded in to buy. By the end of March 1965, GAF had gotten a new Wall Street name: Sweet Aniline.

The US War Claims fund received $189.2 million, plus $17.5 million in back taxes. The stockholders of Interhandel—whoever they were—got a total of $120.9 million.

They and the Swiss government were well pleased at the way it all turned out.

If a country such as Switzerland did not exist, the international business community would probably have to invent one.

All That
Glitters...

IN LATE 1960 a onetime German who had emigrated to South Africa brought an enormous sum of money to a Swiss Big Bank. In addition to a regular drawing account of about $250,000, this man, who can be called Emil Mayer, had half a million dollars he wanted reinvested at large. South Africa was booming; there was money to be made there—but Mayer, who had a keen nose, did not feel secure. He was not interested in the racial or political situation in the Boer Republic, but he felt it might affect his money. For that reason he took all he could get out to Switzerland, and sought Swiss banking advice.

Where Mayer got his money is not important; what happened to it is.

Mayer's procurator went into some detail with him about the instability and insecurity of the US stock market at that time. He did not advise American investments. The bank, like most Swiss banks, was then pulling out of Wall Street. Rather than Wall Street, the bank thought it might be sensible for Mayer to hold some of his reserves in gold. To this Mayer readily agreed.

But Swiss money was also now streaming back into Europe. After the currency convertibility of 1958, European trade was increasing. The Common Market was just beginning to be felt. European exchanges, including the Swiss, were at the start of what was to be a long and feverish boom. The bank told Mayer to invest in Swiss shares, and to do it fast, before it became too late. They were not really supposed to tout domestic investments

—there was no law against it, but banks had agreed not to do it. Mayer, however, was a big and potentially profitable customer, and the bank advised him on the sly.

The stock most praised was CIBA, a huge Swiss chemical complex. At the start of the 1960s this firm, with its rising shares, was Swiss banking's pride and joy.

Mayer, who had heard all his life about the sagacity and sharp noses of Swiss bankers, bit. He went for CIBA big. And for two years he experienced an enormous capital gain as CIBA soared. He did not cash in and realize his gain, because his banker kept smiling and telling him to wait. One share of CIBA finally reached between 6000 and 7000 francs.

Then came Blue Monday, May 28, 1962. In New York the stock market crashed. The over-all losses averaged 25 per cent, though more than a few stocks went through the floor. In a few days the ripples of this disaster reached Europe. It was the old situation: when American financial circles sneezed, Europe caught pneumonia. In June, every European stock price fell. Swiss exchanges dropped by an average 40 per cent. CIBA plunged from 6000 to 2500 Swiss francs.

But there was a difference between the Wall Street and the Swiss reaction. New York prices plummeted in one day. The Swiss just dribbled down, day after day, in desultory trading. The banks and other traders sat on their hands and cried.

Mayer called up his bank and asked them what the hell. The bank told him rather coolly that these things happen, and he was by no means alone. Thousands of investors all over Europe were being hurt. Emil Mayer was of course upset. But he was still a rich man, and he took his losses with a reasonable grace.

But that was only until he happened to talk with an American colleague in New York about two years later. This man, while explaining how the American stock market had come back—most, though not all, losses were regained within two years—also mentioned the stupidity of Swiss bankers in letting CIBA go down. Mayer asked him what he meant.

The American asked him if he had checked the volume on Swiss exchanges as CIBA sank. Mayer said that was none of his business; he left such things to his Swiss bank. The American smiled and told Mayer that while Swiss banks had praised CIBA to the skies and held an enormous amount of the chemical firm's stock, they had in his opinion let it die by default. All they would have had to do was buy in small quantity to hold CIBA high. For a mere $500,000 more they could have held it level. The total transactions on which CIBA sank were always small.

Mayer, intrigued, asked around and found quite a bit of opinion which agreed. When he had time to think, he grew quite annoyed. CIBA in 1964 still sold at around SF 3000 and showed no signs of ever climbing back. He discussed the matter with his banker. He discovered that it was against Swiss bankers' policies to support a falling stock. They considered it a form of rigging the market; Americans did it, but the Swiss disagreed. And now, the bank told him, Wall Street was the place to go again. European exchanges were dead—unlike Wall Street, they did not come back—and Swiss bank money was going to New York.

It took only the sketchiest figuring by Mayer on his own to prove that if he had gone to Wall Street in the first place, in 1960, and stayed there, he would have come out far ahead. A definite coolness developed between him and his bank.

In 1964 Emil Mayer pulled his money out of Switzerland and put it back in South Africa. He told an American friend he still disliked the government and feared the *verdammten* blacks, but he distrusted his Big Swiss Bank more.

Not all people who use Swiss banks secure their future. As the case of Emil Mayer shows, quite a few of them lose their shirts.

The CIBA affair hurt Swiss banking badly. Thousands of Swiss and other investors were ruined, and a certain faith destroyed. CIBA and the stock disasters of 1962 brought up the question Just how competent were Swiss banks?

The answer, of course, depends on what the bank is wanted, or used, for.

Here again, Swiss banks must be broken down into their seven classes or categories. Cantonal, savings, mortgage, and local banks serve the Swiss economy; they are of no interest to outsiders. Informed banking opinion across the world considers these domestic Swiss banks as honest, competent, and well-managed as any in the world, and far better than most. They are inherently conservative. They are helped immensely by the habits and nature of the Swiss people, who in 1964 owned a per capita average of 4000 francs in savings accounts. This figure exceeded the American average by one fourth, even though American incomes averaged about three times as high as Swiss. No other people in the world even approached the Swiss level of individual saving.

The Other Banks are usually thought of as Swiss, and they are becoming immensely important in international trade. The Swiss-Israel Trade Bank, opening new branches in London and Birmingham, and the Banco di Roma of Lugano, influential in Italian affairs, are owned and operated by non-Swiss, with non-Swiss money, and do all of their business outside Switzerland. They are like the thousands of foreign corporations headquartered in the Confederation; being there gives them real advantages. But they are not actually Swiss banks.

The real Swiss banks are the large commercial banks, dominated by the Big Three, and the sixty-odd private banks. These are true Swiss banks, and at the same time the institutions which have importance in the field of international finance.

The Big Banks and the larger private houses do essentially the same things in the monetary world. The big difference is that the Big Banks are large corporate enterprises, run like large corporations, while the private banks tend more to be intimate, family-held affairs. This influences both their respective clienteles and their ways of handling the trade. The man or business who likes to deal with a big, impersonal corporation—who may be impressed or made to feel more secure by bigness itself—prefers the Kreditanstalt or Union Bank. People who prefer more intimate, personal banking will choose Pictet, Gottardo, Vontobel, or Bär.

Both kinds of bank accept deposits and money management from outside. Both act as stockbrokers on all exchanges, form and manage companies, and offer legal and tax advice. But where the Big Three (Kreditanstalt or Credit Bank, Bank Corporation, and Union Bank) are deeply involved in the Swiss economy—in investment companies, utilities, real estate, and insurance—the private houses primarily tend to go outside. The Big Banks handle the bulk of the foreign or international business. They are known by more people, and they are more accessible. They have branches, representatives, or offices in virtually every area of the world. The private banks have a smaller, more select clientele, but their influence in the field of European finance is almost as profound.

Since size is important, these Swiss banks must be put in world perspective. The Big Three's total admitted assets are only 25 billion Swiss francs. This seems large until compared with the Bank of America or Chase Manhattan of New York, whose assets are counted in similar numbers of dollars. Admitted assets put each of the Big Three only in about fiftieth place in the scale of big world banks.

But the figures do not tell the whole story. The real international importance of the large Swiss banks lies in the securities, gold, and currency they hold or manage on private account. Under Swiss law, none of this shows up in their balance sheets. The Swiss banking world is very much an iceberg; only the tip shows. Hans Bär of Zurich has estimated that the Big Banks control approximately 140 billion francs of hidden money—half the entire Swiss total.

Private banks, Bär's included, of course publish no figures at all. But Bär has estimated that all private banks together have resources of about 2 billion francs. The largest, such as Bar or Pictet, must nevertheless be included in the top 3 per cent of all banks by size. These banks control or manage at least 20 billion francs in negotiable securities, or one seventh of the Swiss managed-funds total.

The Big Banks and the *Groupements Genevois* or *Zurichois* provide Europe and America with a unique, mobile pool of ready cash. The same lack of restriction applying to money entering the Confederation applies to loans leaving it. This pool of money gives the Swiss banking industry considerable power in Europe. Because of their store of ready loan money, bankers can influence European corporations or even governments, as was shown during the 1964 British financial crisis. But in world terms the power and the importance is easily exaggerated.

Swiss bankers themselves are awed and fascinated by the monetary power of the United States. The entire Confederation of Switzerland in 1965 had only 6 billion francs in circulation. The Swiss franc is not an international currency, and its power abroad is small. Paul Rossy, former vice-chairman of the Swiss Banking Commission, confronted by accusations of the hidden power of Swiss banks, liked to point out certain facts. A $100-million private loan floated in New York City is hardly mentionable. Such deals rarely even make the newspapers. In 1964, Merrill Lynch, Pierce, Fenner & Smith, after the First Boston Corporation the largest financial underwriter in the United States, handled $75 billion in US government bonds. Swiss loans are measured in millions and tens of millions and, more rarely, in hundreds of millions, when they are made through the Basel World Bank.

But for Swiss banks billion-dollar financing is out of the question. Even the billions they hold on private account are small compared to Washington or New York figures. Swiss financial power in Europe or the world does not even approach New York's.

The entire "Swiss" portfolio held on the New York Stock Exchange, including the $3 billion stemming from Geneva, is less than 1 per cent of the listed values of American stocks. By comparison, Merrill Lynch alone holds more than $14 billion in managed funds or securities in New York.

Switzerland does export more money per capita—SF 100 per head—than any other nation. But there are only 5.8 million Swiss. While Switzerland was investing approximately $500 million abroad in 1964, the United States exported $6.5 billion.

Basel, Zurich, and Geneva are not and never will be financial competition to New York. In the US, General Motors' assets exceed those of the Kingdom of the Netherlands, and the roaring American economy is adding a gross national product equal to France's each two years. While foreign money comes into Switzerland from all over the world, there is more money inside the United States than in most of the rest of the world combined.

The Swiss are competition to European banks, and in a bad moment they can help drive British sterling down. Zurich is a major foreign-exchange center, where thousands of individuals live on the vagaries of or dabble in world moneys. But foreign-exchange manipulation in Zurich can only damage a national currency if it is already on the skids. If a nation is already overdrawn, even a bill for a few pennies more can topple an entire financial structure.

While to New York and Washington money men Swiss bankers are midgets, to Harold Wilson, the Dutch government, and hundreds of European companies they can still be giants.

Actually, when sterling became convertible in 1958, the city of London began immediately to siphon off much of Zurich's money trade. The Swiss had acquired a lot of the business simply because after World War II every other European financial center was defunct. When English bankers could once again receive money and invest it anywhere, houses like Hambro's or Warburg's snapped some of the Swiss business up. Hambro's—this is the opinion of most international bankers—are probably the best merchant bankers in the world. Even a number of Geneva bankers admit this. Hambro's are not so conservative, careful, and therefore so slow as the Swiss. But there is one big difference, not in London's favor: Zurich does not have a British government, or a crumbling empire, like an albatross around its neck.

It is possible that Great Britain, if it could dispose of its imperial past and socialist present, might someday become the "Switzerland" of all time.

No matter how the question is approached, the success of Swiss banking comes down to the peculiar position of Switzerland in the modern world. Neutrality, financial freedom, low taxes, and bank secrecy, far more than Swiss sound business sense, created the unique Swiss financial posture. Few critics contend that the Swiss bankers—with their respect for money, their love of work, and their hard, keen sense of judging men—are anything but good. But to succeed they do not really have to be too good. The endemic social and fiscal chaos of the twentieth century, in which they refuse to take a part, gives them an unbeatable hand.

Swiss banks taking foreign money charge very high custodial fees, pay no interest except on savings accounts, sometimes make serious investment mistakes (as with CIBA, or when they invested in The Belgian Congo), and still get more liquid money than they can use.

There are thousands of Swiss bank customers who would be pleased as Punch if their money in Switzerland *lost* 3 or 4 per cent a year. Just having it there lets them sleep nights. There are thousands more who would willingly take an even bigger loss if necessary—because it would still be less than the tax collector would claim due.

For South American dictators, landowners, and cabinet ministers, for Syrian merchants, for Italian industrialists, for the French bourgeoisie, and Germans who were once wiped out by war, just having gold or assets in Swiss banks is worth almost any price.

For these people and many others, money in a Swiss bank is not just an investment or a habit—it is almost a religion. Any look at the recent history of the world explains why.

Although the buying and selling of securities and investment on world stock exchanges is a major part of Swiss banking business, the Swiss reputation in this field is something of an inflated balloon. The Swiss bankers do have a thorough knowledge of world conditions; they do make money. But they usually make it when everyone else is making money, too. Swiss banks, where stocks are concerned, are rarely what American financial men call "creative." CIBA and similar cases proved that for all time. The Swiss do have one strong feature, however: their emphasis on long-term growth means that the great family fortunes left with them rarely lose. But the average Swiss banker is no one to consult on buying and selling—making money as Baruch or Joseph Kennedy did—from day to day.

Swiss banks built a great reputation for astute investing by going back into Germany immediately after the war. German shares, like those of Daimler-Benz, in some cases gained 5000 per cent. But the German *Wirtschaftwunder*, when the Swiss went in, was by no means assured. The Swiss banks made Germans their largest loans in the 1920s, and in the 1940s for this reason alone two of the biggest banks in Switzerland failed.

The Swiss-German symbiosis, however, cannot be attacked on every ground. The truth in the twentieth century has been that when Germany, the industrial hub, went sour, all Europe itself suffered. While it was true that the Swiss would have gone back into Germany in any case—the Swiss, because of geography, needed a German comeback—their neutrality helped Swiss banks along. Many American corporation executives in the 1950s and 1960s bemoaned their own lack of foresight in not investing in Germany immediately after the war. For a number of years, German shares, even whole German companies, were available for a song. When the American money finally rushed to West Germany, the bargain-hunting days were gone.

Swiss money was there at the vital time, from 1949 through 1953. But it was not all brains. The Swiss were the one people with the money, untroubled by wartime associations, and on the spot. But the Swiss tend to follow world trends, rarely to anticipate them. In this sense the great international corporations, from Caltex to the old I. G. Farben, make better use of Swiss banks than Swiss bankers make of them.

Of course, in the field of stock investment or company formation, it is impossible to measure true skill. As the chairman of Merrill Lynch once said: "I can't tell you what the market is going to do next week, and I don't think anyone can." At any rate, where investments outside the US are concerned, the Swiss foresight has generally been better than the American.

Since most Swiss bank investors are mainly interested in breaking some government's umbilical cord to their money, or keeping it out of unfriendly hands, no amount of criticism of Swiss investment judgment will influence them. Once they have gotten their money safely into Switzerland anything Swiss bankers can make them is so much gravy.

Interest rates also are not a factor, since beginning in 1964 Swiss banks may pay no interest at all on foreign deposits.

For two generations the enormous bank buildup in Switzerland, in relation to the tiny Swiss population, meant only sound money, high gold reserves, quick credit, and ready investment cash—all the benefits of having money in the bank. This made a great many bank owners, bank directors, and Swiss industrialists rich. But as late as 1964 only 13 per cent of all Swiss were employed in banking, insurance, and commerce combined. The overall effect, good or bad, on the average Swiss citizen was very small. The Swiss international financial network did not affect him. The vast majority of Swiss made their livings in industry or crafts, and there were more shopkeepers than banking employees. Banking, to the ordinary Swiss, meant only his personal savings —not checking—account.

There was very little disagreement on economic matters or the basic conditions which made the Big Banks rich. These were not made by the banks, but the other way around. Not only bankers, but workers, hoteliers, and merchants were all likewise doing very well. The Swiss economy, the only one in Europe without controls, invariably ran like a finely-made Swiss watch.

Someday there had to be an end. The Swiss in the 1960s began to be swamped not by overspending or producing too little, all the faults of other nations, but by a surfeit of success.

In 1959 the cost of living started to rise. By 1964 it had risen 11 per cent.

In other nations, or the US, this would not have been a cause for alarm. American living costs averaged a steeper climb most years. Americans grumbled, but had come to accept rising prices as a way of life. Europeans had generally experienced peacetime inflation: in 1963 alone French and Italian prices rose about 20 per cent. But to the Swiss, inflation (except for the deficit financing during World War II) was unknown. The metallic content of Swiss coins, even the design, was basically unchanged since the 1870s. The Swiss National Bank was even coining, though not releasing, gold in the 1950s.

This mildest sort of inflation immediately set all Swiss teeth on edge. It affected every element of the population, since every man, woman, or child in the Confederation had at least one savings account. When the purchasing power of the Swiss franc deteriorated more in 1963 than the interest paid on Swiss government bonds, the issue boiled over bitterly into politics.

What was happening was simple but strange. The Swiss were not creating inflation at home like other peoples through a lack of financial discipline. They were importing it through their booming banks.

Americans, Germans, and people from the Middle East were pouring in. Germans and Levantines, particularly, wanted solid property in a neutral and supposedly safe country. They bought land, office buildings, houses, apartments, anything. They wanted both Swiss property and a Swiss residence permit. They were willing to pay dearly for both. The market was strong; then there was more demand than the limited supply. The market went up. Real estate in Switzerland, a cramped and tiny area, soared.

Swiss banks, particularly the big commerical banks, knew a good thing at home as well as abroad. They had plenty of money, and when they pulled it back from Wall Street in 1958 they began to channel it into domestic real estate. They went further; they organized special real estate investment trusts. Almost every large Swiss bank soon owned or controlled one. Both Swiss and foreigners flocked to buy shares. The pressure of virtually unlimited worldwide money on very limited Swiss space soon put Swiss land prices into orbit. Geneva lots which had sold in 1958 for SF 17 per square meter rose to SF 125 per meter by 1963. Geneva, Vaud, or Ticino estates which could have been had for $50,000 before 1960 sold three years later for a quarter of a million.

Millions of dollars went into elaborate villas or new luxury apartment buildings, mostly for foreigners. Arabs erected glass-and-steel office buildings by the score. All this came at a time when hundreds of thousands of average Swiss, like other Europeans, still lived in inadequate private housing with medieval plumbing. A number of new Swiss and foreign real estate millionaires were made, but hundreds of thousands of Swiss citizens found themselves priced off their native soil. And the boom overbuilt, as all real estate booms eventually do. Even while Swiss householders were hard put to find a place to live, millions of francs were tied up in unproductive property investments—unrented villas or half-empty office buildings.

As land prices rose, they dragged other prices along. Labor was diverted into purely speculative building, and labor costs rose. Costs, as usual, were passed on into the general economy. The Swiss franc, always cool and solid, started to smoke a bit as it was passed from hand to hand. The bulk of the population, which could not participate in the speculative land boom—it did not have the price—began to protest.

All Swiss banks were to some degree responsible for the situation. But the big banks with available foreign funds were the worst. They persisted in jamming it into an already too-tight economy, riding the boom. A flush of prosperity turned into inflation, and a boom which was out of hand.

Swiss banks, and the Swiss people generally, were strongly prejudiced against government controls. No Swiss really trusts his government, and even the poorest farmer or worker is reluctant to allow it any bureaucratic powers. But something had to be done. The National Bank and the Swiss Banker's Association got together in what was called a "gentleman's agreement" that the National Bank or Bern would not press for any controls on banking—but in return the commercial banks would have to stop stoking the land boom with new investment cash. The bankers agreed to get out of land speculation and to start sending *all* foreign money back where it came from.

This was a thoroughly sensible course, and the Swiss banks had a chance to correct their wrongs. But to ask a Swiss banker to stop making money when it was obviously there to be had was like ordering a leopard to change his spots. The voluntary controls did not work. There seemed to be an excess of foreign cash and an unfortunate shortage of gentlemen. The boom, with its excessive speculation, got worse.

Meanwhile, an utterly fantastic situation was developing in other parts of the Swiss economy. Switzerland, exporting more than it ever had in history, and buying no more, began to suffer a serious adverse balance of payments. In 1963 the bad balance amounted to 3.5 billion Swiss francs, resulting in an enormous loss of gold.

Switzerland's problem was just the reverse of England's. The Swiss were selling not too little abroad but too much. The rising demand for fine Swiss goods—watches, metalwork, engineering skills and precision tools—in newly prosperous Europe of the Common Market had at first made the Confederation more highly industrialized than either Britain or Belgium. By 1963 fewer than 10 per cent of the population still worked on the soil. But while the Swiss markets kept expanding, the supply of new Swiss labor had quite run out.

Switzerland had begun to import large numbers of foreign laborers along with foreign tax-dodgers. First came German secretaries and clerks, then Austrian assembly-line producers. Finally, there were Spaniards, Yugoslavs, and most of all, the Italians. At the end of 1963 there were 800,000 foreign workers in the Confederation, 500,000 Italian; all together these made up more than one third of the entire Swiss work force. The highly publicized flow of foreign labor to West Germany was nothing proportionally compared to the Swiss situation.

By any standard, this was alarming. An economist of the

Swiss National Bank wrote that the import of foreign labor could be justified only if the economy built by this flow could still continue to operate after the foreigners went home again. The danger was that foreigners would someday leave, and when they did the whole Swiss economy would be dealt a serious blow. But this stage had already been passed. Thousands of native Swiss had already deserted whole classes of occupations—mostly menial, dirty, or heavy work—for the more lucrative factories. Without thousands of Italians, Zurich could no longer even sweep its streets. Even more dangerous, thousands of the foreigners had already gone into key industries, which would collapse if they were removed.

What caused the terrible balance of payments, meanwhile, was that 800,000 Yugoslavs, Italians, and Spaniards employed in Switzerland were sending most of their wages home. Even in the face of high export levels, and while it seemed to be creating greater profits, the Swiss economic "miracle" was rapidly draining the Confederation's gold.

The National Bank and the beleaguered bureaucrats at Bern were now much worried. As one Swiss newspaper noted, what was discussed was the obvious things: price, wage, and industrial controls to dampen the boom, halt speculation and inflation, and set the economy back on a steady keel. But the government did not have the power to employ such controls in peacetime, nor was it likely to be given them by the Nationalrat. Labor, price, monetary controls were against Swiss nature. The deference to free enterprise put one big stumblingblock in the way of such action, and at the same time the political diversity of Switzerland limited Bern. In these kind of things the separate cantons were still sovereign. Bern dared not encroach on cantonal jurisdiction; it could only work and negotiate with the twenty-five separate states to enlist their support for economic measures in the general interest. But as a result of the fears, the pressures from the little people, and certain delicate negotiations on high levels, in January 1964 Switzerland enacted some federal legislation governing banking and finance.

This was not an agreement but a federal law.

The number of jobs foreigners could hold was immediately frozen at present levels.

Foreign money was forbidden investment inside Switzerland for any reason. A strict quota was given each Swiss bank for inland investment, even on domestic money. The boom was therefore shut off at its source.

A moratorium was slapped on all "unnecessary" construction. This included luxury apartments, high-rent villas, even theaters.

By law, no interest could be paid on foreign deposits in Swiss banks.

Foreigners could no longer organize "Swiss" corporations if their purpose was to invest inside Switzerland.

The National Bank economists believed this would ease the situation—which in the meantime had not been helped by the more than 500 American firms which came in looking for a European headquarters with low taxes. As a result of the new restrictions, four American corporations—Campbell Soups, Carborundum, General Foods, and Grumman—moved out of Switzerland.

Most American businesses which had no interest in adding to the Swiss woes were not affected.

The new laws worked. The punishment—forcing the banks to return the foreign moneys they took in for reinvestment overseas—fit the crime. Banks like Vontobel, Bär, Pictet, Bordier, Gottardo, and the like, which had never been interested in Swiss investment—they were part of the greater European world—hardly cared. Their operations were untouched.

The Big Banks and some banks like Spanish financier Julio Muñoz', were hit hard. The boom ground to a halt, and as always those who had come in late were hurt. Around Geneva in early 1965 at least 600 new luxury villas stood empty. Newspapers carried columns and columns of expensive apartments to let. The Iranian landlords and Syrian merchants who might have rented them (and who in many cases owned them) could no longer get residence permits. Prices began to sink, at first slowly and reluctantly. The crisis in real estate was varied and many-pronged, and the Swiss banks and their customers who had gotten into it were sure to be hurt badly. Julio Muñoz' two banks were the first to fail.

There were other serious side effects. The regulations had been put in hurriedly, through compromise, and in some cases not completely thought out. Swiss citizens themselves put very little money in home mortgages; most of this had always been financed from France. Now this money was cut off, and private housing was dealt a serious blow. Cantonal and city subsidies were raised for cheaper housing, but this in turn created new problems. The housing built in this way was cheap and impermanent, and it might do something which had not occurred in Switzerland. It would eventually create slums, as cheap "temporary" housing always does, and by lumping lower income groups together, as in the US, it was arousing new and highly unfortunate economic class feelings.

After much damage had been done, the Big Banks' golden goose was not quite killed—but the unlimited production of golden eggs was at last forbidden.

The Swiss people had found that all those glittering lire, Deutschemarks, and dollars from abroad were not, as they had thought, pure gold.

The Clearing House
of the World

IN THE early months of 1965, two foreign gentlemen met with a native of the Republic and Canton of Geneva who may be called Philippe. Philippe's specialty was information.

The meeting was held at a quick-lunch café near the lake, in an area much frequented by foreigners in Geneva. The place was crowded with visiting Americans, Arabs, and Japanese on various kinds of business, and two more foreigners, looking uncomfortable in obviously unfamiliar bulky winter clothing, attracted no attention. They were far more private than they would have been at any hotel. Swiss police check hotels and study every registry with frequency and thoroughness.

The two outsiders, swarthy but speaking perfect French, were looking for money. More precisely, they were looking for several million dollars they—and the people behind them—suspected was deposited in a Swiss bank. The two did not resemble ordinary businessmen; one's stance suggested he might be a soldier of some rank. They did not represent any government in being, but they represented one in their native country which might soon be born. The information they were after could materially assist in the birth.

They asked Philippe if it would be possible to put a name and a Swiss bank number together—if part of the information were in hand, could he supply the rest?

Philippe expressed the opinion this could be done. The foreigners, obviously out of their milieu, looked at each other, pleased. They told Philippe they were certain they possessed the number of a certain account. What they needed was the certification of the name and the amount of cash on tap.

Philippe told them frankly that bribery still worked. A man with contacts in Geneva could get them what they wanted. He said such information, illegally supplied, would cost them 200,000 francs. It might not be possible to get exact amounts, but often a name and number could be matched for $50,000 cash. Then he asked them which bank the account was in.

The foreigners didn't know. All they knew was that the money was in some Swiss bank. Philippe explained there were some four hundred Swiss banks, and even if they were prepared to spend millions they had to narrow the field. Any attempt to crack banks wholesale would quickly come to the attention of the federal police. Further, if they were caught, they would be expelled, but their Swiss accomplices would go to jail. What they wanted was against both federal and cantonal law.

The two men told Philippe they could supply information as to the time the money left their country within three months, and possibly some clues as to who brought it into Switzerland. Surely this would help?

Philippe said it would, but only if the amount was significant to have raised a ripple in the financial world. The best way observers knew whose money was in which bank was by who came to Geneva and, afterward, which bank had sudden affluence to invest or lend. Through this kind of evidence, every informed person in Geneva knew that the Trujillo money had flowed through Julio Muñoz' bank.

But after talking with them carefully, Philippe came to a reluctant conclusion. These men were amateurs. They didn't have enough to spend, and the whole affair was always risky. He turned their offers down, and they went home.

The men who have money in Swiss banks, or dream of putting it there, sometimes worry about how secure Swiss banks really are.

Swiss banks, many of them, can be cracked. With enough money, in spite of the law, certain people can be bribed. Fifty or a hundred thousand dollars will often buy interesting information. There is no such thing as a secret which under all circumstances can be kept.

In 1958, the scandal of the Spanish depositors at the Swiss Bank Corporation rocked Swiss circles. Franco's police obtained a little black book with names, numbers, and deposits of some very important Spanish people. This information cost the Spaniards, some high in Falangist or Royalist circles, $5.8 million in all.

Swiss bankers were scandalized because this kind of thing is not supposed to happen, and such little black books not allowed to exist. Several explanations were offered, though not by the Bank Corporation itself.

One was that the Spanish police had caught a Bank Corporation agent in Spain, and under certain threats this man had talked. Any such agent could put together a highly compromising file from memory, and facing years in jail he might have. Another was simply that the same man grew careless, as some Swiss bank agents, particularly the older ones, have been known to do. The informed talk in Geneva was much more blunt. Most bankers stated simply that someone had been paid off.

The bank itself kept quiet, because it was liable, under Swiss law, to its depositors. They could sue for recovery of the entire amounts, because one way or another bank secrecy had surely been breached. And this is exactly what the foreign depositors eventually did.

But this gambit only worked for Spanish agents because in Spain the law and justice are only what the ruling government says. The same kind of evidence would accomplish nothing in American or British courts, where justice requires full disclosure of the facts, and proof beyond a reasonable doubt.

The Internal Revenue Service of the US is not above buying information. It pays out money every year to informers, who get up to 10 per cent of the government's take. But the IRS could not advantageously buy information in Switzerland. In the first place, the diplomatic uproar on discovery would be immense. Second, the information would be expensive, and useless in any case.

The same applies to all democratic governments. It is the

other kind which keep the Swiss security services busy. Every year a number of foreign agents, "diplomats," or information-seekers are expelled. Because of the close cooperation between banks and police very few succeed.

The final problem, which even totalitarian regimes cannot quite overcome, is that even if they locate the money it is not easy to recover. Information can be tortured out of depositors —but this does not always bring cash home. Swiss bankers are extremely cautious. In any case of doubt at all—and there is usually doubt where codes and precautions have been elaborate —they close their eyes and ears and admit nothing. For this reason, few governments try to crack Swiss banks at all.

In this sense, then, money in Swiss banks is quite secure. De-positors need to worry more about their persons than their cash.

And though Switzerland is known as rich, and the interna-tional criminal community know much about Swiss banks, they are extremely hard to rob. In 1958, an Englishman named Brown established himself in Zurich.

Brown's mistake was that on January 30, 1959, he decided to stick up Zurich's Gewerbebank. With a shoebox in one hand and a pistol in the other, he entered the bank before noon. He walked up to the counter, shot a clerk in the body, and scooped up 215 francs in cash. Then he tried to batter open the clerk's locked desk. Another clerk attacked him and was clubbed. In the scuffle the shot bank employee, seriously wounded, pressed the alarm with which all Swiss banks are equipped. The signal flashed to the central police station, and within seconds the Zurich special assault group was in action. But the point of this story is that the police were not the ones who did Brown in.

The ringing alarm frightened Brown, and he ran for the exit. But a sixteeen-year-old apprentice of the bank chased him out onto the street, shouting at the passers-by. A fifty-year-old taxi driver joined the boy. They pounded after Brown.

Snarling, Brown shot the cab driver at close range, killing him. But now a cook from a nearby café took the driver's place, while at a greater distance, a whole mob of people followed the armed and obviously dangerous Brown. They pressed him close.

When Brown turned to threaten the cook and boy with his gun again, the mob closed in. They had Brown disarmed and helpless ten seconds before the steel-helmeted Zurich police arrived.

In September 1959 Brown was sentenced to ten year's loss of civil rights, fifteen years' banishment from the Confederation—to take effect, of course, after he had served his term of life imprisonment. Bank robbery in Switzerland is a very serious offense, and both the courts and the public consider it so.

Unlike in America or England, anyone who robs a bank may have to fight the whole town.

By the 1960s the intrigues and pressures against Swiss banks originated largely in two quarters, the Communist bloc and the third world of the turbulent emerging nations. The nations of Western Europe—France, Italy, Germany—and even the United States of America have grown philosophic about Swiss banks. If money gets to them, that is that, and there is not much investigative agencies can do about it. The panic over Swiss deposits has spread farther east.

The Communist world in the 1960s was slowly ceasing to be a bloc. Polish and Romanian trade increased with the West and other non-Communist nations. Nationalism expanded in satellite eastern Europe; Romanian Ministers have tended to favor Romanian national interests, or their own personal interests, over those of the powerful USSR. To facilitate outside contacts and trade, Swiss banks have become useful for dealing completely outside normal Communist world purposes.

It is extremely convenient to have a nation where foreign exchange or credits do not have to pass through even a central clearing office or national bank. What is good for IBM or General Motors is good for Romania, too. Significantly, in recent years certain Romanian "diplomats" have been expelled from Switzerland. The police caught them trying Gestapo Agent Thomae's old tricks, which no longer work. Swiss banks have grown too smart.

At the same time that East and West Europe seemed to be drawing back together in spite of Russia, a genuine middle class or bourgeoisie was again springing up in Hungary. Doctors, scientists, artists, writers, and musicians were useful to the regime, and had to be treated as a favored class. Interestingly, the Communist bourgeoisie, like the Western moneyed classes, develop a hankering for numbered accounts. However, it is much harder for anyone behind the Iron Curtain to get one. It is difficult to get foreign exchange into Switzerland, and the Swiss are not exactly enthusiastic about this class of trade.

But several Communist parties in East Europe have become highly concerned about some of the people in the ruling hierarchy—the "new class." They are certain some Communist bigwigs, as a hedge to the future, have put substantial sums in foreign exchange or gold in Swiss banks. Free enterprise, even in the Soviet world, is not completely dead.

But this clientele is small. The trade from the Middle East, Africa, Asia, and unstable areas of Latin America is much larger. Gold-smuggling, currency manipulation (except by governments), or taking money out of the country is now punishable by long imprisonment or death in most African or Asian nations. This has only served to accelerate the urge to get money to Switzerland. All the new Arab governments, in Egypt, Syria, Iraq, Algeria, and Pakistan, have tried to bring pressure against Swiss banks, or tried to get information from inside their vaults. Nasser wanted Farouk's private fortune. The Socialist regime in Syria is anxious to run down millions in Syrian pounds which left the country after 1958. Rebels in Iraq—and Feisal's relatives—are determined to repatriate the Royal Iraq treasury. The military regime which ousted Ben Bella in Algeria in 1965 is certain some of Ben Bella's cronies put many millions in Geneva banks. But none of these people has been able to prove a thing—or to get a single dinar back. In fact, there is no chance of the money coming back, or the flow to Switzerland ceasing, until stability in the newer nations is the rule. In this case, the chicken must come before the egg.

The fact that Spanish Fascist, Communist bigwig, and unsavory strongman money stuffs their banks does not openly bother the Swiss conscience. Dr. Schaefer of Union Bank spoke for the whole nation and industry when he said the Swiss could not be their brothers' keepers. Perhaps sensibly, the Swiss refrain from making moral judgments on the world as a whole. But this does not, as some people suppose, mean the Swiss banking conscience is entirely free. Though they would rather die than admit it openly, the fact that Swiss banks have been able to eat the world's cake while keeping their own intact, bothers some Swiss bankers badly.

All of the several strains of Swiss—Germanic, French, Italianate—are remarkably honest and decent people. A traveler is less likely to be cheated in Switzerland than anywhere else in the world, the English-speaking nations included. The banking industry, like the financial structure everywhere in the Atlantic world, is heavily Protestant, and this means that most Swiss bankers deep down are saddled with a Protestant conscience. This has produced a certain dichotomy of talk and practice among them.

The Swiss banker is noted for cool relations with other adults, preciseness, pettiness, extreme frugality—and humanitarian generosity. The same man who argues vehemently that in banking the quality of mercy *must* be strained turns around and donates heavily to the International Red Cross, which Switzerland largely supports. The same man who loves to quote the parable of the good steward (which is increasingly anathema to modern Western social thought) will make enormous donations to charity. It is very difficult for the Swiss, with his rigid Protestant ethic, to understand, much less accept, the concept of the underdog. But this does not mean that his prosperity fails to make him feel guilty. A sense of guilt is completely normal to this kind of mentality, as every European sociologist knows.

The fact that a Zurich banker is not really involved in the troubles of his German, French, or Italian clients, and that he will continue to do well whether Britain's government stands or falls, produces a hardly understood, nagging guilt. All Swiss psychologists who have probed Zurich report the same thing. Being decent people, the Swiss cannot help but be pulled about by decent emotions. But from original practicality they have made neutrality almost a religion. Neutrality for Switzerland makes sense, and all Swiss vehemently defend it.

But neutrality, however sensible or practical, is still a refusal of human responsibility, and every Swiss banker knows this in his heart. Emotionally, it does him a certain damage.

One of the most remarkable things about the Swiss to people who understand their languages is the constant reference to hatreds among the various groups. Zurchers despise Bernese and hate the French. The French openly express fierce dislike of all German Swiss, and both groups are openly contemptuous of the Italians.

Yet this "hatred" never spills over into action. The Genevois treats Zurchers with the same fairness he gives a Frenchman. Zurich courtesy toward Lugano may be cool, but it is always eminently correct. What happens is that Swiss talk their hatreds and frustrations freely—then fail to take the next logical step, which would be to act on them.

This is a form of sanity, perhaps, which the world could use more of. Other peoples tend to be much more hypocritical. They talk brotherhood, then act out their secret frustrations, which all peoples and races have, in other much less pleasant ways. The French historian Halévy wrote before World War I that all Europe would eventually have to choose between something like the federal Swiss model or a bellicose Caesarian empire ruled by force. Events since 1914 have given Halévy a horrifying prophecy. The founders of the Common Market are working against time, and they know it.

Two thousand years of emperors, popes, saviors on horseback, great ideas, and visions of European grandeur have given Europe wars, torturings, burnings, but have not made Europe whole. Some kinds of unity are impossible, since Rome. Napoleon's, Hitler's, or even Hildebrand's concept of Europe failed, as each had to fail. The final peaceful European solution, if one comes, will have to be something like the Swiss' determination not to be their brothers' keeper.

But this severe restraint, which almost no one but the Swiss can practice, has its terrible price. It is emotionally barren. It appalls idealists everywhere. To practice Swiss sensibility, practicality, and restraint, the Swiss banker has had to close his mind to most philosophy, even the implications of his business. He has had to immerse himself in detail. And he has had to make what is probably the freest of all Atlantic societies into something which nearly resembles a well-ordered colony of busy ants. The Swiss banker, who deliberately will not make moral judgments on his neighbor, is increasingly what one sociologist has called "a face in the lonely crowd."

The Swiss immersion in business and detail and refusal to become emotionally involved has made superb watches and immensely successful banks. But it has produced what can only be described as a national inferiority complex. The Swiss has forced himself to think small.

Schwyzerdutch sounds to foreigners like baby-talk. The solid, respected Swiss gold pieces are *Vreneli*—"little" misses. The last silver francs in Europe have become *fränkli*—"tiny" francs. The awesome Alps, some of the most magnificent mountains in the world, are described as *üsere Bärgli*—our small hills. The Swiss mind is almost diametrically the opposite of the American or Russian, which thrives on dreaming big.

But Americans and Russians dabble in other people's business, too. With all their inferiority complex, the Swiss have made a decent domestic world. The world might be an infinitely better place if Britain were always described as a tight little isle; Germany as a quaint, small forest of cuckoo clocks; or France as a comfortable province where the food is good. *Superbia* and terms of grandeur just get nations and people involved in foreign trouble.

A famous Swiss wrote that the Swiss were rich in low things, poor in high things. Depending on the standard, each Swiss banker meets this test. But the problem is that over the years the precise forces which have erected lovely cathedrals have invariably dug torture chambers. The Swiss have never built or created anything superbly grand, and probably never will. But not even the men who hate the cool Swiss nature most can imagine the Swiss nation torturing anyone.

The Swiss force themselves to follow detail and order. It has made them rich, but they pay the inescapable human price.

Unlike France's, Switzerland's society does not permit drinking on the job. But 10 per cent of all the patients in Swiss mental hospitals are alcoholics.

And the general rate of mental illness is one of the highest in the world. Switzerland is one of the few places where men still make and drink absinthe, the mind-destroying, not just mind-blotting, liquor. The Swiss banker holds himself in far higher discipline, but he cracks up mentally far more easily, than his Latin colleagues.

The suicide rate in Switzerland, a half-Catholic nation, is

seventh highest in the world. Prosperity, under the Swiss ethic, has not made for happiness.

Few Swiss deny that they have made money itself a kind of god. But when they began to worship it, almost unconsciously, they made it incumbent upon themselves not to fail their golden diety. Zurich psychiatrists have reported regularly that even a small setback in the financial world can make a man with millions in the bank come unglued. More than one Swiss banker has committed suicide over the loss of only 5000 francs, where American or Roman bankers who lose millions can usually smile and shrug.

The Swiss ethic and discipline have also produced some startling sexual problems. The old Calvinist families of Geneva have been involved in some of Europe's messiest sexual scandals—but this has nothing to do with their banks.

Increasing automation, with its increasing leisure, is only making things worse for the Swiss banker. He prefers working to thinking, and he has been taught from childhood that pure leisure is immoral. Swiss sociologists are concerned about the effects of the inevitably increasing standard of living and leisure upon the Swiss. The recent act of voting down a shorter working week was not one of self-sacrifice or heroics, but desperation. The Swiss cannot spend wealth and they cannot enjoy leisure. If a colony of industrious ants were frustrated in their appointed and traditional tasks, the ants collectively would go mad. If Zurich bankers were forced to conspicuous consumption or to work a six-hour day the discipline of Zurich would collapse. It is not a cheerful prospect.

The increasing prosperity of the banks and economy thus have placed severe strains on the Swiss ethic. Meanwhile, other trends in modern industrialism are straining the anachronistic Swiss Confederation. It is the one European state with almost complete business freedom and without some form of centralized control. But the bank-imported inflation of 1961–1964 and the influx of foreign workers—which may yet create severe social pressures and changes—were developments beyond the limited Swiss government's control.

The important social, industrial, and financial decisions have never come from the federal apparatus in Bern. Bern is an administrative capital, not another Paris. The real direction of Switzerland comes from Zurich. Political power is still diffuse, spreading through the independent states and the banking and industrial octopi which have traced a network across the country. But Zurich, with the most money and with a million people, almost one fifth the whole, tends to dominate. Decisions are made on Bahnhofstrasse and carried out in Bern.

Zurich has thirty-five Nationalrat seats to Uri's one. The cities have traditionally dominated the Confederation since the Middle Ages, but there was always a delicate political balance. The modern exodus from farm to city has destroyed this. The inner cantons like Uri, Schwyz, Obwald, and Nidwald, where Switzerland began, are becoming depopulated. There is nothing which can now offset the concentration of money, people, and political power in Zurich, Basel, and Geneva.

Also, with the phenomenal industrial growth, plants and businesses, and cities and their suburbs are expanding across old medieval cantonal borders. In centralized states this causes no problem; London has expanded for generations. But in Switzerland to step across the line from Canton Zurich to Canton Aargau is to cross a real political frontier. There is no such thing as a Swiss citizen inside the Confederation: this is a term of convenience for use abroad. Swiss refer to themselves as citizens of Zurich, Zug, or Basel, never as Swiss. Thousands of workers in Zurich, for example, come from other cantons. But even thousands who have been born there of "foreign" parentage do not hold Zurich citizenship; they vote in Aargau. Citizenship in Switzerland is grudgingly given. Some Italian or other outside workers may live there for ten generations and not obtain it.

It is difficult for men brought up in unitary nations to understand the problems a confederate system brings. When large industrial concerns straddle cantonal boundaries, it is very much like having half a plant in France, the other in Germany. Every canton has its own industrial laws and separate tax system, and is bitter about enforcing both.

The result politically has been exactly the same as in North America: a forced increase in federal power, which will continue.

In the United States it was not reform movements or men looking to the federal government for certain political acts which forged the immensely powerful American federal bureaucracy. This was originally the product of the American industrialists who, though headquartered in New York, insisted upon regarding the continent as a single economic unit. Ironically enough, American industry did most in the early years to unify the nation, and only later—when the federal apparatus showed signs of getting beyond business or industrial control—did American industry begin to deplore the trend. But any nation which is a single economic unit has to have one basic industrial law, and "national" corporations cannot exist where there is too much local sovereignty. What happened in the US after 1860 began in 1960 to take place in Switzerland.

Some cantons are merging into vast economic units in which the old boundaries make no sense. Thus the sharp division of Zurich into canton and city—when it is really one vast city plus industrial suburbs—is increasingly ridiculous. At the same time, it is also ridiculous to maintain cantons, with cantonal powers, which have only a few thousand people, like Uri's fewer than 33,000. Of Switzerland's old 4000 communes, fully half have lost considerable population. The slowness of political institutions to face or adjust to population changes is becoming a major irritant in some quarters. The cities, already in control, are increasingly impatient with the political power the rural areas still hold.

A mayor of Zurich said: "A political system which treats a vast city of hundreds of thousands in its Senate exactly like a few village hamlets is silly." Interestingly enough, the United States Supreme Court, in its reapportionment decision, thought the same.

The population of Switzerland is still growing. There will be ten million people by A.D. 2050, and most of them will be in the larger cities. The next hundred years will probably accomplish what the power of Austria, Burgundy, Germany, and France could not do. They will undermine and destroy the medieval, communal, and cantonal arrangements of Switzerland in favor of an increasingly powerful central government.

Already the federal bureaucracy sees problems beyond the power of the cantons to solve, and keeps offering advice. In some cases, federal laws are slipped through the Nationalrat. But as in the US, all administration of federal law is normally left to the several states. One major difference, however (though this does happen in the US, too), is that the several states are by no means above ignoring federal statutes when they choose.

Except in times of national crisis, the federal authorities cannot enforce federal law against a canton's will.

In 1963 Zermatt had a typhoid outbreak; the town had ignored federal health and sanitation codes. In the lakes of Zurich and Geneva desirable fish are rapidly becoming extinct. In other cantons the once-sparkling rivers have become polluted. In neither case will the cantonal authorities, conscious of industrial local power, take necessary action. The same forces which made both Roosevelts in the US take federal action are at work in Switzerland, and the end result is apt to be the same. In some cases the cantons do not have the money to solve problems—and the power of the purse gives Bern a powerful tool, just as it makes Washington all-powerful in the United States.

Even more significant, the once-strong sentiments for local government are being undermined in the swollen cities. Bankers find it increasingly irritating to have to vote ten times a year. Switzerland's direct democracy forces almost every issue to popular referendum; Parliament decides nothing. But the city-states have gotten too big for direct democracy to remain coherent. It works in deserted Obwald, because Obwald, like ancient Athens, has only 20,000 citizens. A cantonal election can be held in a city square. But in Geneva or Zurich it is increasingly troublesome and expensive to get hundreds of thousands of voters to the polls.

Any conversation with Swiss bankers—when they are off their guard—reveals their irritation with the system, if not the tradition or sentiments behind it. More and more are saying, "Let Bern handle it"—firmly convinced, of course, that they themselves, in a pinch, can always handle Bern.

But the industrial and financial oligarchy may not keep control. Because of the oligarchy's restraint, fairness, and general blending in with the average population, it has attracted neither attention nor resentment. The Swiss millionaire is quite unlike the Italian, or even the English, much to his advantage. But the overheating of the economy in the 1960s put the public acceptance of the oligarchy's wisdom to some strain. The increasing federalization of Switzerland will not at first affect Switzerland's banks, cartels, or way of doing business. Much later on, if Bern's power is consolidated, it may.

The major reason that Switzerland continues as refuge for international corporations or millionaires is that it is divided into twenty-five sovereign states, each of which puts local profit above a theoretical national general good.

Some day, the slightly graying young rebels who rose with Gottlieb Duttweiler may have their way. But Switzerland will never become another France. Whatever is done will be done with restraint and moderation, because that tradition is too strong. The Swiss may create a genuine nation-state, but it will be more on the American than on the general European model. It is noticeable that in recent years countries with sharply divided ethnic groups, like Canada or Belgium, have been exploring ways of easing tight central government in favor of something more like Switzerland's. Switzerland probably has more to show the world politically than the world has to teach it.

With all its defects and local problems, Switzerland has kept its people politically free. It may yet, as Victor Hugo predicted, in European history have the last word. If that happens, Swiss bankers will be among those who underwrite the brave new world.

Paul Rossy, *Doctor honoris causa*, who was thirty years with the Swiss National Bank and retired as vice-chairman of the Banking Commission, summed it all up in 1964. Rossy, as earthy and as pithy as the Vaudois soil from which he sprang, spent a life trying to see Swiss banking clearly. He lived through two world wars, a great depression, bad times, good times, the Gestapo and American Treasury alike. He was one of the few men in Switzerland who gained the respect and confidence of both big banker and Bern bureaucrat.

A man of severe faith, Rossy said three things:

"Whatever happens in Switzerland, either to banking or to democracy, it will be handled with great restraint. The institution will not be damaged.

"In the world it is not the image, but the substance behind the image which counts. Swiss banks are safe and sane, and all of the financially astute people of the world know it. People who criticize the Swiss system do not understand the nature of Switzerland itself. In Switzerland neutrality comes first.

"Switzerland needs the world—but the world cannot get along without us. God, after all, created Switzerland for one purpose —to be the clearing house of the world."

THE BIG BANKS

The Big Banks handle the bulk of all Swiss international banking business. They also control about half of all marketable securities managed by Swiss banks. The Big Three also do almost all the North American trade.

These banks have branches in every Swiss city and town. Since the names change according to the official language of the community, and since this confuses many foreigners, the names are listed below in the three principal languages:

English	German	French
Swiss Credit Bank	Schweizerische Kreditanstalt	Crédit Suisse
Union Bank of Switzerland	Schweizerische Bankgesellschaft	Union de Banques Suisses
Swiss Bank Corporation	Schweizerische Bankverein	Société de Banques Suisses

Two other smaller banks are members of the Cartel of Big Banks, and are thus considered Big Banks:

Peoples' Bank of Sw.	Schweizerische Volksbank	Banque Populaire Suisse
Leu & Co.'s Bank Ltd.	Bank Leu & Co. A.G.	Leu & Cie.

All of the Big Three have branches and representation in almost every country overseas. The Credit Bank has branches in New York and Montreal, and owns an important securities firm, the Swiss American Corp., in New York. The Bank Corporation has London and New York branches. The Union Bank is represented in all major financial centers and, like the others, maintains approximately 10,000 correspondents across the world.

URI: Member of Confederation since 1291. Area: 1,075 sq.km. Population: 32,400. Cantonal capital: Altdorf.

SCHWYZ: Member of Confederation since 1291. Area: 907 sq.km. Population: 80,600. Cantonal capital: Schwyz.

OBWALD: Member of Confederation since 1291. Area: 491 sq.km. Population: 23,600. Cantonal capital: Sarnen.

NIDWALD: Member of Confederation since 1291. Area: 273 sq.km. Population: 23,000. Cantonal capital: Stans.

LUCERNE: Member of Confederation since 1332. Area: 1,494 sq.km. Population: 260,500. Cantonal capital: Lucerne.

ZURICH: Member of Confederation since 1351. Area: 1,728 sq.km. Population: 1,001,000. Cantonal capital: Zurich.

GLARUS: Member of Confederation since 1352. Area: 684 sq.km. Population: 41,400. Cantonal capital: Glarus.

ZUG: Member of Confederation since 1352. Area: 238 sq.km. Population: 55,300. Cantonal capital: Zug.

BERNE: Member of Confederation since 1353. Area: 6,886 sq.km. Population: 912,100. Cantonal capital: Berne.

FRIBOURG: Member of Confederation since 1481. Area: 1,669 sq.km. Population: 161,000. Cantonal capital: Fribourg.

SOLOTHURN: Member of Confederation since 1481. Area: 791 sq.km. Population: 209,200. Cantonal capital: Solothurn.

BASLE-CITY: Member of Confederation since 1501. Area: 37 sq.km. Population: 230,800. Cantonal capital: Basle.

BASLE-COUNTRY: Member of Confederation since 1501. Area: 428 sq.km. Population: 160,800. Cantonal capital: Liestal.

SCHAFFHAUSEN: Member of Confederation since 1501. Area: 298 sq.km. Population: 69,700. Cantonal capital: Schaffhausen.

APPENZELL A.R.: Member of Confederation since 1513. Area: 242 sq.km. Population: 49,800. Cantonal capital: Herisau.

APPENZELL I.R.: Member of Confederation since 1513. Area: 172 sq.km. Population: 13,300. Cantonal capital: Appenzell.

ST. GALLEN: Member of Confederation since 1803. Area: 2,015 sq.km. Population: 348,100. Cantonal capital: St. Gallen.

GRISONS: Member of Confederation since 1803. Area: 7,108 sq.km. Population: 155,100. Cantonal capital: Chur.

AARGAU: Member of Confederation since 1803. Area: 1,404 sq.km. Population: 374,700. Cantonal capital: Aarau.

THURGAU: Member of Confederation since 1803. Area: 1,006 sq.km. Population: 171,800. Cantonal capital: Frauenfeld.

TESSIN: Member of Confederation since 1803. Area: 2,811 sq.km. Population: 203,700. Cantonal capital: Bellinzona.

VAUD: Member of Confederation since 1803. Area: 3,209 sq.km. Population: 464,700. Cantonal capital: Lausanne.

VALAIS: Member of Confederation since 1814. Area: 5,230 sq.km. Population: 187,000. Cantonal capital: Sitten.

NEUCHATEL: Member of Confederation since 1814. Area: 796 sq.km. Population: 154,500. Cantonal capital: Neuchâtel.

GENEVA: Member of Confederation since 1814. Area: 282 sq.km. Population: 275,900. Cantonal capital: Geneva.

SWITZERLAND IN FIGURES
(1963)

POPULATION (in millions)	5.8
In cities (%)	42.5
LANGUAGES: (%)	
Schwyzerdutch	69.3
French	18.9
Italian	9.5
Reto Romansh	0.9
Other	1.4
WORKING POPULATION (%)	
Employed in Agriculture	10.3
Employed in Industry, Crafts, Construction	50.8
Employed in Commerce, Insurance, Banking	13.7
Employed in Hotels, Restaurants, Travel	10.2
Self-employed	12.9
Wage and Salary Earners	87.1
Working Women	30.2
Foreign Workers (August 1963)	26.5
Registered Unemployment	0.03
Job Vacancies per each unemployed person	7.4
LIVING STANDARDS (per 100 persons)	
Telephones	34.3
Radio Licenses	27.7
Television Licenses	6.0
Passenger Cars	12.0
NATIONAL INCOME (billions of Sw. francs)	
Wages and Salaries	42.4
Business Income of Self-employed	26.0
Income from Investments	8.8
Total Gross National Product	50.9
TRADE BALANCE (billions of Sw. francs)	
Income from Exports	10.5

Spent for Imports 14.0
Deficit 3.5

FEDERAL GOVERNMENT FINANCES (billions of Sw. francs)
Total Revenue 4.2
Total Expenditure 4.1
Fiscal Surplus 0.1
Total Public Debt 5.4

SWISS NATIONAL BANK (billions of Sw. francs)
Notes in Circulation 9.0
Monetary Reserves in Gold 12.2
Percentage of Gold Cover to Paper Money 135.1

TOURIST TRAFFIC
Hotel Nights (millions) 31.0
Hotel Nights by Foreigners (%) 57.4

GEOGRAPHY OF SWITZERLAND
Total Area (sq. km.) 41,288.
Arable Land and Vineyards (%) 6.6
Fit for Fodder-growing only 19.9
Forested 23.8
Alpine Meadows 26.1
Unproductive (includes built-up areas) 23.6

EXCHANGE RATES

Since monetary figures and valuations are quoted in both dollars and other national currencies in this book, the following exchange rates (1965) are listed for convenience:

COUNTRY	USA	UK	Italy	France	Spain	Austria
CURRENCY	$1	£1	L.100	NF 100	Ptas 100	Sch 100
VALUE IN SW. FR.	4.32	12.10	.6950	88.20	7.20	16.75

COUNTRY	W. Ger.	Netherlands	Belgium	Denmark	Sweden
CURRENCY	DM 100	Fl 100	bFr 100	dKr 100	sKr 100
VALUE IN SW. FR.	109.	120.	8.65	62.50	84.

The term *billion* as used in this book refers to the American billion: one thousand millions.

In Switzerland no restrictions exist on the export, import, trade, or exchange of foreign monies, banknotes, or precious metals.